Learning Software Testing with Test Studio

Embark on the exciting journey of test automation, execution, and reporting in Test Studio with this practical tutorial

Rawane Madi

PUBLISHING

BIRMINGHAM - MUMBAI

Learning Software Testing with Test Studio

Copyright © 2013 Packt Publishing

First published: September 2013

Production Reference: 1170913

Published by Packt Publishing Ltd.
Livery Place
35 Livery Street
Birmingham B3 2PB, UK.

ISBN 978-1-84968-890-1

www.packtpub.com

Cover Image by Artie Ng (artherng@yahoo.com.au)

Credits

Author
Rawane Madi

Reviewers
Jim Holmes
Dimo Mitev
Angel Tsvetkov

Acquisition Editor
Amarabha Banerjee

Lead Technical Editor
Susmita Panda

Technical Editors
Krishnaveni Haridas
Shali Sasidharan

Copy Editors
Mradula Hedge
Laxmi Subramanian
Gladson Monterio
Aditya Nair
Kirti Pai
Adithi Shetty

Project Coordinator
Shiksha Chaturvedi

Proofreader
Lesley Harison

Indexer
Monica Ajmera Mehta

Graphics
Abhinash Sahu
Yuvraj Mannari
Ronak Dhruv

Production Coordinator
Conidon Miranda

Cover Work
Conidon Miranda

About the Author

Rawane Madi has a Bachelor's degree in Computer Science and around five years of experience in software testing and automation. She started her career as a Quality Control Engineer at a multinational company that provides both web and Windows applications' solutions. She is a holder of the ISTQB Certified Tester Foundation Level certification and the author for article reviews on automated testing tools published online on DevPro.

"No one can whistle a symphony. It takes a whole orchestra to play it." by *Halford E. Luccok*

With this, I would like to start by thanking Packt Publishing for offering me the generous opportunity of sharing my experience in this book. I would also like to thank Telerik's team support, and particularly *Jim Holmes* for providing his important contribution and critical review.

A lot of gratitude goes to my employer and the management who were always ready to offer their kind support and technical help. These include *Raed Gharzeddine*, *Imad Koussa*, and *Bilal Haidar*.

Finally, special thanks to my family and friends, especially, *Liliane Madi*, *Nadim Mohsen*, *Layal Abi Farraj*, and *Jad Al Deeb* for their continuous encouragement.

About the Reviewers

Jim Holmes is the Director of Engineering for Test Studio at Telerik. He has over 25 years of experience in the IT field in positions including PC Technician, WAN Manager, Customer Relations Manager, Developer, and Tester. Jim has held jobs in the US Air Force, the Department of Defense (DOD) sector, the software consulting domain, and commercial software product sectors. He has been a longtime advocate of test automation and has delivered software on a wide range of platforms. He coauthored the book, *Windows Developer Power Tools*, and blogs frequently at `http://FrazzledDad.com`. Jim is also the President of the Board of Directors for the CodeMash conference held in the middle of winter at an indoor waterpark in Sandusky, Ohio.

Dimo Mitev has almost 10 years of experience working in the IT industry in various international companies, and roles such as Test Consultant, QA Engineer, QA Lead, and Team Lead. Dimo has gained variety of experience in different software testing types, including functional, web service, performance testing, and automation testing. He is currently working as a QA Architect for Telerik Corp., a leading market provider of end-to-end solutions for application development, automated testing, Agile project management, and reporting and content management across all major Microsoft development platforms. Dimo always tries to share his knowledge and at the moment, he is a lecturer in one of Telerik's academies, specialized in teaching young people on software testing discipline. His favorite credo is that quality is more than the lack of bugs. Dimo is currently working on his first book about software testing and is expecting it to be released very soon.

Angel Tsvetkov is an experienced, goal-oriented Quality Assurance Engineer with proven ability in test automation. He has an exceptional ability to enter new environments and produce immediate results through the use of flexible test techniques with excellent communication skills. Driven by challenge, his excellent interpersonal skills provide the ability to operate effectively at all levels and across all test activities. Angel established a QA process in one of the teams and helped in the improvement of automation testing across the Telerik company. While working with IBM, he set up the automation testing as a main approach for testing and spread the knowledge even to the customers to increase their confidence. He worked with Musala Soft and took part in the establishment of service, performance, and functional testing across different teams dealing with the development of web solutions as well as standalone and mobile solutions. Also, he was involved in one of the biggest company projects such as Johnson Controls for a huge client. His main responsibility was the development of automated test scripts for testing of the devices integrated in vehicles. His strong knowledge of electronics was beneficial for the success of the project.

To know more about Angel, visit his blog at `http://qaagent.com`.

www.PacktPub.com

Support files, eBooks, discount offers, and more

You might want to visit www.PacktPub.com for support files and downloads related to your book.

Did you know that Packt offers eBook versions of every book published, with PDF and ePub files available? You can upgrade to the eBook version at www.PacktPub.com and as a print book customer, you are entitled to a discount on the eBook copy. Get in touch with us at service@packtpub.com for more details.

At www.PacktPub.com, you can also read a collection of free technical articles, sign up for a range of free newsletters and receive exclusive discounts and offers on Packt books and eBooks.

http://PacktLib.PacktPub.com

Do you need instant solutions to your IT questions? PacktLib is Packt's online digital book library. Here, you can access, read and search across Packt's entire library of books.

Why Subscribe?

- Fully searchable across every book published by Packt
- Copy and paste, print, and bookmark content
- On demand and accessible via web browser

Free Access for Packt account holders

If you have an account with Packt at www.PacktPub.com, you can use this to access PacktLib today and view nine entirely free books. Simply use your login credentials for immediate access.

Instant Updates on New Packt Books

Get notified! Find out when new books are published by following @PacktEnterprise on Twitter, or the *Packt Enterprise* Facebook page.

Table of Contents

Preface

Test Studio is a tool that offers a variety of features to build custom automated solutions for desktop and web applications. It hosts and simplifies the testing process by supporting manual test creation, automation, and execution. Additionally, its reporting capabilities help in conveying to managers the quality status of the application under test. Test Studio can be extended with bug tracking tools, thus bringing the developers into the loop by seamlessly combining bug reporting within the testing process. This tool is tightly integrated with Team Foundation Server and Visual Studio, which provide the user with a wider set of benefits related to version controlling, management, development, and other powerful software test development characteristics.

Test Studio has two editions for testing desktop and web applications, the standalone and the Visual Studio plugin. Along with these editions, it supports an extended version intended for mobile testing.

Throughout this book, testers will learn how to use Test Studio features in order to create automated tests using interface recording and how to customize these tests by adding functionalities from the underlying test framework library. The different chapters cover the available built-in templates, such as manual, WPF, web, performance, and load test templates, where each chapter elucidates the underlying features that constitute the testing type implied by the template. Therefore, this book helps in learning manual test creation, automation, and execution against a WPF application, in addition to performance testing, benchmarking, workload designing, load testing, result analysis, and reporting against a web application. Furthermore, it contains an overview of Test Studio integration with Team Foundation Server and Visual Studio. A section is also dedicated to revealing the usage of Test Studio extension for automating, executing, reporting, and managing the tests for iOS applications in the cloud.

This book presents hands-on examples, code snippets, and snapshots to conduct the implementation, execution, and reporting phases pertaining to the software testing process inside Test Studio. It makes use of the available tools to present solutions for testing the functional and nonfunctional aspects of an application.

What this book covers

Chapter 1, Introduction, explains what software testing is, introduces some important concepts, and the comprised phases. The introduction also provides a summary of Test Studio features and the chapters in which they are reflected. This chapter also introduces the applications that will be used in the examples and how to properly set up their environment.

Chapter 2, Automating Functional Tests, introduces Test Studio, its architecture, and the supported technologies. It explains how to use its features to automate functional tests using simple recording, coding, execution, debugging, and logging. This chapter also provides an overview of test integration with Visual Studio.

Chapter 3, Data-driven Tests, demonstrates the usage of the data source features in order to create and execute data-driven automated tests. It covers the entire list of supported file system and database management sources to craft independent and embedded data-driven tests.

Chapter 4, Maintaining Test Elements, introduces Test Studio concepts on test element creation, recognition, finding, and editing using the tool IDE and framework library. This chapter also explains some techniques to help in sustaining the test repository and referencing it from within the automated tests.

Chapter 5, Manual Testing, demonstrates manual test creation, integration with MS Excel, execution, and transitioning to automated tests. Test Studio provides a managed process for converting manual testing into a semiautomated version through hybrid tests and then to a fully automated version. Furthermore, this chapter covers source and version controlling functions in Team Foundation Server, managed from Test Studio and Visual Studio IDEs.

Chapter 6, Test Lists and Reports, presents Test Studio's support for test suites through its test lists. It explains and demonstrates the creation and grouping of tests under static and dynamic lists. This chapter also dwells on the reporting side in this tool, its integration with Visual Studio, and customization with MS SQL server.

Chapter 7, Performance Testing, covers the nonfunctional aspects of an application's performance. It explains Test Studio's mechanism for carrying out performance testing by using the specific test template. The built-in capabilities are revealed through simulating real user requests, measuring performance counters, calculating metrics, comparing executions for the same test, and benchmarking the desired instance.

Chapter 8, Load Testing, demonstrates the steps to replicate real-life user loads. Using the load test template, virtual users can be employed to simulate any number of users, automated tests can be executed via different browsers, agents can be installed to initiate requests in a sparse environment, performance counters can be profiled on target machines as well as the networks, and user activity can be designed and tuned. Test Studio also offers a built-in mechanism to chart and compare the results collected for the multiple test runs.

Chapter 9, Mobile Testing, uses Test Studio extensions for iOS to demonstrate functional testing for a mobile application. The chapter explains UI test recording, execution, failure debugging, and accessing of test elements in order to automate the desired tests. Other Test Studio collaboration and reporting features are also exemplified. These features are supported in the feedback and crash reports modules that are viewable from the registered application web portal, which hosts a dashboard enabling other management and tracking testing functionalities related to test execution progress, quality monitoring, and users' collaboration.

Chapter 10, Tips and Tricks, presents some ideas resulting from the combination of different Test Studio features in order to provide useful solutions that enhance test reusability, maintainability, and flexibility in test functions.

Appendix A, Configuring BugNet, contains step-by-step instructions to configure the BugNet project and underlying objects for testing purposes.

What you need for this book

This book assumes basic knowledge in C# in order to comprehensively follow the examples pertaining calls to the test framework library. Test Studio integration with the Team Foundation Server and Visual Studio requires familiarity with these tools' IDEs and features. This book contains material related to iOS testing, which also requires familiarity with the XCode development IDE. The reader must have prior knowledge of software testing concepts. The following is a list of the required tools in order to execute the examples in the book.

For functional and automated web performance and load testing:

- Test Studio
- MS SQL Server 2008
- Visual Studio Ultimate 2010
- Team Foundation Server 2010
- A File Comparer WPF application
- The BugNet Issue Tracker open source application

For mobile testing:

- Mac OS X 10.7
- iOS SDK 6
- XCode 4.6
- Test Studio extension for iOS
- Test Studio bundle
- The Switchy open source application

Who this book is for

This book is for any person motivated by software testing who wishes to exploit and apply Test Studio features in order to manage an automated testing environment from test case creation to reporting.

It assumes a prior knowledge with the testing concepts in addition to having a basic C# knowledge and familiarity with Visual Studio IDE.

Conventions

In this book, you will find a number of styles of text that distinguish between different kinds of information. Here are some examples of these styles, and an explanation of their meaning.

Code words in text are shown as follows: "Clicking on the `FileComparer.Test` node it will display its properties in this pane."

A block of code is set as follows:

```
[default]
exten => s,1,Dial(Zap/1|30)
exten => s,2,Voicemail(u100)
exten => s,102,Voicemail(b100)
exten => i,1,Voicemail(s0)
```

When we wish to draw your attention to a particular part of a code block, the relevant lines or items are set in bold:

```
[default]
exten => s,1,Dial(Zap/1|30)
exten => s,2,Voicemail(u100)
exten => s,102,Voicemail(b100)
exten => i,1,Voicemail(s0)
```

Any command-line input or output is written as follows:

```
# cp /usr/src/asterisk-addons/configs/cdr_mysql.conf.sample
    /etc/asterisk/cdr_mysql.conf
```

New terms and **important words** are shown in bold. Words that you see on the screen, in menus or dialog boxes for example, appear in the text like this: "On the startup window, click on **Create New Project**".

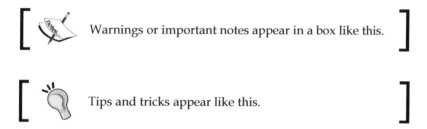

Warnings or important notes appear in a box like this.

Tips and tricks appear like this.

Reader feedback

Feedback from our readers is always welcome. Let us know what you think about this book—what you liked or may have disliked. Reader feedback is important for us to develop titles that you really get the most out of.

To send us general feedback, simply send an e-mail to feedback@packtpub.com, and mention the book title via the subject of your message.

If there is a topic that you have expertise in and you are interested in either writing or contributing to a book, see our author guide on www.packtpub.com/authors.

Customer support

Now that you are the proud owner of a Packt book, we have a number of things to help you to get the most from your purchase.

Downloading the example code

You can download the example code files for all Packt books you have purchased from your account at `http://www.packtpub.com`. If you purchased this book elsewhere, you can visit `http://www.packtpub.com/support` and register to have the files e-mailed directly to you.

Errata

Although we have taken every care to ensure the accuracy of our content, mistakes do happen. If you find a mistake in one of our books—maybe a mistake in the text or the code—we would be grateful if you would report this to us. By doing so, you can save other readers from frustration and help us improve subsequent versions of this book. If you find any errata, please report them by visiting `http://www.packtpub.com/submit-errata`, selecting your book, clicking on the **errata submission form** link, and entering the details of your errata. Once your errata are verified, your submission will be accepted and the errata will be uploaded on our website, or added to any list of existing errata, under the Errata section of that title. Any existing errata can be viewed by selecting your title from `http://www.packtpub.com/support`.

Piracy

Piracy of copyright material on the Internet is an ongoing problem across all media. At Packt, we take the protection of our copyright and licenses very seriously. If you come across any illegal copies of our works, in any form, on the Internet, please provide us with the location address or website name immediately so that we can pursue a remedy.

Please contact us at `copyright@packtpub.com` with a link to the suspected pirated material.

We appreciate your help in protecting our authors, and our ability to bring you valuable content.

Questions

You can contact us at `questions@packtpub.com` if you are having a problem with any aspect of the book, and we will do our best to address it.

1
Introduction

Some of the reasons why you would want to achieve software quality are to make sure that the system does what it's supposed to do; uncover errors and/or to provide assurance for your software user. This chapter will explore some general terminologies and processes in software testing to shed light over some concepts used in this book, and briefly introduce the tool automation features that are covered in the next chapters.

If you are already familiar with the following testing concepts, you can jump to Test Studio uncovered in the later chapters of this book.

Testing concepts

The following is a conceptual overview of some fundamental testing terminologies and principles. These are used in day-to-day testing activities and will be directly referred to in the chapters when explaining the business case for our examples.

Test case

A test case is a scenario that will be executed by the tester or by an automation tool, such as the Test Studio for any of the software testing purposes, such as uncovering potential errors in the system. It contains:

- **Test case identifier**: This identifier uniquely distinguishes a test case.
- **Priority**: The priority holds a value to indicate the importance of a test case so that the most important ones are executed first and so on.

- **Preconditions**: The preconditions describe the initial application state in which the test case is to be executed. It includes actions that need to be completed before starting the execution of the test case, such as performing certain configurations on the application, or other details about the application's state that are found relevant.

- **Procedure**: The procedure of a test case is the set of steps that the tester or automated testing tool needs to follow.

- **Expected behavior**: It is important to set an expected behavior resulting from the procedure. How else would you verify the functionality you are testing? The expected behavior of a test case is specified before running a test, and it describes a logical and friendly response to your input from the system. When you compare the actual response of the system to the preset expected behavior, you determine whether the test case was a success or a failure.

Executing a test case

When executing a test case, you would add at least one field to your test case description. It is called the actual behavior and it logs the response of the system to the procedure. If the actual behavior deviates from the expected behavior, an incident report is created. This incident report is further analyzed and in case a flaw is identified in the system, a fix is provided to solve the issue. The information that an incident report would include are the details of the test case in addition to the actual behavior that describes the anomalous events. The following example demonstrates the basic fields found in a sample incident report. It describes a transaction carried out at a bank's ATM:

- Incident report identifier: ATM-398
- Preconditions: User account balance is $1000
- Procedure: It includes the following steps:

  1. User inserts a card.
  2. User enters the pin.
  3. Attempts to withdraw a sum of $500.

- Expected behavior: Operation is allowed
- Actual behavior: Operation is rejected, insufficient funds in account!
- Procedure results: Fail

The exit criteria

The following definition appears in the **ISTQB (International Software Testing Qualification Board)** glossary:

> *"The set of generic and specific conditions, agreed upon with the stakeholders, for permitting a process to be officially completed. The purpose of exit criteria is to prevent a task from being considered completed when there are still outstanding parts of the task, which have not been finished. Exit criteria are used to report against and to plan when to stop testing. [After Gilb and Graham]"*

The pesticide paradox

Software testing is governed by a set of principles out of which we list the pesticide paradox. The following definition appears in the ISTQB glossary:

> *If the same tests are repeated over and over again, eventually the same set of test cases will no longer find any new defects. To overcome this, "pesticide paradox", the test cases need to be regularly reviewed and revised, and new and different tests need to be written to exercise different parts of the software or system to potentially find more defects.*

Element recognition

Element recognition is a pillar of automated test execution as the tool used can't perform an action on an object unless it recognizes it and knows how to find it. Element identification is important in making the automated scripts less fragile during execution. This topic will be reflected in this book.

Testing phases

The following set of fundamental testing phases is based on their definition by ISTQB. Other organizations might name them differently or include different activities in them.

- Test planning and control: Test objectives and activities are set during test planning and a test plan is created. It can include:
  - Test strategy: The general approach to testing the application
  - Test tools: Reporting tools, automated testing tool, and so on

- Test techniques : Will be discussed in the next section
- Human resources: The personnel needed to carry out the testing

As for test control, it should be exercised during all the phases to monitor progress and amend the test plan as needed.

- Test analysis and design: During this phase, the system specifications are analyzed and test cases, along with their data, are designed. They are also prioritized and the testing environment is identified.

- Test implementation and execution: When implementing your tests and before executing them, you should set up your environment, generate the detailed test cases, run them, and then log and report the results of your findings.

- Evaluating the exit criteria and reporting: Evaluating exit criteria is important in order to know when to stop testing. Occasionally, we find that more tests are needed if the risk in one or more application areas hasn't been fully covered. In case it is decided to stop that test implementation and execution, reports are generated and submitted to the implicated persons.

- Test closure activities: The test closure activities are designed to facilitate reusing of the test data across different versions and products, as well as to promote evaluating and enhancing the testing process. These activities include saving all the test data and testware in a secure repository, evaluating the testing process, and logging suggested amendments.

Testing techniques

Ranging from easy and straightforward to complex and machine-computed, many testing techniques guide the design and generation of your test cases. In the this section, we will describe the most basic of these techniques based on the ISTQB standards:

- **Equivalence classes**: By definition, an equivalence class is a single class of inputs generating an equivalent output. Vice versa, it could be a single class of outputs generated from equivalent inputs. For example, imagine you need to test a simple numeric field which accepts values from 0 to 100. During your testing, you cannot possibly exhaust all the values, hence we would identify one valid equivalence partition and three invalid partitions as follows:

For valid partitions:

- ° Values between 0 and 100 inclusive

For invalid partitions:

- ° Values less than zero
- ° Values greater than 100
- ° Nonnumeric inputs

As a result, you now choose tests from the four equivalence classes instead of testing all the options. The value of equivalence classes analysis lies in the reduction of testing time and effort.

- **Boundary values**: When choosing boundary value analysis, you study the limits of your system input. Typically, they are the logical minimum and maximum values in addition to technical or computational limits, such as register sizes, buffer sizes, or memory availability. After determining your logical and technical limits, you would test the system by inputting the actual boundary, the boundary decremented by the smallest possible unit, and the boundary increment by the smallest possible unit.

  Assuming our system is an application form where you need to enter your first name in one of the fields, you can proceed with a boundary value analysis on the length of the first name string. Considering that the smallest input is one character, and the largest input is one hundred, our boundary values analysis will lead to a test for strings having the following number of characters: zero (empty input), one, two, ninety-nine, one hundred, and one hundred and one.

- **Decision tables**: In certain systems, many rules may be interacting with each other to produce the output, such as a security matrix. For instance, let's assume your system is a document management system. The possible factors determining whether a user will have view rights or not are as follows:

  - ° Belonging to user groups with a permission set for each group
  - ° Having an individual permission for each user
  - ° Having access to the documents' file path

These factors are called the conditions of the decision table, where the actions might be reading, editing, or deleting a document. A decision table would allow you to test and verify every combination of the listed conditions. Certain rules might simplify your table, but they are outside the scope of this book. The resulting decision table for the previous example of document management system is illustrated as follows:

Test Case ID	1	2	3	4	5	6	7	8	9	10
Conditions										
User group permission	Read	Edit	Delete	Read	Edit	Delete	Read	Edit	Delete	Delete
Individual permission	Read	Read	Read	Edit	Edit	Edit	Delete	Delete	Delete	Delete
File path accessible	Yes	Yes	Yes	Yes	Yes	Yes	Yes	Yes	Yes	No
Actions										
Resulting Permission	Read	Read	Read	Edit	Edit	Edit	Delete	Delete	Delete	None

Decision table for user rights

- **State transition diagram**: In some systems, not only do the actions performed determine the output and the routing of the application, but also the state in which the system was in before these actions. For such systems, a state transition diagram is used to generate test cases.

    1. Firstly, the state transition diagram is drawn with every state as a circle and every possible action as an arrow. Conditions are written between square brackets and the output is preceded by a forward slash.

    2. Secondly, each action represented in the diagram is attempted from an initial state.

    3. Thirdly, test cases are generated by looping around the state transition diagram and by choosing different possible paths while varying the conditions.

The expected behavior in state transition test cases are both the output of the system and the transition to the next expected state. In the following sample diagram, you will find the state transition diagram of a login module:

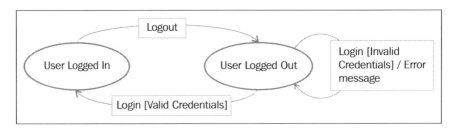

State transition diagram for user authentication to the system

Test Studio uncovered through the chapters

This section gives the list of features provided in Test Studio and the chapters in which they are reflected:

1. Functional test automation: The Test Studio solution to functional test automation is going to be discovered through the following topics: building automated tests, using translators and inserting verifications, adding coded steps, executing tests and logging, adding custom logging, inserting manual steps, assigning and reading variables in tests, debugging errors, and integrating automated test creations with Visual Studio. These topics will be found in *Chapter 2, Automating Functional Tests* and *Chapter 10, Tips and Tricks*.

2. Data-driven architecture: Test Studio offers built-in integration with data sources, allowing you to apply the data-driven architecture during test automation. This feature includes binding tests to SQL, MS Excel, XML, and local data sources, creating data-driven verification, and integrating data-driven architecture with normal automated execution contexts. These topics will be found in *Chapter 3, Data-driven Tests* and *Chapter 10, Tips and Tricks*.

3. Element recognition: Element recognition is a powerful feature in Test Studio from which it derives additional test reliability. Element recognition topics will be covered through Test Studio Find expressions for UI elements, element repository consolidation and maintenance, and specialized Find chained expressions. These topics will be found in *Chapter 4, Maintaining Test Elements* and *Chapter 10, Tips and Tricks*.

4. Manual testing: In addition to automated testing, Test Studio guides the manual testing process. Manual testing includes creating manual test steps, integrating with MS Excel, converting manual tests to hybrid, and executing these two types of tests. These topics will be covered in *Chapter 5, Manual Testing*.

5. Organizing the test repository and source control: Tests within the Test Studio project can be organized and reorganized using the features embedded in the tool. Its integration with external source control systems also adds to this management process. The underlying topics are managing tests under folders, setting test properties, and binding your test project to source control from both Test Studio and Visual Studio. The best practices on test repository organization will be encountered throughout the examples of the first four chapters, where the source control topic will be discussed in *Chapter 5, Manual Testing* since we will have covered all the types of tests offered by the tool by then.

6. Test suites execution and reporting: Grouping tests under test suites is achievable through the Test Studio test lists. This feature comprises creating static and dynamic test lists, executing them, logging their execution result, viewing standard reports, and extending with custom reports. These topics will be covered in *Chapter 6, Test Lists and Reports*.

7. Extended libraries: Extending testing framework automation functionalities for Test Studio is an option available through the creation of Test Studio plugin libraries. This topic will be covered in *Chapter 10, Tips and Tricks*.

8. Performance testing: In Test Studio, nonfunctional testing is firstly addressed with performance testing. This feature covers developing performance tests, executing them, gathering performance counters, and analyzing and baselining execution results. These topics will be covered in *Chapter 7, Performance Testing*.

9. Load testing: Nonfunctional testing in Test Studio is augmented with another type of test, which is load testing. This topic covers configuring Test Studio load testing services, developing load tests, recording HTTP traffic, creating user profiles and workloads, monitoring machines, gathering performance metrics, executing load tests, and creating custom charts. These topics will be addressed in *Chapter 8, Load Testing*.

10. Mobile testing: Test Studio is extended with a version specialized in iOS web, native and hybrid apps testing. It includes preparing applications for testing within Test Studio, creating automated tests, inserting verifications on UI elements, registering applications on the web portal, syncing test projects, sending and viewing built-in feedback messages, sending and viewing crash reports, and managing and monitoring registered applications through web portals. These topics will be addressed in *Chapter 9, Mobile Testing*.

Approach

While reading this book, you will find a problem-based approach to automating tests with Test Studio.

The following general approach might vary slightly between the different examples:

- General problem: We will start by stating the general problem that you may face in real-life automation

- Real-life example: We will then give a real-life example based on our previous experience in software testing

- Solutions using the Test Studio IDE: Having described the problem, a solution using the Test Studio IDE will be provided

- Solutions using code: Finally, some solutions will be provided by writing code

At any point, you can refer to the accompanying Test Studio solution for each chapter, which contains all the examples!

Setting up your environment

You will get a list of files with this book to help you try the examples properly. The following is an explanation on how to set up the environment to practice the automation examples against the applications under test.

The File Comparer application

Chapters 2 through 6, as well as *Chapter 10, Tips and Tricks*, revolve around the `File Comparer` WPF application. To configure this application environment, you need to:

1. Run the `FC_DB-Database Scripts.sql` files in the SQL Management Studio.

2. Open the `settings.xml` file from the solution bin and edit the `ConnectionString` parameter.

Reports

Chapter 6, Test Lists and Reports, gives examples on custom reports that can be found in the `File Comparer - Reports.xlsx` workbook. The data source files for these reports can be found in the `ODCs` folder. In order to properly display the charts in the workbook:

1. Edit the `ConnectionString` parameter inside the `ODC` extension files.

2. Bind the pivot tables inside the excel workbook to these files as follows:

   ○ The **Execution Metrics for Last Run** sheet to the `FC_DB-L-EMLR.odc` file

   ○ The **Execution Metrics over Time** sheet to the `FC_DB-MOT.odc` file

   ○ The **Feature Coverage** sheet to the `FC_DB-FC.odc` file

   ○ The **Test Execution Duration** sheet to the `FC_DB-TED.odc` file

Alternatively, you can create these charts with the queries provided in *Chapter 6, Test Lists and Reports*.

Additional files

The following are the additional files used in this book:

- The `Test Studio Automated Solutions` folder contains the Test Studio automated solution for the examples in the book. For each chapter, there will be an incremental solution holding the examples for this chapter and the ones before.

- The `TestStudio.Extension` folder is a Visual Studio solution and it corresponds to the Test Studio extension library demonstrated in *Chapter 10, Tips and Tricks*.

As for the remaining files, such as the data sources, external tests, and the fiddler SAZ file, they will be referenced by their names within the chapter examples.

Other reference sources

Refer to Telerik online documentation for:

- Test Studio standalone and VS plugin editions found at `http://www.telerik.com/automated-testing-tools/support/documentation/user-guide/test-execution/test-list-settings.aspx`

- Mobile testing using Test Studio extension for iOS testing found at `http://www.telerik.com/automated-testing-tools/support/documentation/mobile-testing/testing.aspx`

Also, for software testing and automation concepts you can refer to:

- ISTQB-BCS Certified Tester Foundation Level book, *Foundations of Software Testing* by *Dorothy Graham, Erik Van Veenendaal, Isabel Evans,* and *Rex Black*
- ISTQB glossary of testing terms 2.2

2
Automating Functional Tests

You have been recently working on an application as part of the Quality Control team. It's been a month since the project has started where as quality control engineers you work with have been designing and generating test cases.
The project test leader calls the team for an urgent meeting early in the morning.

"Test case coverage is low and the manual testers' effort in regression testing is insufficient knowing the degradation impact from developers' bug fixes. Testing is falling behind" says the team leader.

Two hours of discussion went on before a decision was taken. Automation seems to be the solution to the problem at hand and knowing your usual high commitment and performance, you are going to be part of the team carrying out this task. All the attendees already knew that lots of factors related to the problem at hand are working against the team's benefit: the lack of knowledge in automation and the tool technology, the time constraint to meet the release deadline along with the frequent project requirement changes. So, the first reaction you welcome the news with is complete panic.

As a solution to the preceding problem, Test Studio, a test automation tool, is adopted to organize testing, increase coverage, and enhance the accuracy of execution. In principle, part of the manual test repository is going to be converted into autonomously executing scripts. These scripts should take over mechanical human tasks distinguished by their repetitiveness or need for intricate calculations. Knowing that the resulting automated scripts are characterized by their speed of execution, precision, and consistency, automation will in the long run achieve substantial time saving considered as a risk related to the application's success.

Test Studio enables a rich toolkit to proficiently automate the procedures of the manual test cases. Its features comprise UI recording, logic insertion, specialized verification, and other test development functionalities that require no coding; however, optionally, Test Studio's test automation library can be invoked to perform further functions through the addition of customized coded steps within the recorded test.

In the execution phase, the test's reliability is derived from Test Studio's advanced UI object recognition. Being a tool that identifies target UI controls based on their nature rather than their coordinates, the scripts can be repetitively replayed while excluding the possibility of an object misidentification failure.

Based on these given reasons, by the end of this chapter, you would have learned how to realize the following tasks with Test Studio:

- Proper test repository design
- Functional test automation and verification
- Proper automated test case design
- Test execution
- Failures debug
- Visual Studio integration

Getting started with automation

Many tasks underlie the testing process of the software life cycle. They fall under the different testing activities, which slightly vary based on the company's development life cycle strategy and sometimes based on the project criticality. Despite the different names attributed to these tasks or their classification and grouping, we can still denote a fundamental relationship between testing activities and their tasks.

The test plan activity comprises planning tasks related to testing strategy, skills, timelines, tools, environment, and others.

The design activity comprises tasks with purpose to design tests and environment based on the strategy and approach adopted in test planning. It consists of choosing and applying design techniques on the software specifications in order to prepare for the manual test case generation, test data generation, test case automation, the environment, and others.

The implementation and execution activity is closely tied to the design phase where it extends it by elaborating on each of the precedent tasks. Hence, during this activity, the test cases for the prepared designs are generated, the test data is produced, the automation is scripted, and the environment is implemented. At the end of this stage, the test cases are executed in the testing environment and the results are logged.

The reporting and evaluation activity is responsible for assessing the results against the objectives and exit criteria and producing test reports afterwards.

In this chapter, we are interested in test automation, which participates in the test implementation and execution activities, but when and what to automate?

Where does automation fit best?

Test automation solves the problem of software high quality with less cost. This statement is relative to the project under test and the work environment's maturity. Therefore, subduing factors with negative impact shifts the automation outcome to our benefit. If we succeed, the advantages that test automation offer us in comparison with manual testing are in terms of efficiency and time duration.

Efficiency includes less error vulnerability during execution, automatic repeatability, objectiveness in test verification, automatic test parameter tuning in order to increase defect detection coverage, and realistic load tests.

In terms of time duration, the automation is capable of running a greater number of tests in the same period of time compared to manual testing. For regression testing purposes, the automated solution can run continuously and repetitively against the incrementing builds of the application under test.

Out of the risks that threatens the success of the automation comes the training cost, the unrealistic expectations as to what the automation tool is capable of doing, the nonaccountability of the startup time after which the automation return is much higher than that of the resources needed, the proper choice of the tests to automate, and the development of non-maintainable test scripts.

These factors are not to be underestimated since they have a direct effect on failing automation and inflicting damage on the cost and delivery deadline. The next examples give you an idea about the areas where making use of test automation benefits you the most. The typical test types to be automated are as follows:

- Tiresome to be performed by human such as those which are repetitive in nature; for example, when executing the same test case with 100 different inputs

- Complex tasks necessitating high accuracy such as tasks which involve computations having decimal numbers with n-digit precision

- Requiring highly consistent results if they are to be repeated the same way such as those calculating code coverage after executing the same test suite consecutively against the same source code

This list is not limited to these test types. All these examples are more error prone when they are performed by humans where on the other hand they become more efficient with automation tools.

The following table illustrates the advantages versus the disadvantages of test automation:

Advantages	Disadvantages
Reduction of repetitive tasks	Unrealistic expectations
Accuracy	Necessary time for learning and automating tests
Objectiveness and repeatability	Maintainability effort and time
Organized test repository and traceability	
Time saving and increased efficiency in the long run	

Having said all this, automation is still a losing case if the underlying automated tests are not designed with long term vision and maintainability in mind. For this purpose, the next section talks about a few automation strategies, which we are going to apply throughout this book.

Test strategies

Software quality has functional and nonfunctional characteristics. The functional tests are used to verify that the software abides by its functional specifications. In other words, they are used to make sure that the software succeeds in performing what it is supposed to do. Alternatively, the nonfunctional tests are concerned with testing software attributes, which are not related to the functionality by testing how the software is performing the needed functionalities rather than what are the needed functionalities. Out of the nonfunctional testing types we list:

- **Performance testing**: It measures the degree to which the application performs in terms of time and resource usage when exposed to predefined user and activity rates

- **Load testing**: This measures the application's behavior when subjected to an increasing load of parallel users and transactions while varying the last two factors within the boundaries of the defined specifications

- **Stress testing**: This measures your application's behavior beyond the limits of the defined concurrent users and transactions

- **Usability testing**: This measures how easy it is for a new user to understand and intuitively find the means to achieve the wanted operations

Test strategies provide solid designs for functional tests where the nonfunctional ones build on these tests by repetitively executing them during a time period, with high user load and perhaps scarce resources.

Capture and playback

The first approach to start automating functional tests is by capture and playback. The outcome of this task is an automated test with specialized steps built on top of the test execution tool language. It is usually done by the tool's automatic recording during the manual execution of the test case.

If you got the impression that this type of automation is brittle, it's true. During recording, capture and playback records the UI interactions performed within the context of the system's state at that time. The system state is known to vary based on some factors, such as environment or components upgrade, where after all we automate the test cases to rerun them when we doubt that the system has regressed. System changes could, for example, result in unexpected windows, UI component changes, or unreachable data. From here emerges the need to improve our tests in order to cater for such situations by inserting some validation and default handling steps.

Other steps could also be inserted to offer generic functionalities related to formatting data, verifying against databases, or others. As these steps are inserted, we find ourselves repeating them in all the automated tests since they all revolve around the same set of UI elements. Therefore, you start to feel the need to:

- Unify the call to these steps whenever possible since duplication is not favored in development practices
- Add common data source utilities to interact with databases or Excel sheets
- Add string utilities to parse strings based on specific business logic within an application

Eventually, these customized functions grow into modular reusable test libraries, which will come in between the test scripts and the tool automation framework.

Data-driven architecture

Another problem in capture and playback tests is that they have their input values tied to them. Hardcoded input values also promote repetitive test UI functionalities. In addition, it is exhaustive and time consuming to create one more test for each input parameter. The lack of data scalability suggests another form of evolution to a data-driven architecture. The purpose of data-driven testing is to cover massive data combination for the same test procedure. Instead of having one test for each data combination we end up having one test for all data. During execution, these tests populate the UI elements on the screen by reading their input from data sources containing the data-driven data in tables.

Keyword-driven architecture

Among the listed application development risks, is the cost. Automation maintenance is one of the costs recurring whenever the application's specifications change. The preceding two architectures expand the test scripts' durability with respect to requirements volatility. They can also be pushed to a higher level where a function inside the application under test or even a whole test will take part in the procedure of another test. As an example, we will take two scenarios for an online shopping application.

The first scenario comprises this sequence of actions: user logs in, adds items to the cart, buys the items, and logs out. The second scenario comprises a different sequence: user logs in, adds items to the cart, cancels the operation, and logs out. Both the scenarios share a common function, that is, adding items to a cart. It is very probable that the way to add items to a cart changes during the project's life cycle. Therefore, if we have 100 test cases that include adding items to the cart, all 100 test cases will have to change!

Some atomic functions can be extracted from the preceding two scenarios such as: logging in/out, adding items to cart, and cancelling. Had we automated each of these functions independently in its own test and let the other tests build on it, then we would have had only one change to do, which is on that atomic function's automated test. So imagine each of the preceding scenarios, representing the main test, calling within its procedures the subtests responsible for executing the needed atomic functions. This approach is called keyword-driven architecture. At the end of this chapter, there is a section that illustrates this approach through the call of random keyword tests.

About Test Studio

There exists a wide set of automation tools to automate the tasks belonging to the testing activities we have seen earlier. For instance, test management tools, modeling tools, test data preparation tools, test execution tools, bug tracking tools, comparators, and others.

Test Studio is a test execution tool provided to us by Telerik, which offers automated solutions in the software quality assurance field. Test Studio's first version was released in March 2009 as WebUI Test Studio. It was the outcome of joint efforts of ArtOfTest, leaders in software quality assurance, and Telerik. ArtOfTest materialized the automated testing functionalities in a testing framework library called WebAii library upon which Telerik has built the WebUI Test Studio IDE. This tool has evolved today into Test Studio's standalone and Visual Studio's plugin editions where they both communicate with the free Telerik testing framework and at the same time extend it with other handy automation features.

Test Studio is primarily a test execution and logging tool for functional and nonfunctional testing. Functional tests are firstly created through its record feature where they can be further customized in code. Performance and load testing are also available for nonfunctional quality characteristics. Test Studio is capable of simulating the functional automated tests with virtual users, under real life workloads and stress situations. Instead of taking assistance from external tools to capture performance data during nonfunctional test execution, it is equipped with a monitoring mechanism to collect performance measures related to network traffic, SQL, and IIS metrics.

Test Studio is also a management tool for manual test cases where it bridges the gap of separately storing manual and automated test scripts in order to promote traceability between them.

Finally, it integrates with other tools such as Team Foundation Server, which, out of many other benefits, allows scheduling of the automated tests to run against the project's updated builds. As for incident management, bug reports can be directly created from within Test Studio into Team Pulse Server, for example. Also, thanks to the fact that Test Studio integrates with Microsoft Visual Studio, features such as code coverage and unit testing are also available.

Supported technologies

Test Studio is primarily an automation tool for web, desktop, and mobile applications. In case of the web, HTML5, ASP .NET MVC, Silverlight, PHP, AJAX, and JavaScript are the supported technologies. In case of desktop applications, it supports WPF, and finally iOS for native, web, and hybrid mobile applications.

Architecture

Test Studio's standalone application is aimed at QA engineers. It has its own record and playback mechanism where the automated test script generated from the record feature is composed of test steps with various functions. The steps cover UI operations, verification expressions, and logical branching, which constitute the toolset for automation. Customizing these steps in code is optional where the supported languages are .NET, C#, and Visual Basic.

As shown in the following diagram, Test Studio is built on top of the free Telerik testing framework. It consists of .NET libraries providing the UI element retrieval functionality and their corresponding wait methods, the UI interactive actions, the supported application controls, and the browser abstraction for web tests. The additional functionalities such as the integration with the external tools mentioned previously, the element repository, the DOM Explorer, and the Telerik RadControls translators are solely contained in the Test Studio IDE.

All the test drivers created inside Test Studio, whether coded or not, are based on the Telerik testing framework. Eventually, when the tests are executed, their test steps are compiled and interpreted into various framework method calls.

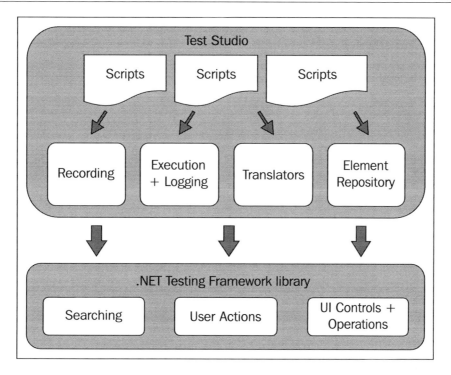

Test Studio's architecture

Functional test automation

In this section, we will convert manual functional test cases into automated tests using the record feature, edit these tests based on emerging automation needs, perform dynamic verifications, customize test steps in code, and log intermediate as well as overall test execution results. The application for testing is called `File Comparer`. It is a WPF application that does some basic file comparison and saving functionalities. So, let's open Test Studio and get started.

Recording an automated test

The largest unit of work to deal with inside Test Studio is a project. A project usually maps to the whole application under test and creating it is simple, just perform the following steps:

1. On the startup window, click on **Create New Project**.

2. From the **New Project** window, enter `FileComparer.Test` in the **Project Name** text field.

3. Click on **OK**.

   The project is created and Test Studio now displays three panes: **Data Sources**, **Properties**, **Project Files** as shown in the following screenshot:

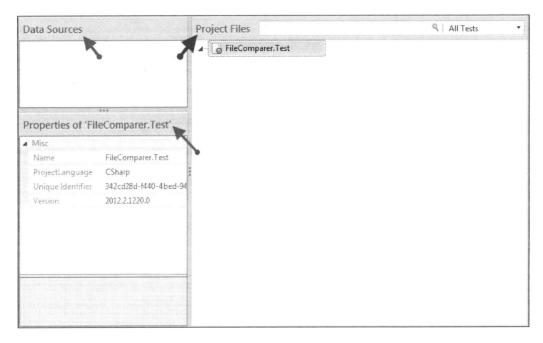

Test Studio's project tab

To the upper left, **Data Sources,** designated with a red arrow, lists the database and file connections that are used in the project by the automated tests. Since none are created, the pane is currently empty.

To the right, the **Project Files** pane designated with a blue arrow shows the project folders and tests hierarchy. At the root of this hierarchy comes the project node as shown.

Finally, to the lower left of the window, the **Properties** pane designated with a green arrow is going to display the properties for any selected automation. The object can represent a project, folder, test, data source, or anything that appears inside the other panes. For example, clicking on the `FileComparer.Test` node will display its properties in this pane.

Before we jump on to create our first automated test, let's first shape things up by performing the following steps:

1. Right-click on `FileComparer.Test` and click on **Create Folder**.
2. Rename the created folder under the project node to `Automated Test Scripts` and press *Enter*.
3. Right-click on the previously created folder and choose **Create Folder** again from the context menu.
4. This time rename the folder to `Functional Tests`.

Nested folders provide the first way to neatly group tests based on a logical criterion, which is a type of test strategy in our case. This nested folder is going to contain all subsequent automated tests that we are going to create in this chapter.

No need to wait more, we are ready to start creating automated tests.

Right-click on the `Functional Tests` folder node and then **Add New Test**. In the **Select Test Type** window, we have an option to choose between the following test types:

- **Web Test**: It is used to automate functional tests for web applications encompassing ASP .NET, AJAX, Silverlight, and HTML5
- **WPF Test**: It is used to automate functional tests for WPF applications
- **Manual Test**: It is used to create tests having instructions to be executed manually by the tester
- **Load Test**: It is used to design tests, which involve virtual users and workloads in order to measure the application's performance during load testing

Since this chapter deals only with automated tests and our application is WPF, we are going to choose **WPF Test**. Change the test name to `Func-1_FileCompare_Equal_Successful`.

The **Project Files** pane now has the hierarchy shown in the following screenshot:

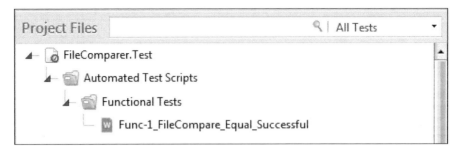

Creating a new test

Record and playback

In order to see the `File Comparer` application running, open Visual Studio and run the application. The interface shown in the following screenshot will be launched:

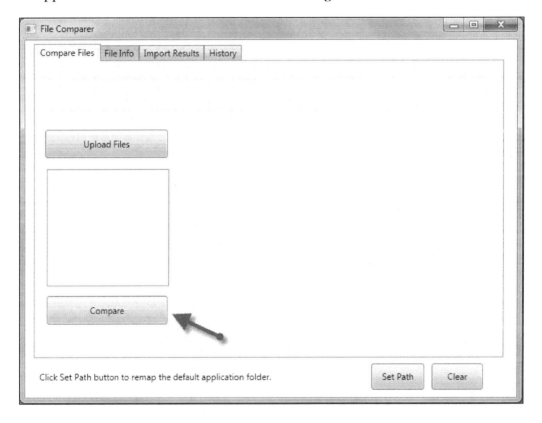

The File Comparer application

The first tab, **Compare Files,** has the functionality to compare two files with XML content depending on some criteria. For the time being we are not interested in the method of comparison so we will skip it.

The files to compare are fed after clicking on the **Upload Files** button. The **Compare** button designated with a red arrow launches the comparison and the result is displayed in a textbox above it. Close the application by closing the window and then create a folder called `File Comparer Files` under your `C:`. The purpose of this folder is to contain the files which the application will compare, so place all the files inside it.

The first test case we are going to automate is a test-to-pass generated to verify the comparison of two identical files. It ascertains that we get an output stating that the two files are equal in case if they are identical. The manual steps of test case one are as follows:

1. Prerequisites are two XML files with same content
2. Test procedure:
    1. Start the `File Comparer` application.
    2. Click on the **Compare Files** tab.
    3. Click on the **Upload Files** button.
    4. Enter `C:\File Comparer Files\"Func-1_FileCompare_ Equal_Successful_In1.trx" "Func-1_FileCompare_Equal_ Successful_In2.trx"` in the **File Name** field of the **Upload Files** window and then click on the **Open** button.
    5. Click on the **Compare** button.
    6. Close the application.
3. The expected result displayed is: **The files resulted in equal comparison!**

Now we know the feature to test and the test case, let's start automating the test case steps.

Double-click on the `Func-1_FileCompare_Equal_Successful` test node. Test Studio navigates you to its **Test** tab, where the following screenshot shows the **Steps** toolbar:

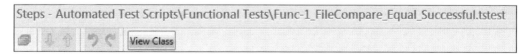

The Steps toolbar

Firstly, the test needs to be bound to the application under test, so click on the **Configure** button from the **Application** ribbon, which is the button on the right in the following screenshot. The **Configure WPF Application Path** window will take care of instructing Test Studio to attach its recorder to the `File Comparer` application once the test is started.

There are two configuration options, either browse for an executable application or choose from any of the running WPF applications. Since none are currently running, let's click on the **Browse** button and choose the `File Comparer.exe` file contained in the application's debug folder. Finally click on **OK**.

 Test Studio has the option to record window actions such as resizing. It is enabled by selecting the **Record Window State Changes (Maximize, Minimize, Restore, Close)** checkbox from the **Configure WPF Application Path** window. We will not be using this feature in our tests.

In the upper-left side of the screen, a button called **Record** appears in the **Application** ribbon, which corresponds to the left button in the following screenshot. We need to click on this button to start the recording:

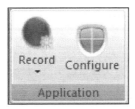

The Application ribbon

As you can see in the following screenshot, an instance of the `File Comparer` application is started with a recorder toolbar attached to it. The recording toolbar allows us to manage the recording of our test steps. Therefore, any action contained outside the application window will be disregarded by Test Studio.

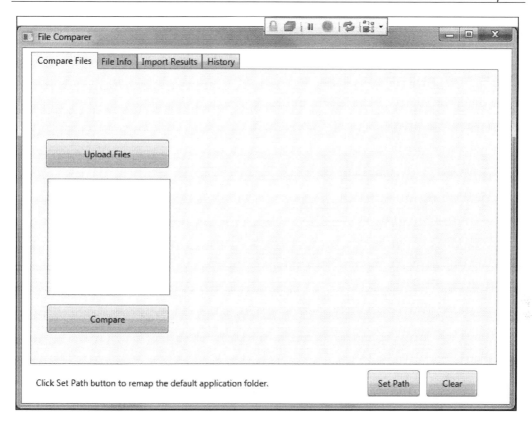

Test Studio's recording toolbar

On the launched application, execute the actions as listed in the manual test case procedure and then close the application. During test recording, Test Studio inserts an automated test step for each manual step that you are performing. The recording outcome is as follows:

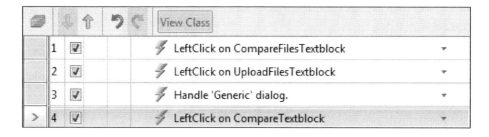

Steps of the Func-1_FileCompare_Equal_Successful test

Let's walk through the steps. The first step says **LeftClick on CompareFilesTextblock**; by decomposing this sentence we can map the following: **LeftClick** to the UI operation and **CompareFilesTextblock** to the UI object name as named inside Test Studio. In other words, the recorder detected a left click on a label containing the **Compare Files** text. If we follow the same logic on the other two similar steps 2 and 4, we find that there were two other left clicks on **UploadFilesTextblock** and **CompareTextblock**. Step 3, the **Handle 'Generic' dialog,** deals with handling file dialogs where this step waits for the appearance of a generic dialog. Test Studio has an internal mechanism for handling dialogs and one of them is managing **Open File** windows, which is exactly what is needed in this test case. Right-click on step 3 and choose **Delete** from the context menu. We will use the add step feature to handle the specific kind of dialog that we are dealing with.

From the **Add** ribbon, click on **Dialogs** and choose **Open File**. A step is added to the **Steps** pane and Test Studio notifies you that you should edit the properties of the step. Click on **OK** in the ensuing window, and then in the **Steps** pane click on the dropdown icon [▼], which is present at the end of the newly added **Handle 'OpenFile' Dialog** step to expand its properties. We will fill them in using the following values in order to cater to our situation:

- **FilePath** value: `C:\File Comparer Files\"Func-1_FileCompare_Equal_Successful_In1.trx" "Func-1_FileCompare_Equal_Successful_In2.trx"`

- **DialogTitle** value: `Upload Files`

- **HandleButton** value: `OPEN`

While the step is still selected, click on this icon [⬆] from the test toolbar to move it to the third position.

It is time to see our first automated test running. Click on the **Run** button in the **Quick Execution** ribbon and watch Test Studio playing back the recorded steps.

Editing tests

The next day you come to work and retrieve the latest build of the `File Comparer` application. Proud of your automation efforts, you open Test Studio then you hover over the `Func-1_FileCompare_Equal_Successful` test until the **Run** button appears, and then you click on it. Crash! An error has occurred!.

The execution was interrupted because the **Upload Files** button is now disabled. After you inquire more about the issue, the result is as follows. File Comparer now supports a default file comparison for the file found under the application's default folder. To specify the default folder a button has been added to the bottom of the window. Consequently, the application now operates in two modes, either by providing two files for comparison or by using the newly added feature. For this purpose, two radio buttons have been added to the main window. As it turns out out, in order to make our test pass again we need to check the radio button corresponding to the **New Files** option.

In order to simulate the preceding story, open the solution in Visual Studio and go to the MainWindow.xaml file. Click on the **Upload Files** button and comment the statement that gets highlighted in the **Design** panel by wrapping it in a comment tag as follows:

```
<!--<Button Content="Upload Files" Height="38"
HorizontalAlignment="Right" Margin="0,82,581,0" Name="uploadFilesBtn"
VerticalAlignment="Top" Width="170" Click="uploadFilesBtn_Click"
IsEnabled="True" Grid.ColumnSpan="2" />-->
```

Uncomment the block appearing in green as follows:

```
<Button Content="Upload Files" Height="38" HorizontalAlignment="Right"
Margin="0,82,581,0" Name="uploadFilesBtn" VerticalAlignment="Top"
Width="170" Click="uploadFilesBtn_Click" IsEnabled="False" />
            <Grid Height="56"   HorizontalAlignment="Left"
Margin="15,11,0,0" Name="grid1" VerticalAlignment="Top" Width="168"
Opacity="1" ShowGridLines="False" Visibility="Visible">
            <Grid.ColumnDefinitions>
                <ColumnDefinition Width="44*" />
                <ColumnDefinition Width="124*" />
            </Grid.ColumnDefinitions>
            <Label Content="New Files" Height="26"
HorizontalAlignment="Left" Margin="9,2,0,0" Name="label1"
VerticalAlignment="Top" Width="62" Visibility="Visible" Grid.
Column="1" />
            <Label Content="Default" Height="31"
HorizontalAlignment="Left" Margin="10,25,0,0" Name="label2"
VerticalAlignment="Top" Width="62" Grid.Column="1" />
            <RadioButton Content="newFilesRB" Height="17"
HorizontalAlignment="Left" Margin="28,9,0,0" Name="newFilesRBEdited"
VerticalAlignment="Top" Width="16" Checked="newFilesRB_Checked"
IsEnabled="True"/>
```

```
                    <RadioButton Content="defaultRB" Height="17"
    HorizontalAlignment="Left" Margin="28,31,0,0" Name="defaultRB"
    VerticalAlignment="Top" Width="16" Checked="defaultRB_Checked" />
                    </Grid>
```

From the `MainWindow.xaml.cs` file, uncomment the methods `newFilesRB_Checked` and `defaultRB_Checked` as follows and then build the applications to update solution's `.exe`:

```
private void newFilesRB_Checked(object sender, RoutedEventArgs e)
    {
        if ((bool)newFilesRBEdited.IsChecked)
            uploadFilesBtn.IsEnabled = true;
    }

    private void defaultRB_Checked(object sender, RoutedEvent
            Args e)
    {
        if ((bool)defaultRB.IsChecked)
            uploadFilesBtn.IsEnabled = false;

    }
```

Should we delete the automated test and start over again! Luckily, we can use Test Studio's add new steps feature to add functionality to an already created test by performing the following steps:

1. Right-click on the first step and choose **Record Next Step** from the context menu.

2. Since the radio button selection option comes after clicking on the **Compare Files** tab, we will choose the **After Selected** option.

3. To record the step, click on the **Record** button.

4. The latest application version is started and connected to the recorder toolbar, so all we need to do is select the radio button corresponding to the **New Files** option.

5. Close the application.

As a result, a step is added with the **Click on NewFilesRBRadiobutton** description.

Until now we have seen how to mechanically convert manual procedure steps into automated ones. So far so good, however, automation is usually left to run without human monitoring, anyhow watching them is a boring sight especially after the tenth test onwards!

Given that tests should be autonomous as much as possible, the method that we applied to automate the first test case has no way to verify the result displayed by the `File Comparer` application following the comparison of any two files. So let's see what Test Studio has to offer!

Translators and verification steps

In this section, we will see how to create evaluation points inside the automated tests in order to learn about the execution result without the need to actually watch the screen events.

This section explains how to add verification expressions around any UI element. Given that the portal to add any new automated step is through the **Record** button, click on it. After the application launches, enable the hover over highlighting feature

by clicking on the second icon in the recorder toolbar [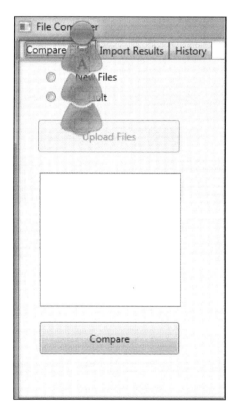] to enable the surface highlighting feature. As you position the mouse on top of the `File Comparer` text, a blue nub appears, which fans out into what is called translators.

Translators around the Comparer Files text

We are now operating with a powerful Test Studio feature, which is at the core of UI components recognition. The translators show us how the UI components are open for Test Studio to work with. There is a specific translator for each element, which knows all about its actions and properties. Let's take the example of the preceding screenshot, traversing the translators from inside out dictates the UI object hierarchy starting from the leaf all the way up to the root level. Each translator is represented by a fin and thus the three depicted fins correspond to the following chained objects:

- Tab text content, Compare Files
- Tab item
- Tab control

Clicking on any of the translators will invoke verification steps and other automation actions specific to the involved object. Using the highlighting feature over any other UI object reveals the entire hierarchy from that object to the root in the manner of fanned out translators just as we have seen in this example!

Many advantages are brought and we are seamlessly benefited in our automation by this feature. Firstly, during execution, the UI element is retrieved based on its properties, which are transparent to Test Studio rather than its coordinates with respect to the application window. This fact brings up the idea of reliability where, for example, finding a button on the screen with its static ID confirms to us that this will work no matter how many times we repeat the scripts, or no matter the location to which this button will be moved to. Secondly, generally in automation, the object recognition is the first obstacle preventing UI element actions from taking place. So, at least the translators eliminate the cause for such malfunctioning. Thirdly, it is given that any required verification, which happens to be related to a screen object, is based on the profound knowledge of the automation test tool with the UI controls' internals. Provided that, we appropriately choose the verification expressions, and verification reliability inside Test Studio also comes to our advantage.

Going back to our test, as you place the mouse pointer on top of the translators of the tab, the tool tips will display the type of the corresponding object in the hierarchy. So, note that not only the focused object is translated but also all the objects hierarchy ending by that object. Hover over the **Compare Files** tab, and click on the translator that has the tabItem tool tip. An Element Menu window appears as shown in the following screenshot:

Element menu

While we are not on it, let's look at all the available icons:

- Add To Project Elements

- Locate in DOM

- View 3D

- Build Verification

- Quick Tasks

- Drag & Drop

- Mouse Actions

- Image Verification

- Add a Manual Step

The Build Verification and Quick Tasks buttons relate to to verification steps.

Build Verification allows us to construct advanced verifications with composite expressions. A verification expression is composed from criteria and operators. The criteria are chosen from the UI element attributes whereas the operators are rendered based on the attributes' types. The attributes cover a wide area of UI elements content, visibility, UI rendering and styles, item selection, properties, and others.

Quick tasks, as its name suggests, has ready-made quick access to key tasks. Some of them are verification tasks also accessible through the advanced verification mode mentioned previously such as **Verify – element visibility is visible**. Others are **Wait** steps such as **Wait - element visibility is visible**. These steps will wait on the evaluation expression following the **Wait** keyword to be satisfied before resuming the execution such as waiting for a text field to become visible on the screen before typing inside it. From an automation design's perspective, these steps can be used for verifications prior to UI actions whereas the verification steps follow them later to indicate whether the execution status is pass or fail. Finally, the **Extract** steps are used to extract a property value for later usage such as **Extract – Element Visibility is collapsed**, which will make the `collapsed` value of the control's `visibility` property available for other test steps.

Inserting a verification step

Let's shift our attention to the expected results. According to our manual test, after comparing files a text will appear in the `File Comparer` application textbox as: **The files resulted in equal comparison!** This is what we need to insert as a final verification in the test by performing the following steps:

1. Right-click on any test step and choose **Record next step** and then **After Last Step** since post conditions' verifications should execute as the last step.

2. Click on **Record** to launch the recorder.

In order to get the expected result label, we should execute all the steps listed in the test case procedure. However, we do know that as we execute the UI actions the corresponding test steps will be added and therefore the existing automated steps will be doubled! In order to instruct Test Studio to disregard the steps that we are about to perform, click on the Pause button from the recorder toolbar and execute the manual test case procedure again until you get the result, and then perform the following steps:

1. Toggle on the hover over highlighting feature and place the mouse over the result label displayed in the textbox.

2. Click on the translator for TextBlock to open the element menu.

3. Click on the **Quick Tasks** button.

4. Double-click on the **Verify – verify text** content's match **'The files resulted in equal comparison'** to add it to the test steps.

5. Hover over the result label again and enable the TextBlock element menu again.

6. This time we will construct the text verification expression using the advanced verification feature by clicking on the Build Verification button.

7. In the **Sentence Verification Builder** window, click on the **Property** button.

8. For the added entry in the **Selected Sentences** section, open the **Property** combobox and scroll down to see the available properties.

9. Choose **Name** while keeping the operator and the value intact.

The verification expressions are depicted in the following screenshot:

A new verification step based on the Name property

Before we confirm our verification, it is a good practice to go over it and verify that the expressions are correct. At the beginning of each step a Validate icon [ ] is available to actually execute and verify the step against the current object state. Click on the Validate icon for the verification step.

Test Studio informs us that the evaluation is successful and a **Validation Passed** label is displayed. Change the operator to **NotEqual** and validate again.

The yielding result is failing with a **Validation Failed** label accompanied with an additional description about the cause. Let's revert the operator to **Equal**. Click on **OK**, toggle off the surface highlighting feature, and stop the recording by closing the application.

Let's look at these properties: textBlock and Name from another perspective. Open the File Comparer solution in Visual Studio and locate the properties of the text block's XAML tag, notice the Name property that appears in the following code:

```
<TextBlock Height="361" HorizontalAlignment="Left" Margin="248,7,0,0"
Name="comparisonResultTB" Text="" VerticalAlignment="Top" Width="491"
Opacity="3" Visibility="Visible" ToolTip="Execution results area" />
```

Hence, the verification expressions are another way of seeing the preceding object's attributes!

The final test steps are as follows:

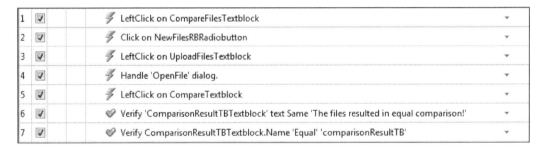

1	☑		⚡ LeftClick on CompareFilesTextblock	▼
2	☑		⚡ Click on NewFilesRBRadiobutton	▼
3	☑		⚡ LeftClick on UploadFilesTextblock	▼
4	☑		⚡ Handle 'OpenFile' dialog.	▼
5	☑		⚡ LeftClick on CompareTextblock	▼
6	☑		❤ Verify 'ComparisonResultTBTextblock' text Same 'The files resulted in equal comparison!'	▼
7	☑		❤ Verify ComparisonResultTBTextblock.Name 'Equal' 'comparisonResultTB'	▼

Steps of the Func-1_FileCompare_Equal_Successful test

Test Studio's built-in log

The overall test and step results can be directly accessed by clicking on the **View Log** link, which appears in the test toolbar after the test's execution completes.

Therefore, run the Func-1_FileCompare_Equal_Successful test and click on the **View Log** to open the **Test Log** window shown in the following screenshot:

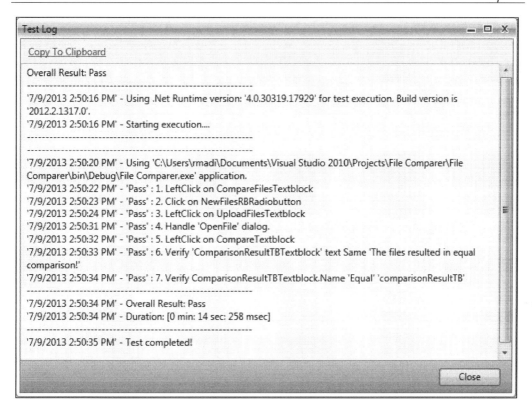

The log shows the following details:

- The overall status of the test cases which comes in the first line
- The components that were loaded initially comprising the executable application and the automated test class
- The execution status for each step comprising the test step's status, number, and description
- The overall test duration
- The time at which the test completed execution

Custom logging

So far we have seen how to record UI interactions, add verifications, execute the test, and access the automatically generated logfile. However, sometimes you might want to add some custom logging for many reasons, such as logging messages specific to the application's business rules. Hence, you want to collect this information while the test is running, log them in a file and access them afterwards. In this section, we will see how to create customized logfiles, which enable us to learn more about the execution flow.

In this example, we will permanently save the results of the verification steps in a customized log message. For this purpose, we are going to extend our steps with a coded step to log the result on a local file. As mentioned at the beginning of this chapter, a coded step extends the functionalities provided in the Test Studio IDE with others directly accessible from the underlying Telerik testing framework and .NET libraries. The code examples in this chapter are in .NET and C#.

From the **Add** ribbon, click on **Script Step** and choose **C#** from the combobox of the **Select Scripting language** window. A panel opens to allow editing of the routine name and signature. Edit the **Routine** and **Description** values to `Func1_FileCompare_Equal_Successful_LogPCVerification` and `Log post-condition verification` respectively. Click on the **View Class** button from the test steps toolbar and notice the method signature added to the underlying code class:

```
[CodedStep(@"Log post-condition verification")]
public void Func1_FileCompare_Equal_Successful_LogPCVerification()
    {


    }
```

Insert the following code inside the `Func1_FileCompare_Equal_Successful_LogPCVerification` test's body:

```
string data = "The files used in this test have the same content. The
actual behavior is: " + Applications.File_Comparerexe.File_Comparer.
ComparisonResultTBTextblock.Text + Environment.NewLine;

using (System.IO.FileStream fileStream = new System.
IO.FileStream(@"C:\File Comparer Files\Log.txt", System.IO.FileMode.
OpenOrCreate, System.IO.FileAccess.ReadWrite, System.IO.FileShare.
Read))
{
fileStream.Seek(0, System.IO.SeekOrigin.End);
byte[] buffer = new byte[data.Length];
buffer = Encoding.UTF8.GetBytes(data);
fileStream.Write(buffer, 0, buffer.Length);
fileStream.Close();
}
```

There are two things that we can denote in the preceding code snippet. The first thing is accessing code through the `File Comparer` result text block element, which holds the comparison result. The second thing is that while the test recording was in process, Test Studio was building a repository for the UI elements that were involved in the UI interaction. Each UI object participating in the definition of any test step under the `File Comparer` project has a unique entry under this element repository. Thus, elements for all tests belong to the same hierarchy and can be later on referred to from the test's code without having to redefine them. Some operations, for example editing element names are granted to the user in order to render the element's list more descriptively and comprehensively. This repository is refreshed as steps are recorded or deleted from the tests. The repository elements are listed inside the **Elements** pane as depicted in the following screenshot:

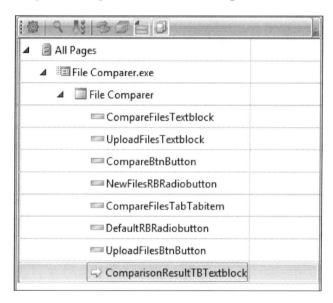

The Elements pane

The hierarchy starts with the **All Pages** node, which is going to be the parent for all the UI elements that are going to be eventually stored. Right under it comes the application node, `FileComparerexe`, and then the main WPF application window, **FileComparer**. The other UI objects that we dealt with so far are children of the **FileComparer** node including the result text block, which is in our current interest. It is the highlighted entry in the preceding screenshot and is called **ComparisonResultTBTextBlock**. We made use of this hierarchy in order to hold an instance of the text block object inside the coded step, where we accessed its text property.

In the preceding code, the line that initializes the `data` string takes care of referencing the `ComparisonResultTBTextBlock` object based on the hierarchy we just described.

The second thing that the code does is saving the content of the `data` string inside a file that is going to be created on your local `C:` under the `File Comparer Files` folder.

Make sure that the scripted step is the last one to execute and then click on the **Run** button. Open to see the content of the log text file, and verify that it contains the text displayed inside the textbox: **The files resulted in equal comparison!**

Code refactoring

Let's imagine that we have used a replica of the code discussed previously to insert other customized log messages inside this and other tests. One day, we realize that the requirements have suddenly changed and, in order to support text formatting, the destination log text file should be replaced with an HTML file. This change will then incur changes on each and every log method!

Therefore, since we are devoted to developing automated scripts with maintainability in mind and in order to avoid duplicate code inside our class, we will do some refactoring first.

Click on the **View Class** button on top of the steps. In the class code panel, add the following method signature before the last two closing brackets:

```
private void LogResult (string text)
{
}
```

Edit the implementation of the `Func1_FileCompare_Equal_Successful_LogPCVerification` and `LogResult` methods to get the following code:

```
public void Func1_FileCompare_Equal_Successful_LogPCVerification()
{
string data = "The files used in this test have the same content. The
actual behavior is: " + Applications.File_Comparerexe.File_Comparer.
ComparisonResultTBTextblock.Text + Environment.NewLine;
    LogResult(data);

}
private void LogResult (string text)
{
text = text +  Environment.NewLine;
```

```
using (System.IO.FileStream fileStream = new System.
IO.FileStream(@"C:\File Comparer Files\Log.txt", System.IO.FileMode.
OpenOrCreate, System.IO.FileAccess.ReadWrite, System.IO.FileShare.
Read))
        {
                fileStream.Seek(0, System.IO.SeekOrigin.End);
                byte[] buffer = new byte[text.Length];
                buffer = Encoding.UTF8.GetBytes(text);
                fileStream.Write(buffer, 0, buffer.Length);
                fileStream.Close();
        }
}
```

Instead of duplicating the same code that handles writing to the text file, we will call the `LogResult` method with the customized message passed in the `text` parameter.

The test case preconditions were satisfied early on when the two files with the same content were placed in the `File Comparer Files` folder under `C:`. Thus, for the time being, we will add manual steps to handle the preconditions, in case they were not executed, which is as follows:

1. Click on the **More** button from the **Add** ribbon and choose **Manual Step**.

2. Edit the added step description to instruct the tester, who is going to carry out the manual preconditions, what is supposed to be done.

3. Move the step upward to the very beginning of the test and add a step to the log that the preconditions have been manually executed.

Automated test case design

The following is a suggested model to use when designing a test for automation. It mainly aims at covering the different components of a test case during automation in addition to providing useful logging where needed:

- Preconditions' execution consists of executing necessary steps to guarantee an initial correct state of the test

- Preconditions logging takes care of logging the precondition status

- UI element verifications validates whether the UI elements are in a proper state before using them

- UI element actions consist of performing the actions on the UI elements, as appearing in the test case

- UI element action result logging takes care of logging the outcome of executing the operations against the UI elements in case they fail

- The third and fourth features are repeated

- Postcondition verification validates whether the expected application behavior after executing the test case steps is met

- Postcondition logging takes care of logging the outcome of the postcondition verification step

Properly automating a test to handle itself suggests a better understanding of a test case structure. So what is a typical test case? It starts by executing certain preconditions. The kind of preconditions could be related to creating initial data, resetting a form, navigating to a window, rolling back database to a previous state, or many others. Once we have passed this, we can log a custom message and then move to the subsequent steps contained in the test case procedure. These steps are somewhat identical in nature as we will see.

Generally procedure steps are going to perform an operation on a UI element. However, this operation should not be done blindly because it hides in itself some implicit preconditions depending on the test case context. These preconditions should be verified and logged in case if they fail. We are going to call the preconditions on a UI element with the corresponding UI action and custom message, a subprocedure block.

Lastly after a test finishes executing the procedure, we want it to make sure that the system is in the state that we want it to be in. These are the postconditions against which a final verification step should be added. The outcome of this verification will have the greatest weight in calculating the overall execution result of the test.

The following diagram illustrates an automated test case structure:

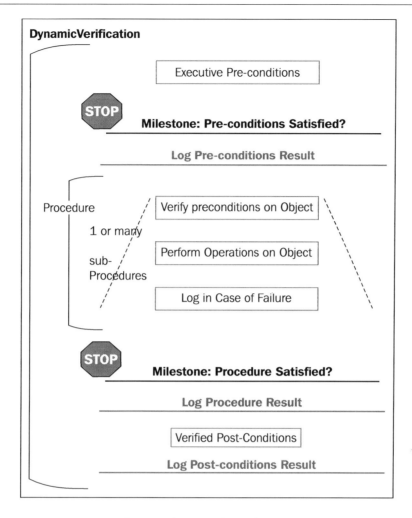

DynamicVerification

Executive Pre-conditions

STOP **Milestone: Pre-conditions Satisfied?**

Log Pre-conditions Result

Procedure

1 or many

sub-
Procedures

Verify preconditions on Object

Perform Operations on Object

Log in Case of Failure

STOP **Milestone: Procedure Satisfied?**

Log Procedure Result

Verified Post-Conditions

Log Post-conditions Result

Automated test case design diagram

Following our preceding definition of a subprocedure block, a procedure is made of one or more subprocedure blocks. The diagram also has the notion of a **Milestone**. A **Milestone** is the point at which continuing the test case execution, in case the preceding block has failed, is useless. The first one appears after the preconditions. For example, if the preconditions responsible for logging into the application under test were not satisfied, what is the point of continuing the test case? Exactly, there is no point so we are fine to break the test here.

Similarly, if the UI element did not pass the verification criteria to ascertain that the object is entitled of receiving the UI actions required by the test cases, it is needless to continue the execution. Thus, again, we can break the execution at this point because recursively a subprocedure block is in itself a precondition for the next subprocedure block.

Provided that all the subprocedure blocks have successfully executed, we encounter another milestone. This milestone is generally important in automation, since if the execution has passed it and the overall result is failing, the chances that a bug resides in the application under test is high.

The milestones we have seen so far are static in a sense that we expect them to be important execution turning points. Other dynamic events could alter the execution flow and they constitute important verifications as well. We are talking about any unexpected situation such as an unplanned window that could disrupt UI actions.

Recognizing the critical test case milestones is not enough, so collecting information at these points is very useful. Therefore, logging can be used here to save results in a filesystem.

The main benefits that we get from this approach or any an adapted form of it are conformity and readability. When all of our functional tests map to one design they are, firstly, easily understood by new testers reading them where they also represent an automation guide for future manual test cases waiting on the automation list. Secondly, interpreting the log result becomes much easier since it will contain the critical information captured at the test case joints, knowing that the tests are in themselves smarter in interpreting the situations.

According to the preceding model, handling unexpected windows is still not covered in the test that we automated. Unexpected windows could pop up sporadically during execution. Their causes are unpredictable, otherwise we would target specific steps to handle them. They emerge because of a changing condition in the system state, which wasn't the same at the time of recording. Such unexpected windows will remove focus from the application windows, where the actions can no longer be applied on the UI elements and therefore interrupt the execution. What we practically want in such a situation is to gracefully solve it by closing the unexpected window, logging an error, and continuing the execution of the tests.

The Telerik team offers us a handy solution to the preceding problem. It can be found on their Test Studio online documentation page `http://www.telerik.com/automated-testing-tools/support/documentation/user-guide/code-samples/general/log-error-dialogs.aspx`.

Using tests as steps

Test Studio offers a powerful feature that allows using tests as steps. During execution, the inserted test is called to execute within the context of a parent test. As we will see, tests as steps also enhance test maintainability. In this section, we will continue with automating the second test-to-pass on the list, which deals with the default file comparison feature. The manual test steps of test case two are as follows:

1. Prerequisites:
    1. Map the default application folder
    2. Check whether the folder contains identical XML files

2. Procedure:
    1. Click on the **Compare Files** tab.
    2. Click on the **Default** radio button.   ❧
    3. Click on the **Compare** button.

3. The expected result displayed is: **The files resulted in equal comparison!**

Before we can automate the test procedure we have to execute the preconditions section. We could execute them manually, similar to what we did in the previous test; however, this has a disadvantage. The preconditions are frequently shared between test cases. In our case, every scenario that involves a default comparison needs to make sure that the application already has a mapped folder. Now suppose for a second that in our agile environment, a requirement change comes to alter the way the application folder mapping is currently done. This change would require us to modify every automated test that uses this folder mapping feature and thus would cost a considerable time. It is true that changes always happen; however, it is essential that we anticipate such situations and design our tests in a loosely coupled way. This means not to tie scenarios and conditions which are not inherently related.

Having said that, let's automate the preconditions instead of executing them manually. So start by creating a separate WPF test and name it `Func-3_FileCompare_MapFolder_Successful`. Perform the following steps:

1. Click on the **Set Path** button.
2. In the window that pops up enter: `C:\File Comparer Files`.
3. Click on **OK**.

Notice that, during the recording when the **Set Path** window pops up, another recorder toolbar is attached to it. Therefore, we need to use the latter recorder in case we want to add UI element verification steps on the objects that the invoked window holds.

Also notice how the objects underneath the invoked window along with the window itself are added as children to the **All Pages** node, as shown in the following screenshot:

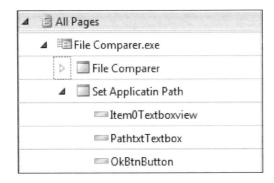

File Comparer UI objects inside the Elements pane

The resulting steps are shown in the following screenshot:

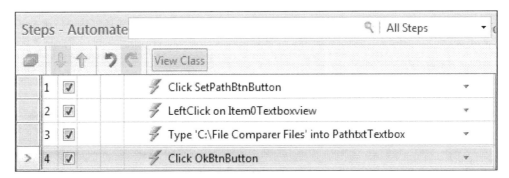

Steps of the Func-3_FileCompare_MapFolder_Successful test

Now let's record the default folder comparison. Create a WPF test and name it `Func-2_FileCompare_DefaultComparison_Successful`.

From the **Add** ribbon, click on the **Test as Step** option. A window pops up displaying all the available tests inside our project. Choose `Func-3_FileCompare_MapFolder_Successful` and click on **Select**. We can now add the other steps from our procedure, which will result in the test steps depicted in the following screenshot:

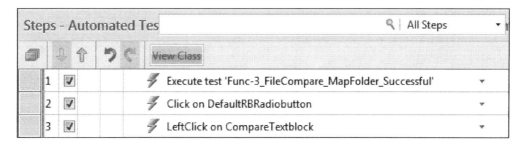

Steps of the Func-2_FileCompare_DefaultComparison_Successful test

Run the test and notice how the first step will call the map folder test to execute within the context of the parent.

Logical branching

Our test is passing but is not efficient because we are mapping the application's default folder regardless of whether the folder is actually already mapped. We can use the clue that the application gives us in this matter. If no folder is mapped, a label with the **Click Browse button to map the default application folder** content is displayed to the left of the **Set Path** button; whereas if the folder is mapped, the label changes to **Click Browse button to remap the default application folder**. Therefore, we need to introduce logical branching, which saves us from the trouble of mapping the default folder again in case it is already mapped. The time savings may seem small, but they will mount up when this test case has to execute 100 times overnight.

The branching will go as follows. If the displayed label is equivalent to c**lick Set Path button to map the default application folder**, execute preconditions and jump to procedures, else log that the preconditions are satisfied and continue with procedures. The expression label **Click Set Path button to map the default application folder** is the equivalent of a verification step inside Test Studio. For this purpose perform the following steps:

1. Add an **if...else** construct located in the **Logical** combobox at the top of the **Add** ribbon.

2. Click on the **Record** button.

3. Use the surface highlighting feature on the target label to build the expression depicted in the following screenshot.

4. Close the application.

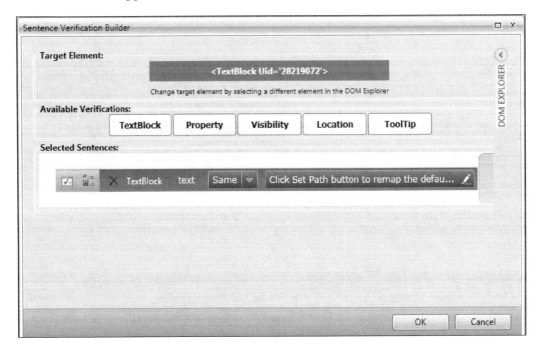

Verification on text content in verification builder

As any `if-else` block, Test Studio's `if-else` block comprises two elements: the condition and execution block for each branch. The condition corresponds to any verification step whereas the execution block can be a combination of any automated steps.

In order to combine a verification step to the condition of the `If` statement, hover over the **If (...) THEN** step and click on the **Choose Verification** button as follows:

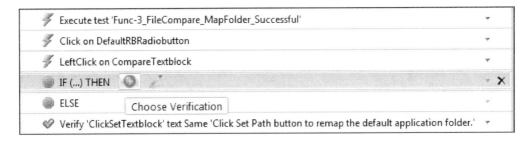

Choosing verification for an If statement

Once clicked, all verification steps will have the same button enabled inside the column preceding the text description, but this time in the select verification mode. Click on the **Verification** button for the verification step shown in the preceding screenshot. Both the steps are merged and this verification step now constitutes the condition statement where the description is changed to: **IF (Verify 'ClickSetTextblock' text Same 'Click Set Path button to remap the default application folder.') THEN**. To complete the branching condition, drag the **Execute test 'Func-3_FileCompare_MapFolder_Successful'** step and hold it on top of the **ELSE** step until the **Drop inside ELSE** tool tip appears and then release it. Move the **if-else** block to the beginning of the test and add a log script step as follows:

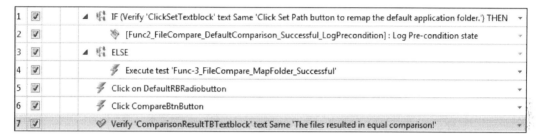

Steps of the Func-2_FileCompare_DefaultComparison_Successful test

Let's run to see the changes. Since the default folder is already mapped, the IF step implementation will not execute.

Extracting values to variables

The purpose of the following test case is to discover the automation of another more complex WPF UI elements such as comboboxes and grids and to see how we can retain some values shared in variables between the test steps.

The comparison method has a byproduct, which is keeping a history of the compared files in terms of filenames, comparison results, and dates of comparison. The **History** tab of the application allows the retrieval of the comparisons based on the date chosen from the combobox. The **Choose date from** label instructs the user from where to select the date to filter on. The date combobox is populated with the dates during which there have been file comparisons. The user has the option to choose between a certain date and all dates. The manual steps of test case three are as follows:

1. The precondition is that at least one comparison should be made
2. Procedure:
   1. Click on the **History** tab.
   2. Choose the date **2/8/2012** from the combobox.

3. The expected result is:
   - ○ The data grid displays three rows
   - ○ All the data grid entries have 2/8/2012 in their Date column

4. Executing this test case requires some implicit steps as follows:
   1. Click on the **History** tab.
   2. Select date value **2/8/2012** from the combobox.
   3. Store value **2/8/2012** for later use
   4. Store the number of rows in the grid.
   5. For every row inside the grid, verify that the Date column contains the stored value 2/8/2012.

Test Studio has a built-in mechanism to save a UI element's property value, accessible throughout all the test steps. The feature was previously mentioned very briefly when listing the **Quick Tasks** section of the **Element** menu, and it's called **Extract**.

In step 4, we use this feature to temporarily save the value chosen from the combobox. This value is used for comparing the date column content of the data grid. In step 5, we also need to extract the number of rows that the data grid currently holds in order to specify the loop's upper bound for step 6.

The automation procedure goes as follows:

1. Create a WPF test.
2. Rename to Func-4_History_SingleDate_Successful.
3. Click on the **Record** button.
4. Execute steps 1 to 3 from the detailed procedure.
5. For step 4, click on the hover over highlighting button and place the mouse on top of the date combobox.
6. This time we will click on the translator with the ComboBox tool tip.
7. In the **Element** menu, click on **Quick Tasks** and choose **Extract- selected item has index '1'**.
8. Use the hover over highlighting feature to extract another value related to the data grid, so from **Quick Tasks** choose **Extract-dataGrid row count equals '3'**.
9. Stop the recording.

Let us first expand the properties for step 4 as follows:

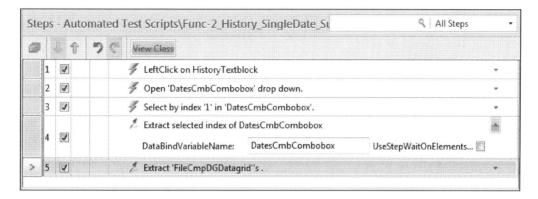

Steps of the Func-4_History_SingleDate_Successful test

`DataBindVariableName` contains the variable name where the selected value, 2/8/2012 is stored. Similarly, for step 5, **Extract 'FileCmpDGDatagrid"s**, the `Value` property holds the number of rows loaded inside the grid.

Until this point, we created the steps to interact with the UI in addition to those that will hold the necessary key values. It is time to implement the post condition verification. For this purpose, add a loop construct from the **Logical** button of the **Add** ribbon. Expand the added step and edit the value for the `Count` property to 3, since the expected result states that three data grid rows will appear. Add a script step with a target to validate a single value of the date column at a specific row. Drag the latter step and place it inside the loop block. Edit the underlying method for the script test:

```
[CodedStep(@"Verify cell has date")]
public void Func4_History_SingleDate_Successful_VerifyDate()
{
int selectedIndex = Int32.Parse(GetExtractedValue("DatesCmbCombobox").
ToString());

ArtOfTest.WebAii.Controls.Xaml.Wpf.ComboBoxItem cbItem =(Applications.
File_Comparerexe.File_Comparer.DatesCmbCombobox.Items[selectedIndex]);

string rowContent = Applications.File_Comparerexe.File_Comparer.
FileCmpDGDatagrid.GridData[gridIndex][0].ToString();

bool pass = rowContent.Contains(cbItem.Text);
gridIndex++;
```

```
Log.WriteLine("Selected text is : " + cbItem.Text);
Log.WriteLine("Data Grid row number is : " + GetExtractedValue("FileCm
pDGDatagrid").ToString());
Log.WriteLine("Cell Verification result: " + pass );
}
```

The first instruction stores the selected value extracted from the combobox. The `GetExtractedValue` method takes as a parameter the name of the variable that was bound in the **Extract selected index of DatesCmbCombobox** step.

The second instruction creates an object to hold reference to the item of the date combobox. The text property of the combobox item represents the value of the selected date that will be used for comparison.

The third instruction reads the value of a data grid row, which is the index number that is going to be read from the variable called `gridIndex`. This variable is instantiated at the beginning of the class as a global variable. Each time the condition of the loop is satisfied and the loop block is traversed, `gridIndex` is incremented by one.

The fourth instruction evaluates the row content against the selected value and saves the result in the `pass` Boolean variable.

Finally, the code calls the `Writeline` method. This method belongs to the `BaseWebAiiTest` class. We can call this method at any time to log information to Test Studio's executing logfile.

Initialize the `gridIndex` variable at the beginning of the class code as follows:

```
public int gridIndex;
```

Run this test and click on the **View Log** button from the steps toolbar. The following screenshot shows the content of the test case execution log:

```
Overall Result: Pass
--------------------------------------------------------
'2/15/2013 11:57:15 AM' - Using .Net Runtime version: '4.0.30319.296' for test execution. Build version is '2012.2.1317.0'.
'2/15/2013 11:57:15 AM' - Starting execution....
'2/15/2013 11:57:18 AM' - Detected custom code in test. Locating test assembly: FileComparer.Test.dll.
'2/15/2013 11:57:18 AM' - Assembly Found: C:\Users\rmadi\Documents\Test Studio Projects\FileComparer.Test\bin\FileComparer.Test.dll
'2/15/2013 11:57:18 AM' - Loading code class: 'FileComparer_Test.Func_2_History_SingleDate_Successful'.
--------------------------------------------------------
--------------------------------------------------------
'2/15/2013 11:57:18 AM' - Using 'C:\Users\rmadi\Documents\Visual Studio 2010\Projects\Test Studio\Test Studio\bin\Debug\File Comparer.exe' application.
'2/15/2013 11:57:20 AM' - 'Pass' : 1. LeftClick on HistoryTextblock
'2/15/2013 11:57:21 AM' - 'Pass' : 2. Open 'DatesCmbCombobox' drop down.
'2/15/2013 11:57:23 AM' - 'Pass' : 3. Select by index '1' in 'DatesCmbCombobox'.
'2/15/2013 11:57:24 AM' - 'Pass' : 4. Extract selected index of DatesCmbCombobox
'2/15/2013 11:57:25 AM' - 'Pass' : 5. Extract 'FileCmpDGDatagrid''s .
'2/15/2013 11:57:25 AM' - LOG: Selected text is : 2/8/2013
'2/15/2013 11:57:25 AM' - LOG: Data Grid row number is : 3
'2/15/2013 11:57:25 AM' - LOG: Cell Verification result: True
'2/15/2013 11:57:25 AM' - 'Pass' : 6. LOOP (3) Times
Logical step encountered. Executing branch => LOOP (3) Times, Iteration (1):
--------------------------------------------------------
'2/15/2013 11:57:25 AM' - Using 'C:\Users\rmadi\Documents\Visual Studio 2010\Projects\Test Studio\Test Studio\bin\Debug\File Comparer.exe' application.
'2/15/2013 11:57:25 AM' - 'Pass' : 7. [Func2_History_SingleDate_Successful_VerifyDate] : Verify cell has date

'2/15/2013 11:57:26 AM' - LOG: Selected text is : 2/8/2013
'2/15/2013 11:57:26 AM' - LOG: Data Grid row number is : 3
'2/15/2013 11:57:26 AM' - LOG: Cell Verification result: True
'2/15/2013 11:57:26 AM' - 'Pass' : 6. LOOP (3) Times
Logical step encountered. Executing branch => LOOP (3) Times, Iteration (2):
--------------------------------------------------------
'2/15/2013 11:57:26 AM' - Using 'C:\Users\rmadi\Documents\Visual Studio 2010\Projects\Test Studio\Test Studio\bin\Debug\File Comparer.exe' application.
'2/15/2013 11:57:26 AM' - 'Pass' : 7. [Func2_History_SingleDate_Successful_VerifyDate] : Verify cell has date

'2/15/2013 11:57:26 AM' - LOG: Selected text is : 2/8/2013
'2/15/2013 11:57:26 AM' - LOG: Data Grid row number is : 3
'2/15/2013 11:57:26 AM' - LOG: Cell Verification result: True
'2/15/2013 11:57:26 AM' - 'Pass' : 6. LOOP (3) Times
Logical step encountered. Executing branch => LOOP (3) Times, Iteration (3):
--------------------------------------------------------
'2/15/2013 11:57:26 AM' - Using 'C:\Users\rmadi\Documents\Visual Studio 2010\Projects\Test Studio\Test Studio\bin\Debug\File Comparer.exe' application.
'2/15/2013 11:57:26 AM' - 'Pass' : 7. [Func2_History_SingleDate_Successful_VerifyDate] : Verify cell has date

--------------------------------------------------------
'2/15/2013 11:57:26 AM' - Overall Result: Pass
'2/15/2013 11:57:26 AM' - Duration: [0 min: 7 sec: 599 msec]
--------------------------------------------------------
'2/15/2013 11:57:26 AM' - Test completed!
```

The Func-4_History_SingleDate_Successful log

For each iteration, the log shows the following:

- The **Logical step encountered** expression that holds the iteration number at the end

- The comparison status after the **Cell verification result** expression

Additional automation tweaks in the code

What we have learned so far in this chapter is enough to get us started with automating any functional test case. We have seen how to analyze and breakdown a test case, how to start the process by recording a stepwise test, how to change the direct flow of execution by using logical branching constructs, and how to customize our steps in code where needed.

The following two paragraphs discuss some additional capabilities that we can implement in our test solution. These examples revolve around handy code tweaks that fit in the context of every automated test.

Normally, it is very useful to automatically add specific handling after executing the last step. The testing framework enables this flexibility by implementing the `OnAfterTestCompleted` method for the `BaseWebAiiTest` class.

Each test has an object of type `TestResult`, which holds the test execution's overall result in a property called `Result`. To dynamically log the value of this property, open the `Func-1_FileCompare_Equal_Successful` test and add the following code after clicking on the **View Class** button:

```
public override void OnAfterTestCompleted(TestResult result)
    {
if(result.Result ==
ArtOfTest.Common.Design.ResultType.Fail)
            Log.WriteLine("The overall result is fail.");
        else
            Log.WriteLine("The overall result is pass.");

        base.OnAfterTestCompleted(result);
    }
```

Run the test and notice how the built-in Test Studio log now contains our message describing the overall test result as follows: LOG: The overall result is pass.

This type of example is useful to be adopted in the overall automation strategy, since it is effortless and helpful in the test result analysis. It can also be applied for overriding the other built-in Test Studio framework methods such as `OnBeforeTestStarted()`.

Another similar practical functionality is related to logging. The test case design model talks about the importance of logging custom messages at certain key points. More important is their availability after the test has been executed. Just think how convenient would it be if each time we make a call to the `Writeline` method, Test Studio is smart enough to replicate the message also in our logfile! In fact, this can be done if we subscribe to the log event.

Each test has a reference to a `Manager` instance responsible for managing the test execution. So, the `Manager` instance is the observer and actor that handles the main flow of the tests by being the intermediary between the framework and the application instance.

The `Log` class of the test `Manager` object has an event called `LogWrite`. We will subscribe to this event by attaching a custom method to the event handler of the `LogWrite` method. In order for this operation to precede any `Writeline` method call inside the automated test, insert a coded step at the very beginning of the test binding to the `Log` event:

```
[CodedStep(@"Attach To Log Event")]
public void AttachToLogEvent()
{
this.Manager.Log.LogWrite += new EventHandler<LogWriteEventArgs>(LogH
andler);
}
```

Create a custom method called `LogHandler`, which will take care of calling the `LogResult` method and eventually log the messages to the physical logfile. Therefore, enable the class code by clicking on the **View Class** button and then add the following method:

```
public void LogHandler(object sender, LogWriteEventArgs e)
{
    LogResult("Text is: " + e.Message + Environment.NewLine);
}
```

The class does not compile until we add a reference to the event argument's namespaces inside the `using` block as follows:

```
using ArtOfTest.WebAii.EventsArgs;
```

Run the test again and then open our custom log and notice how an additional line is added to the log: `Text is: [Trace] : The overall result is pass.`

You might also want to implement those functionalities in separate tests and call them using the **Test as Step** feature. The purpose of such refactoring is to avoid having the code repeated in each automated test.

Functional random keyword-driven tests

All the test cases so far address one type of operation in the application. We have seen how to compare two new files, map the application folder, filter on history, and compare using the default feature. On the whole, we have four main operations. Generally, the user will rarely start the application to perform one operation and then close it. Furthermore, we might want to automate the requirement's use cases that describe user scenarios composed from many operations. The two use cases are illustrated as follows:

- Use case one:

    1. Open an application.
    2. Map the application folder.
    3. Compare files using the default feature.
    4. Check history.

- Use case two:

    1. Open an application.
    2. Compare files using the new files option.
    3. Check history.
    4. Map the application folder.

These use cases are nothing but a rearrangement of the basic application functions we listed previously. They also form keyword sets where each numbered bullet maps to one `File Comparer` function. So we are going to address each function as an atomic unit. Any unique combination of the atomic functions could serve as an automated keyword test and this is exactly what we are going to see in this section.

Let us picture for a second the keyword test structure. The first task is to generate the sequence of random keywords. The second task is to loop over this sequence and call the corresponding tests.

The three new notions that we need to take care of are as follows:

- Introducing the random factor in the test
- Saving the randomly generated output into a structure that will be visible to all the test steps
- Dynamically calling the random tests

Theoretically, we are going to map each basic test from the atomic functions to an integer that starts with 0 and increases by 1 as follows:

- Value 0 represents `Func-1_FileCompare_Equal_Successful`
- Value 1 represents `Func-2_FileCompare_DefaultComparison_Successful`
- Value 2 represents `Func-3_FileCompare_MapFolder_Successful`
- Value 3 represents `Func-4_History_SingleDate_Successful`

Create a folder under the `Automated Test Scripts` folder called `Keyword Tests` and then add a WPF test called `KeywordTests_Random`. Open the test and add a coded step called to it and then edit the underlying function's name to `KeywordTests_Random_KeywordTestManager`. This function will, as its name suggests, produce the random number sequence. In the following way, we would have catered the preceding first notion:

```
[CodedStep(@"Generating random number sequence")]
        public void KeywordTests_Random_KeywordTestManager()
        {
            Random random = new Random();
    InfoHolder.tests = new int[]{random.Next(3), random.Next(3), random.
Next(3), random.Next(3)};
        }
```

The generated number sequence is saved in the `InfoHolder.tests` structure. This structure is accessible inside all the subsequent coded steps since it will be created in a static class, meaning that there will be only one instance of it throughout the life span of the test. Add this code to the beginning of the class right before the `public class KeywordTests_Random` statement:

```
public static class InfoHolder
        {
            public static int[] tests = new int[4];
            public static int testNum;
        }
```

The `tests` integer array will be populated with the random numbers generated when the `KeywordTests_Random_KeywordTestManager` method executes. The `testNum` variable is going to hold the index of the loop that will dynamically call the tests based on their mapped number. At any time, this variable is strictly less than four. With this, we have implemented the second notion.

From the **Logical** button of the **Add** ribbon, add a loop after the **[CodedStep(@"Generating random number sequence")]** test step and set the value of its count to 4. Finally, add the following coded step, which is responsible for dynamically calling the keyword test and dragging it inside the loop block:

```
[CodedStep(@"Execute Random Test")]
        public void KeywordTest_RandomTest()
        {

            string testToExecute = String.Empty;

            switch (InfoHolder.tests[InfoHolder.testNum])
                {
                case 0:
                    testToExecute = "Automated Test Scripts\\
Functional Tests\\Func-1_FileCompare_Equal_Successful.tstest";
                    break;
                case 1:
                    testToExecute = "Automated Test Scripts\\
Functional Tests\\Func-2_FileCompare_DefaultComparison_Successful.
tstest";
                    break;
                case 2:
                    testToExecute = "Automated Test Scripts\\
Functional Tests\\Func-3_FileCompare_MapFolder_Successful.tstest";
                        break;
                case 3:
                    testToExecute = "Automated Test Scripts\\
Functional Tests\\Func-4_History_SingleDate_Successful.tstest";
                        break;
                }

InfoHolder.testNum++;

            Log.WriteLine("Executing Keyword test");
            this.ExecuteTest(testToExecute);

        }
```

The `switch case` block assigns the physical file path to the `testToExecute` variable, based on the theoretical numbering of the atomic functions. This variable is the parameter of the built-in Test Studio framework's `Execute` method. When it executes, it will call the automated test, which will run under the `KeywordTests_ Random` scope. With this step we have finalized the preceding three notions.

Set up the test, so that it launches the `File Comparer` application using the **Configure** button and then run it.

Test execution settings and debugging

Rarely is an automated test going to execute successfully from the first hit, and if it does, we should be careful for logical hidden problems. The automation errors fall under the following three categories:

- The first category holds the syntax problems that do not allow your code to compile in the first place and therefore the test cannot be executed.

- The second category holds problems dormant inside the automated steps and will not come out until execution. We can list, for example, problems in recognizing an object at runtime.

- The third category holds problems that are not even necessarily revealed during runtime. These are the most malicious types of problems, since the symptoms are not as flagrant as the preceding two categories.

In the third case, the test executes normally until the person verifying the automation becomes suspicious about the executed test result. The root cause of such problems is an embedded logical error in the translation of the manual test. At this point, it is good to remember that automation in itself is building logic on top of the application under test, which leaves an open field for the testers' mistakes in addition to those of the developers'. This fact dwells on one of the automation overheads.

In this section, we are going to see examples based on the preceding categories and how we can address them inside Test Studio.

Syntax errors

In the class code of the `Func-1_FileCompare_Equal_Successful` test, it would have been more convenient to simply name the `LogResult` method as `Log`. Let's do it and see what happens. The method signature now looks as follows:

```
private void Log (string result)
```

Click on the **Run** button. The test does not start and a compilation error is displayed as shown in the following screenshot. All the steps are not executed as shown in the following screenshot:

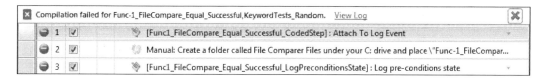

The Func-1_FileCompare_Equal_Successful test with compilation error

Click on the **View Log** link. The error description will be displayed as follows:

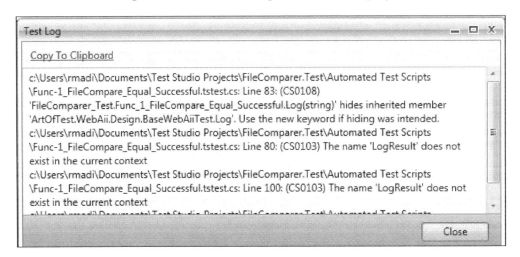

Error log of the Func-1_FileCompare_Equal_Successful test

Technically, the error is telling us that the `BaseWebAiiTest Log` class already has a function with the same signature. Instead, if our aim is to really let our definition to execute the `Log` method, we should add the `new` keyword.

We have just seen an example of the syntax error and how to collect details about it. We will next look into the execution errors.

Execution errors

Execution errors appear after passing the syntax verification stage, and as mentioned previously, they will be shown during test execution runtime. The first clue we get about these errors is that their corresponding step in the logfile starts with `Fail`. Could the cause be a bug inside our script? Or, could it be a failing verification or a blocked UI operation? To resolve it, we need to dig in more into this problem by means of the collected information made available to us at the level of the failing step.

Let us first introduce the error in the test. We can try something like preventing the object recognition on the screen such as the **New Files** radio button. To do so we will first explore how Test Studio finds it during execution. Click on the **NewFilesRBRadiobutton** option from the **Element** pane to display its properties inside the **Properties** pane. Locate the **FindLogic** property:

```
[Name 'Exact' newFilesRB] AND [XamlTag 'Exact' radiobutton]
```

We deduce that Test Studio is recognizing the element by the value `newFilesRB` found in the `Name` property. Let's break this! In Visual Studio, edit the `Xaml` tag corresponding to the **New Files** radio button to the following:

```
<RadioButton Content="newFilesRB" Height="17"
HorizontalAlignment="Left" Margin="28,9,0,0" Name="newFilesRBEdited"
VerticalAlignment="Top" Width="16" Checked="newFilesRB_Checked"
IsEnabled="True"/>
```

Before compiling the solution, edit all the occurrences of the `newFilesRB` word to `newFilesRBEdited` inside the `MainWindow.xaml.cs` file.

Now run your test inside Test Studio. Did you get an error?

Step 4 fails because the radio button cannot be found. Of course, we quickly made this conclusion because we intentionally implanted the error. However, in cases where it wasn't intentional, to inquire more about the error, double-click on the red and white cross to open the **Step Failure Details** window:

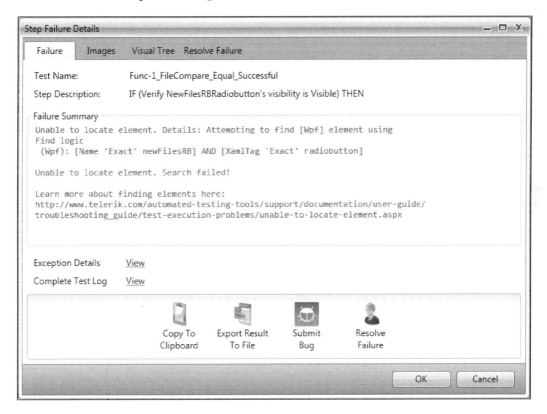

Troubleshooting failure in the Step Failure Details window

The first tab called **Failure** summarizes the problem. It says that Test Studio is unable to locate the radio button. Exception trace is found in the **View** link of the **Exception Details** window.

The second tab called **Images** is the equivalent visual interpretation of the failure summary. It holds the application snapshots taken at the time of execution.

The third tab called **Visual Tree** is a snapshot of the object hierarchy at the time of error. It provides additional information, in case the problem is not clearly visible in the UI. If we expand the hierarchy tree to the tab control, we can spot the problem which caused the radio button's recognition to fail:

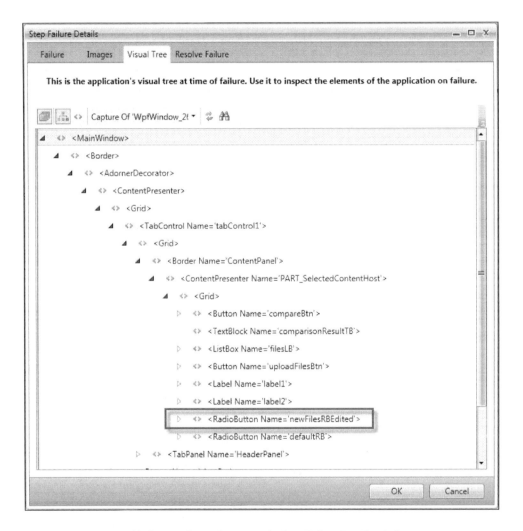

Troubleshooting hierarchy tree in the Step Failure Details window

Finally, the fourth tab called **Resolve Failure** is there to guide you on the solution for it.

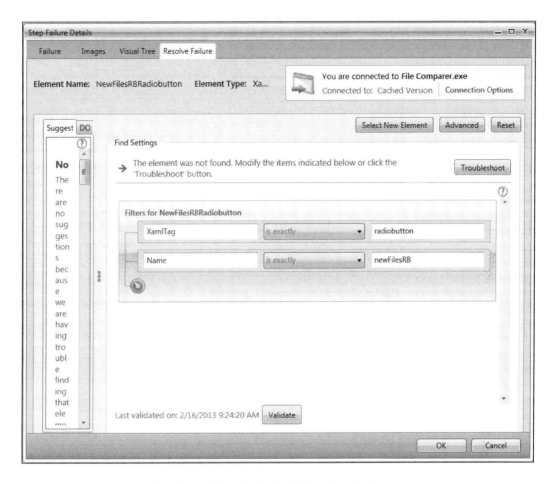

Resolving failures in the Step Failure Details window

Now we will see how interesting the tab is. To the left is displayed the element tree that we have seen in the tab before. It is worth noting that it reflects the object model for the application during the last run and not during the time of recording. To the right, the **Find Settings** pane directs us to the root of our problem described in the label highlighted in red before the **Troubleshoot** button. You can imagine how much debugging time we have just saved. Not only that, it also gives the opportunity to fix the problem right away. In the **Filters for NewFilesRBRadion** section, update the **Name** operator to **contains** and click on the **Validate** button. The label now changes to: **Great! We are able to find your element using the settings below**.

If we decide that the failure problem does not have to do anything with our test and we wish to escalate the issue to the developer's team, we need to go back to the **Failure** tab and click on the **Submit Bug** button. We could either export the result to an Excel file or submit it to any of the two integrated systems, which are: TeamPulse Server and Team Foundation Server. Click on **OK**. A window pops up and asks us whether we want to update the find logic of this element for all its occurrences in the test.

Selecting steps after editing element find expression

Select everything as depicted in the preceding screenshot and click on **Select**.

Note that to configure the TeamPulse Server and Team Foundation Server, go to the **Project** tab and click on the **Bug Tracking** button from the **Extensions** ribbon.

Execution settings

The automation of our test cases is complete. What remains now are some settings related to the execution. For example, deselecting the box that is tied to a test step will cause the latter to be ignored during execution and Test Studio's execution log will hold an entry describing it.

During the automation of our manual test cases, we decide that the test case execution does not have to be interrupted upon slight nonbusiness failures. In order to instruct Test Studio not to break execution at a certain step, enable the Continue on Failure option as shown in the following screenshot. The green arrow indicates that now this step is not going to abort the execution in case it fails.

Toggle the Continue on Failure setting on the attach to event step

Suppose that in the `Func-1_FileCompare_Equal_Successful` test, after clicking on the **Compare** button, the file comparison is taking some time to finish, and suppose this time is greater than what the verification on the result text block is giving us, then in this case, Test Studio will wait on the label inside the text block for 10 seconds before it marks it as failing and proceed to the next step.

Perform the following steps to avoid such problems:

1. Add **While(...)THEN** from the **Logical** button of the **Add** ribbon and drop it right after the step that clicks on the **Compare** button.

2. Add to the loop body an execution delay from the **More** combobox menu of the **Add** ribbon and edit the value of its `WaitTime` property to `1000` milliseconds.

3. Finally, create a verification condition that is passing for any displayed text and add it to the loop body. So, during execution as long as no text is displayed in text block, the execution will be delayed by 1 second.

All of this is offered out of the box in Test Studio. Either add a **Wait** step from the text block's quick tasks or expand the **"Verify 'ComparisonResultTBTextblock' text Same' The files resulted in equal comparison!'"** step's properties and select the **UseStepWaitOnElments** box. This feature overrides the default waiting time, which is 10 seconds. In the **Properties** panel, increment the **WaitOnElementsTimeOut** box to `20000` as shown in the following screenshot:

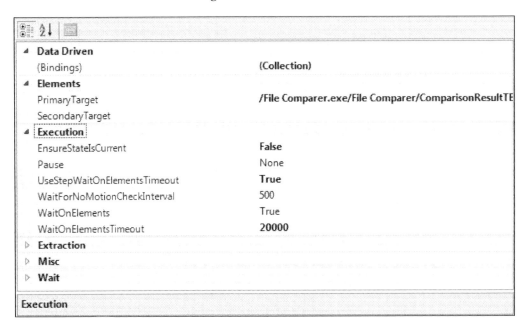

Wait step properties

Debugging

Debugging is our means to pause the test execution when a certain situation needs evaluation. The outcome could be identifying and removing flaws from the application or just learning more about that situation.

We have two ways to pause the execution inside Test Studio. Either by toggling a breakpoint or inserting an inspection point. When a breakpoint is reached, the execution will pause and a **Debug** window will be displayed through which we can explore the available information.

In the `Func-1_FileCompare_Equal_Successful` test, in the **Verify 'ComparisonResultTBTextblock' text Same 'The files resulted in equal compare**

son!' step, change the value of the extended property, `Value` to `The files resulted in unequal comparison!` in order to enforce a failure. Let us toggle a breakpoint and the Continue on Failure option as follows:

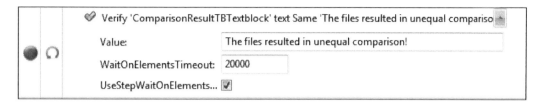

Inserting a debug breakpoint

 Had there not been a step to log the result after this comparison, it would not be recommended to toggle the Continue on Failure option. Instead, we want the test to halt execution after this failure. This option is enabled to demonstrate all debug functionalities.

Run the test. The execution breaks before executing the step to debug. We are going to shift our attention to the debug window, which appears to the lower-right corner of the screen:

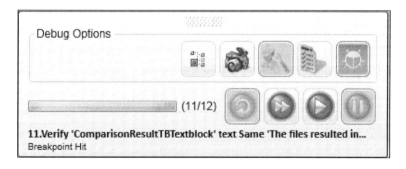

The Debug window

Click on the first button to open the DOM Explorer window, which, as we have seen previously, shows us the tree of UI elements of the application. If we expand the hierarchy until we reach the corresponding tag of the textbox, we notice that it contains the text value currently showing on the application as follows:

```
<textblock Name="comparisonResultTB" Uid="66471715">The files resulted
in equal comparison!</textblock>
```

Let us go through all the available debug functionalities in order to further troubleshoot and solve the error:

1. Close the **DOM Explorer** window and click on Execute one step at a time icon [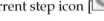].

2. The step at which we stopped will now be executed.

3. Click on the Diagnose currently failed step icon [].

4. The outcome is the **Sentence Verification Builder** window (which we are already familiar with), so edit the value of the verification sentence to **The files resulted in equal comparison!** and then click **OK**.

5. In the **Debug** window, click on the Re-run current step icon [].

6. Click on the Execute one step at a time icon again.

7. Let's open the execution log by clicking on the View Execution log icon [] and notice how the comparison is now passing.

8. Close the **Execution Log** window.

9. Click on the Continue Execution icon [] to finish the test.

10. The **Apply test updates** window prompts us to make a decision regarding the changes we have done; since they did solve the problem so we will click on **Apply** and then on the **Close** button.

Also, inspection points are useful in case we want to pause the execution and examine the DOM hierarchy. They are added from the **More** button of the **Add** ribbon. When the execution pauses, the **DOM Explorer** window pops up so we can drill down in its hierarchy.

Integration with Visual Studio

When Test Studio is installed, a plugin is added to Visual Studio, this section will exhibit how the previewed features in this chapter are integrated inside the Visual Studio IDE. The examples are also based on the File Comparer application.

Inside Visual Studio, the `File Comparer` solution contains only one WPF project. Test Studio projects can be added as any other project type by right-clicking on the solution node and choosing **Add** and then clicking on **New Project**. In the **Add New Project** window, select **Telerik** from the list displayed in the **Installed Templates** pane. Then expand the node and click on **Test**. Make sure that the **.Net Framework 4** option is selected from the combobox at the top of the window:

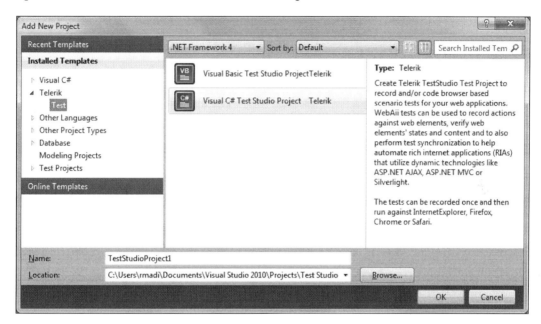

Creating a new project inside Visual Studio

Two templates are displayed to give the user a choice to develop the application either in Visual Basic or C#. We are going to continue our examples in C#, so select **Visual C# Test Studio Project** and name the project `VSFileComparer.Test`.

By default, a web test is created, but since our application is in WPF we are going to add a WPF test. Right-click on the `VSFileComparer.Test` node and choose **Add** and then **New Test**. From the **Add new Test** window, choose the Test Studio WPF Test template and rename the test to `VS_MapFolder_Successful.tstest`. A Test Studio WPF test file is added under the test project and it opens directly in the edit mode.

The test toolbar enables all the functionalities that we have already covered in addition to the feature supported to convert all steps to code.

Similar to the Test Studio's standalone version, set the configuration settings for the test by clicking on the **Configure WPF Application** button and browsing for the File Comparer.exe file.

Let's record the test first inside Visual Studio. Record the Func-3_FileCompare_ MapFolder_Successful test by clicking on the **Set Path** button, entering C:\File Comparer Files inside the text field for the **Set Path** window, and then clicking on **OK**.

Click on the Convert all steps to code icon depicted in the following screenshot:

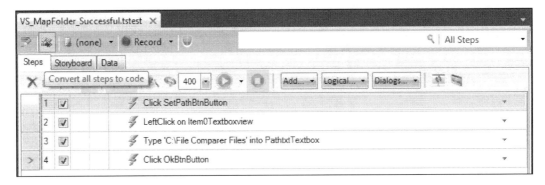

The Convert all steps to code button in the test toolbar

A window pops up and prompts us to choose the unit tests frameworks that we want the test steps to get converted to. Choose **MSTest** that corresponds to a Visual Studio unit test and click on **OK**. In the VS_MapFolder_SuccessfulUnitTest.cs file that we created, the VS_MapFolder_Successful method corresponds to the recorded test and is marked with the [TestMethod()] method attribute. The method's body contains the translation of the recorded steps into Test Studio's automation framework calls.

We don't need to create the tests all over again because this integration enables us to import existing tests. Right-click on the `VSFile Comparer.Test` node and choose **Add** and then **Existing Item**. Browse to the Test Studio's `File Comparer.Test` solution inside the Test Studio's `Projects` directory, then to the `Functional Test` folder, and select all the files after displaying files with all extensions. These tests are now accessible from the Test Studio's `File Comparer.Test` solution inside Visual Studio. In order to successfully compile these tests, add the using `VSFileComparer.Test` inside the `.cs` files.

Open the **Test** menu, click on **Windows** and then **Test View** to open the window with the Visual Studio tests. Right-click on the `VS_Map_Sucessful` test and choose **Run Selection**:

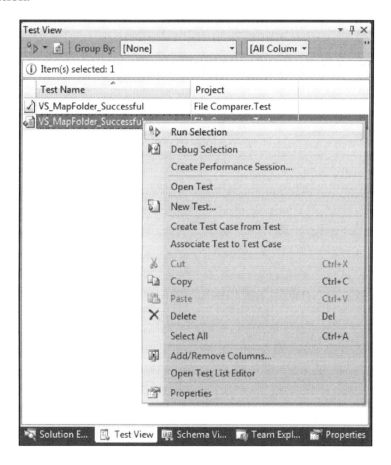

Running the tests of Visual Studio

After the test executes, enable the **Test Results** window through the **Windows** option of the **Test** menu again and verify the execution results:

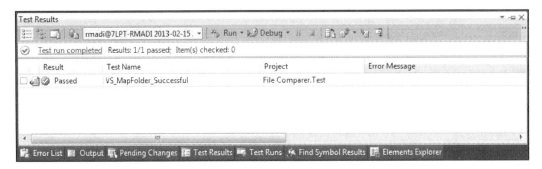

Test Results in Visual Studio

Summary

In response to the problem raised at the beginning, this chapter summarized the creation of automated function tests inside Test Studio. We have seen how to create a stepwise test using the record and playback feature. Once the steps became ready, Test Studio's quick tasks feature was tackled to firstly insert verification on the UI elements properties at key points inside the test. Test Studio offers handy features accessible from the elements menu, out of which we have just mentioned quick tasks and used some others throughout the chapter such as adding elements to the repository, building advanced verifications, and viewing the DOM hierarchy.

In order to endow the tests with some logical reasoning, constructs such as `if` statements and loops were used to control the execution of the tests based on suitable conditions. In case where more advanced logic was necessary, direct calls to the test framework library were inserted among the steps in order to implement more complex scenarios.

This chapter has also introduced the keyword-driven architecture and implemented a test which randomly calls major functionalities available in `File Comparer`.

The next step in automation was to verify the validity of the automated tests. Hence, the developed scripts were executed where afterwards the resulting built-in log was examined. As it is the case in real life, some of the steps succeed and others fail. Troubleshooting the failures is essential in identifying the root cause problem. Identification and resolution of a problem is guided in Test Studio, thanks to some integrated helpful features contained in the step failure details window.

All of the preceding information was part of the standalone version of Test Studio. The last section of this chapter covers, the Visual Studio plug-in edition, which offers the same automation features in addition to an extremely helpful functionality. This functionality is the ability to instantly convert all recorded steps into an equivalent code based on several test frameworks.

The next chapter will extend on this knowledge to demonstrate how to create data-driven tests and bind their input and verification steps to various data sources.

3
Data-driven Tests

The second meeting took place a few days later. The overall feedback was positive since the automation has started off faster than expected. Bugs were being caught faster and more code was tested. The remainder of the meeting revolved around the new features that were recently added. After giving a few demos to the client, the data preparation for the application was the subject of most of the meetings. Setting up initial data for the application was hardly controllable, since the operation is allowed from different portals; and thus, data integrity was threatened. This is very critical not to mention the time and effort needed to establish it. Thus, the client highly preferred to incorporate data creation in the application.

From the development point of view, the new component that will cater to this feature consists of a form that accepts user inputs and commits them to the database after validating their integrity. This is where your mind couldn't but digress to count the huge time needed to develop a test case for every data combination in the test data that will be generated!

Accordingly, in this chapter, you will learn how to avoid the explosive growth of your automated test scripts by:

- Creating data-driven tests using MS Excel, CSV, and XML file data sources
- Creating data-driven tests using databases sources
- Binding UI elements to data columns
- Creating embedded data-driven tests

Data-driven testing architecture

The fulfilment of a testing deficiency is that, in any testing environment at the origin of adopting automation the testing environment is driven by the need to satisfy the augmenting speculations and concerns revolving around whether or not a project is going to be delivered at the agreed date, and if so, whether or not enough confidence exists to go live. One obsession starts to outweigh choices and trade-offs, which is cost. This is when numbers related to time versus cost, quality versus time, usability versus functionality, resources versus budget start inflicting decisions. Test automation is brought in to balance risks, costs, and quality. With fewer budgeting resources, automation increases your code coverage and uncovers the bugs early within less time. These facts flatten cost, as it is needless to speak about the importance of fixing bugs early in the development life cycle. After automation is adopted, the general atmosphere is happy, the ROI increases, and you start welcoming new tests to make the most out of it.

The first set of worries fades out only to be replaced by new and new ones. How to respond to change, how to maintain the scripts, or how to avoid repetitive work in automation? So you start getting creative in the implementation. Ideas and designs might slightly differ from each other, but eventually they are all oriented towards allowing your automated solution to grow in a healthy way while dealing with your worries. Practically, this is where you get to create a backend library for your tests or test framework extensions. The solution disciplines the effect of requirement changes, enforces maintainability, and promotes components' reusability.

But again, just as you manage to sort out your second problem a third one arises, and this time, it is data scalability. How to add more scripts that test the same functionality with varied input by spending the least effort? You notice that the solution is as follows: the greater number of test cases you cover with less number of scripts, the more the automation is beneficial for your problem.

So, you sit around for a bit and observe your tests. You conclude that your test is doing the same XYZ operations for the various inputs, and you realize that the steps to work around this problem are as follows:

- Separate the functionality from the input
- Allow the input to grow in a dynamic way with respect to your tests
- Make your scripts operable regardless of the input source

There you start remodelling your test scripts and end up styling them in what is called as a data-driven architecture. This process of evolving from normal test recording to data-driven is self imposing in the sense that it calls upon itself with the rising of testing needs.

Throughout the coming examples in this chapter, Test Studio capabilities are going to be exhibited to demonstrate how it contributes in solving the data scalability problem described earlier. Each test is going to start with simple recorded steps having one integrated set of inputs and will end up in a parameterized test reading its input from external data sources.

Binding tests to data sources

In this section, we will explore through examples, how to redirect reading test input using various data sources. Five scenarios are going to be used to explore configuring datafiles and connections, assigning connections to automated tests, and binding test variables to data source columns. Each scenario is going to connect to one out of the four data source types which are: Excel file, XML file, built-in Test Studio table, and SQL database.

Excel data source binding

The `File Comparer` application has a tab called **File Info**, which we have not discovered yet. **File Info** is used to create application data. In our case, these are documents with their corresponding metadata. After opening the **File Info** tab of the `File Comparer` application, the user enters text in the two input fields which are **File Name** and **Creator Name**. In addition, there exists a checkbox called **Reviewed**, that explains about the readiness of the file to a concerned party, who also needs to be aware whether the file was examined previously. A combobox is also available to specify **File Extension** from a list of predefined extensions. Finally, a slider is used to determine the amount of **Effort** that was employed to finish the document. The **Effort** scale changes from one to 10. The following screenshot illustrates the aforementioned fields:

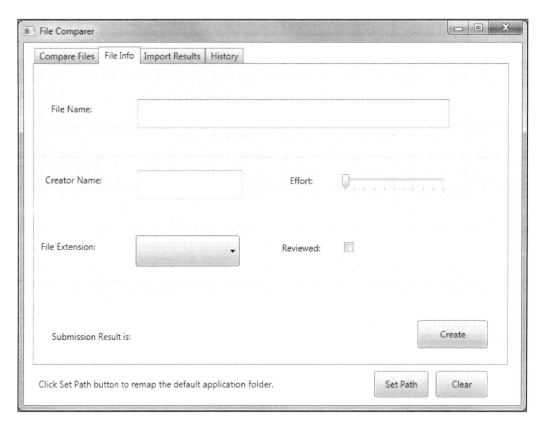

The File Info tab

As you can see there are a variety of UI elements, where each has its own specific set of UI actions. What is common between them is that these actions will not have their values hardcoded inside them, but rather they are going to be fed at runtime. The mechanism through which a UI element receives its data is by binding one of its properties to a column from a data source.

The following example demonstrates the usage of MS Excel sheets as data sources. In general, the following preparatory steps need to be performed before binding the UI element's properties to columns:

1. Automate the scenario to be converted to a data-driven test.
2. Design the data source.
3. Set up the data source connection.
4. Bind the test to the data source.

In this chapter, a folder called `Data-Driven Tests` contains all the data-driven examples. Hence, perform the following steps:

1. From the **Project** tab, create a folder under the `Automated Test Scripts` folder.
2. Rename it to `Data-Driven Tests`.
3. From the context menu of the newly created folder, add a test based on the `WPF Test` template.
4. Rename the test to `Func-6_FileInfo_Create_Successful`.

This test is supposed to enter values in various form fields to create a sample document and then submit it. Double-click on the `Func-6_FileInfo_Create_Successful` test and then perform the following steps:

1. Configure it by clicking on the **Configure** button to connect to the `File Comparer` executable file.
2. Clicking on the **Recorder** button, create test steps to simulate the creation of a file, with the following sample file metadata:
   ○ **File Name**: `File Comparer Test Plan Document`
   ○ **Creator Name**: `Mark Moore`
   ○ **File Extension**: **XML**
   ○ **Effort**: `3`
   ○ **Reviewed**: `true`

3. After completing the list and while the recording is still going on, click on the **Create** button.

4. After the submission, the result appears.

5. Click on **OK**.

Record the operations for the preceding sample file metadata, and then add a few verification steps on controls availability results in the final test, as shown in the following screenshot:

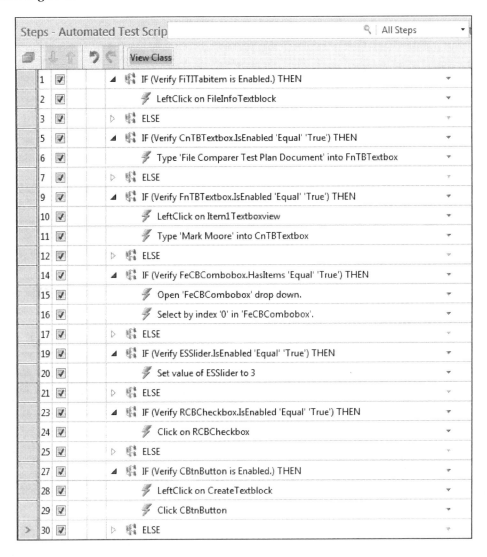

Steps of the Func-6_FileInfo_Create_Successful test

Importing an Excel data source

As we are done with step one, now step two is to decide on the design of an Excel table. The two restrictions to be kept in mind while designing Excel tables are that, firstly, a test can only be read from one Excel sheet, and secondly, the data-driven feature of Test Studio works by binding a UI element property to a single column inside the Excel table. The most straightforward design to adopt is to create a column for each UI control in the preceding test case, and name it after the control preceding the label present on the **File Info** tab in order to preserve test readability. The Excel workbook called `FileInfo_DS` is based on this design, which is depicted in the following screenshot:

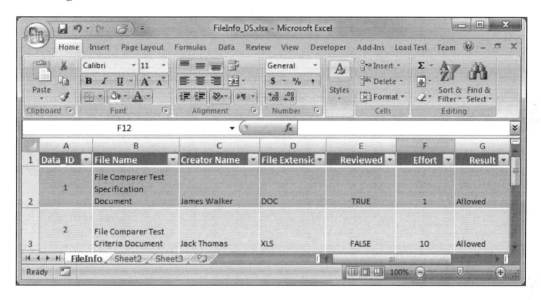

The Excel data source

If you look at the screenshot carefully, you will realize that in addition to the columns that are related to the controls, there exist two others called `Data_ID` and `Result`, which are located in the first and last positions respectively. The first column, `Data_ID` is solely there as test case metadata. This column holds an identifier denoting one row in the data-driven test, which means it references one test case data combination set. And in automation terms, it holds the input for one iteration. As for the second column, it holds the expected submission status with respect to input integrity and we will also see that it will be used to validate the execution status for each iteration. Once the test is bound to the data source, Test Studio is going to execute the recorded steps for the `Func-6_FileInfo_Create_Successful` test a fixed number of times (equal to the number of rows contained in the table) while running the test. Hence, the execution will stop only after covering all the rows of data inside the table.

It's time to transform this workbook into a test data source. Inside Test Studio, a data source is created at the project level, so it belongs to the same scope, and therefore any of the underlying tests can bind to it. Make sure that the `FileInfo_DS` workbook inside the `File Comparer Files` folder is present in your `C:`. Click on the **Project** tab outlined in red in the following screenshot, and from the **Data Sources** ribbon, click on **Add** and then select the **Excel File** option designated with an arrow:

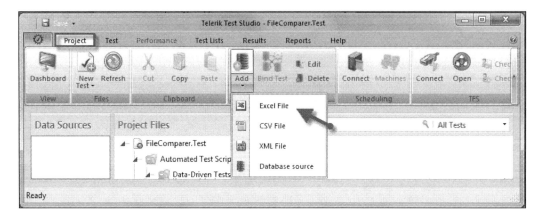

Importing the Excel data source

In the invoked **Create new data source** window:

1. Click on the ellipsis button to browse for the `FileInfo_DS` directory.

2. Select the workbook.

3. Click on **OK**.

By default, after creation, the data source is named after the filename, and an entry for it is added to the **Data Sources** pane of the **Project** tab, which we are currently on.

This would be enough to import an Excel data source to Test Studio and with that we have completed the third step.

The fourth step requires binding the test to `FileInfo_DS`. From the **Project Files** pane, right-click on the `Func-6_FileInfo_Create_Successful` test and choose **Data Bind**, as shown in the following screenshot:

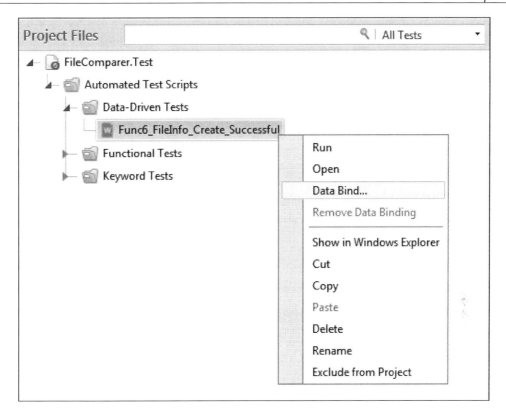

Binding a test data

In the **Bind test to data source** window that opens, choose `FileInfo_DS - (excel)` from the **Data Selection** combobox for the data source we have just created. On selecting this option, the **Select Table** combobox is populated with all the worksheets that the workbook currently holds. Each worksheet is equivalent to a data table, so select `FileInfo$`, which holds the data table for the `File Info` test.

The following screenshot shows the **Preview Data** grid, which is a snapshot of the content in the first sheet and encloses the data rows that the test will execute:

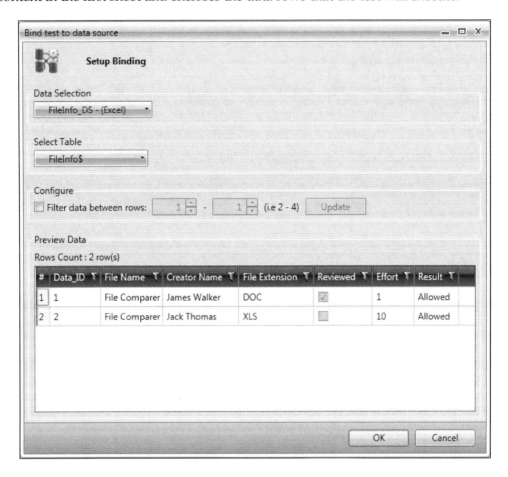

Choosing data table from the Excel data source

Binding to a data source also offers the option to filter out some rows based on ranges using the **Configure** section. By selecting the checkbox and specifying the numbers representing the start and end boundaries of the rows we want to include, we can instruct Test Studio to run the test only for the filtered rows. Since we want the test case to run for both the rows in the sheet, we will just click on **OK**.

Binding columns to Excel columns

Now double-click on the test to open it for editing. We are going to perform binding for the following UI elements:

- The **File Name** text field
- The **Creator Name** text field
- The **Reviewed** checkbox
- The **File Extension** combobox
- The **Effort** slider

Binding to controls is straightforward and simple. It only requires assigning the element property to a column contained inside the `FileInfo_DS` data source. Starting with the **File Name** text field, click on step with description Type '**File Comparer Test Plan Document' into FnTBTextbox** to display its properties in the **Properties** pane. From the **Data Driven** section in the properties window, locate the **Bindings** property. This property is responsible for specifying the column header of the data for this step. As shown in the following screenshot, click on the arrow to open the binding window and select the **File Name** value from the `TypedText` property, and then click on the **Set** button:

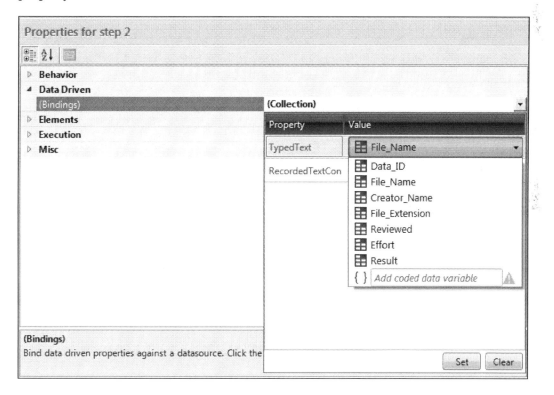

Binding free input fields to data column

The `DataDriven: [$(File Name)]` text is appended to the step description as follows:

> ⚡ Type 'File Comparer test plan document' into FnTBTextbox - DataDriven: [$(File_Name)] ▾

Step description for data bound columns

Repeat the same procedures to bind step with the **Type 'Mark Moore' into CnTBTextbox - DataDriven: [$(Creator Name)]** description to the **Creator Name** Excel column.

Binding the **Reviewed** checkbox consists of the same steps, however, the property name is `IsChecked` instead of `TypedText`. This is because the UI operation is different from that of text fields, where it consists of a select action rather than a typing action. So perform binding actions as shown in the following screenshot:

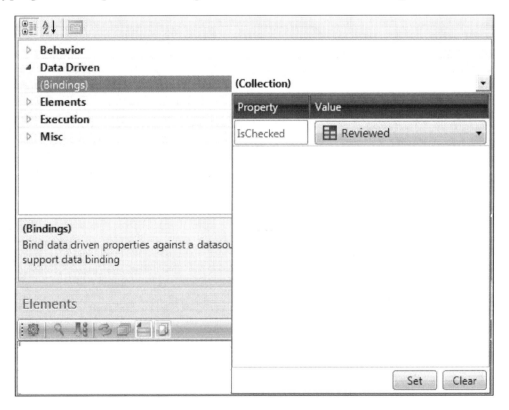

Binding checkboxes to data columns

So far, we have attached the data columns and the checkbox to the text fields, we are still left with the combobox and the slider.

There are two ways to perform a selection from a combobox, either with the item index or with the item text. Hence, selecting the XML value for the file extension can be either instructed through the item index, 0, knowing that it's loaded as the first position in the drop-down list, or the item text XML of the combobox. The following screenshot shows two properties of the combobox, SelectedIndex and SelectedText, which respectively map to the aforementioned index and text values. During execution, only the bound property is going to be used to perform selection for the **File Extension** option.

From the **Properties** pane, locate the **Bindings** property for the **'Select by index '0' in 'FeCBCombobox'.** step. As expected, when trying to bind the Excel column to the **File Extension** value, we have the choice between two values: SelectedIndex or SelectedText. Since the FileInfo_DS sheet has the values of the File Extension column filled with text, we will choose mapping the SelectedText property as shown in the following screenshot:

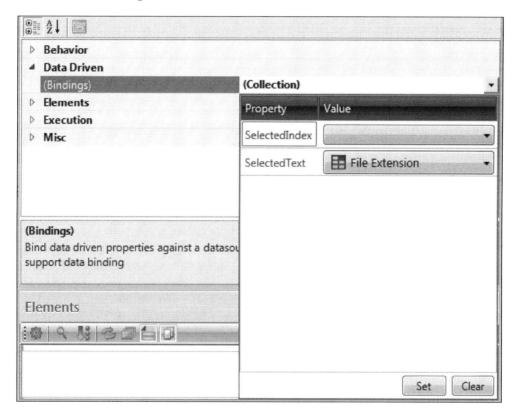

Binding a combobox to a data column

Expand properties for this step, by double-clicking on it. Notice that here selecting the value of the combobox can also be done either through the index or text. Change the SelectMode property to ByText as shown in the following screenshot:

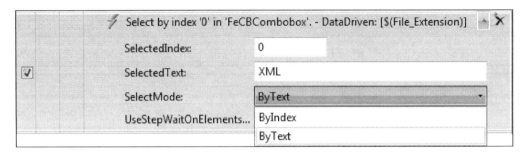

Changing the SelectMode combobox

Finally, for the slider control, map the Effort Excel column to the slider's Value property.

Data-driven verification

With this, we would have finished binding all the UI operations to data input read from the Excel data source. Save your test and click on the **Run** button to start its execution. The test is going to iterate twice by invoking the UI actions with the two data rows.

The test case procedure automation and data are completed but not the output verification resulting from file creation. This is where the Result column from the Excel workbook comes into picture.

The file creation has two expected values based on the form input. After clicking on the **Create** button, the data on the form is validated, where none of the **File Name**, **Creator Name**, and **File Extension** field values are empty, the creation is allowed. In the Excel workbook, the value of the Result column for this scenario is allowed, signifying that we are expecting the notification message to contain this word. If one of the preceding condition is violated, an error will be displayed to the user mentioning that the creation was not successful with details on the offending UI element. Instead, the value of the Result column is going to hold the name of the UI control that has failed the submission.

As you might have guessed, after submission, we must add a step to compare the **Result** label against the current `Result` data row value. To implement it, perform the following steps:

1. Click on the **Record** button and pause the recording from the recorder toolbar.

2. Click on the **File Info** tab.

3. Toggle the hover over the highlighted button to add the verification step as shown in the screenshot.

4. Stop the recording.

5. Change the verification step's position such that it executes before the last step which performs a single left-click on the **OK** button.

6. Right-click this step and choose **Customize step in code** from the context menu.

Adding verification steps on submission of result

The method body contains a call to the `ArtOfTest Assert` method, which belongs to the `UnitTesting` namespace. This method is responsible for performing the following activities:

- Evaluating the screen text by calling the `String.Compare` method as its first parameter.
- Setting the step `Result` status to either `pass` or `fail`.

Hence, in the current verification example, if at runtime the displayed value for the submission result is equal to **Submission result is:**, the `Assert` method will evaluate to `true`, which means that the step has passed.

The `String.Compare` method in its turn takes three parameters:

- The string to be evaluated
- The expected string value
- The string to log in case if the verification fails

The string to be evaluated represents, in our case, the content of the result submission label in the **File Info** tab whose value is retrieved at runtime.

The second is the expected value for this label. Currently, it is the label that was present during recording, which is equal to **Submission Result is:**.

The third is the type of operator with which the `String.Compare` method is going to perform the comparison. It is still `ArtOfTest.Common.StringCompareType.Same`.

When the test executes in the data-driven mode, the combination of values passed in each row in the table is going to trigger different results. Hence, we want the verification to be performed against the value passed in the `Result` column that we have previously added to the table. For example, if for the data row values we expect the submission to be allowed, the `Result` column is going to contain the word `allowed` and the verification should take place on the word `allowed`. Whereas if for the data row values we expect the submission to fail due to missing text in the **Creator Name** field, the `Result` column will contain the name of the creator and the verification should take place on the word `Creator Name`.

Ultimately, we are going to replace the parameter for the `String.Compare` method's expected result with the value extracted from the `Result` column's currently executing row. Also, we will update the search operator from `Same` to `Contains` since the comparison logic has been modified to look for the `Result` column keyword inside the submission result label.

For all the preceding reasons, update the code by making the following replacements:

1. Occurrence of `ArtOfTest.Common.StringCompareType.Same` with `ArtOfTest.Common.StringCompareType.Contains`

2. Occurrence of `"Submission Result is: "` with `this.Data["Result"].ToString()`

3. Occurrence of the word `Same` with `contains` in the third parameter of the `Assert` method to comply with the new comparison logic

The final method body will look like this:

```
Assert.IsFalse
    (
Assert.IsFalse
((ArtOfTest.Common.CompareUtils.StringCompare (Applications.
File_Comparerexe.File_Comparer.SubmissionTextblock.Text, this.
Data["Result"].ToString(), ArtOfTest.Common.StringCompareType.
Contains) == false),
string.Format("Verify \'SubmissionTextblock\' text Contains \'" +
this.Data["Result"].ToString() + "\' failed. Actual v" +
"alue \'{0}\'", Applications.File_Comparerexe.
File_Comparer.SubmissionTextblock.Text));
```

Edit the verification step description to `[Func6_FileInfo_Create_Successful_Verify] : Verify 'SubmissionTextblock' text` by clicking on the icon [ ], enabled after hovering over the step.

Before we run the test, notice how the code uses `this.Data["Result"]`, a special Test Studio feature to access the data row at runtime through code. During execution, the test holds a `Data` object. This object represents the data table, which the test is bound to. In order to access a specific column in the table, the `Data` object takes the column name `Result` as the parameter. As for the row number, it corresponds to the iteration number of the executing step.

There still exists a problem in the test case. If the verification step does not logically pass, for example, if the submission should be allowed but the verification step yields to false, the click on the **OK** button step will not execute, and in this case the application will not enable the UI elements on the form. Therefore, when the next row executes, all the attempts to set the UI controls will fail and subsequently the remaining iterations of the test case. This behavior masks the actual results that should have resulted after executing the row with a proper initial state.

In real life, when this data-driven automated test executes overnight, we ought to gracefully handle logical errors by logging them and enabling the execution for the next row to resume. To cater for such handling, enable the Continue on Failure option for the verification step, as shown in the following screenshot:

Enable Continue on Failure on the test step

Click on the **Run** button to execute the test. The test execution log contains all test iterations appended to each other. The following screenshot shows the log snippet for the third iteration around the verification step for the last data row:

Execution log showing the verification step's result

Data-driven verification binding

The data binding feature in Test Studio does not stop at the steps that perform UI operations; this means that not only steps similar to setting text in free input fields can be bound to the data-driven output, but verification steps can also be bound. `Func-6_FileInfo_Create_Successful` is a suitable example that can be used to demonstrate the data-driven verification.

For this purpose, we will data bind the verification step for the submission result as follows:

1. Disable the coded step added in the previous example by deselecting its corresponding checkbox.

2. Build a verification step using the advanced verification over the **Submission Result is** label, as shown in the following screenshot.

3. Click on the step to enable its properties and then from the **Binding** property of the **Data Driven** section inside the **Properties** pane, specify **Result** from the **Value** combobox.

4. Click on the **Set** button.

5. Place the verification step under the disabled step.

6. Run the test.

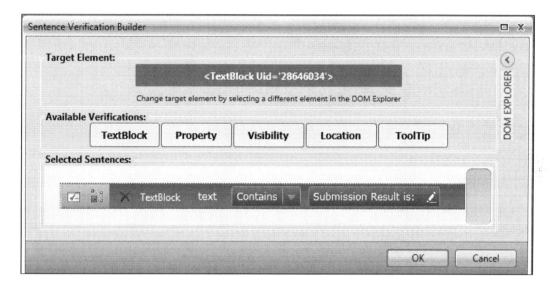

Verification result on the submission label

The passing status for all steps indicates that the Result column values were effectively changed with each iteration of the test.

CSV data binding

CSV files can also be used inside Test Studio as a data-driven source. Using them necessitates the same procedure steps seen with Excel binding.

Editing a data source

The data source does not contain data to test the application behavior upon an illegal input. For example, what happens if we set the slider to its lower boundary 0? Of course, since we only wish that any document would cost us zero effort, the system should reject such value. Consequently, if we were to insert an additional row inside the data table, changes on the Excel workbook from outside Test Studio are not going to be reflected during the test execution. Thus, to edit the data source, go to the **Project** tab, select the `FileInfo_DS` entry from the **Data Sources** panel, and click on **Edit** from the **Data Sources** ribbon. In the Excel sheet that opens, add an extra row with the following values and save it:

Parameters	Attributes
Data_ID	3
File Name	File Comparer Test Cases Design Document
Creator Name	Mary Smith
File Extension	XLS
Reviewed	False
Effort	0
Result	Effort

Click on the **Run** button again. The test iterates three times and the evaluation on the `Result` column's value should be successful for all.

Logging the test metadata

Finally, suppose that you want to log to a physical file, a unique ID is generated upon entering each iteration of the test. In this case, the test name is not sufficient since it denotes no difference between the multiple iterations. An indicative iteration ID would be to append the data row ID found in the `Data_ID` column of the test name.

The test name can be attained from the `Test` property of the `ExecutionContext` class pertaining to the executing test. Whereas the data row ID of the Excel table can be accessed through the test `Data` property as we have seen with the `Result` column.

Click on the **View Class** button from the test toolbar and add the following code, which makes use of the `LogResult` method we saw in *Chapter 1, Introduction*:

```
CodedStep(@"Logging Test Name")]
public void Func6_FileInfo_Create_Successful_LogName()
{
        LogResult(this.ExecutionContext.Test.Name.ToString() + "_"
        + this.Data["Data_ID"].ToString());
```

```
    }

    private void LogResult (string text)
    {
        text = text + Environment.NewLine;
        using (System.IO.FileStream fileStream = new System.
        IO.FileStream(@"C:\File Comparer Files\Log.txt", System.
IO.FileMode.
        OpenOrCreate, System.IO.FileAccess.ReadWrite, System.
IO.FileShare.
        Read))
        {
                fileStream.Seek(0, System.IO.SeekOrigin.End);
                byte[] buffer = new byte[text.Length];
                buffer = Encoding.UTF8.GetBytes(text);
                fileStream.Write(buffer, 0, buffer.Length);
                fileStream.Close();
        }
    }
```

Click inside the test steps pane in order to force Test Studio to create an entry for the method added through code. Drag the newly added method to the very beginning of the test.

This function makes use of the `System.Runtime.Serialization` library. In order to add a library reference to the project, execute the following steps:

1. Go to the **Project** tab.
2. Click on the **Show** button in the **Settings** ribbon.
3. In the **Project Settings** invoked window, click on **Script Options**.
4. Using the **Add Reference** button, browse for the `System.Runtime.Serialization` library in the .NET framework.
5. Click on **OK**.
6. Run the test again.

The log file found in the `File Comparer` folder of the `C:` contains entries for each iteration as follows:

- `Func-6_FileInfo_Create_Successful_1`
- `Func-6_FileInfo_Create_Successful_2`
- `Func-6_FileInfo_Create_Successful_3`

The integer suffix stands for the `Data_ID` value, whereas `Func-6_FileInfo_Create_Successful` is the test name.

XML data source binding

The test that we are going to create in this section demonstrates binding an automated test to an XML data source. It extends the capabilities of one of the tests created in *Chapter 1* by attaching its input and output verification to a datafile. `Func-4_History_SingleDate_Successful` in the `Functional Tests` folder tests the selection of a date from the combobox and verifies that the selected value appears in every row of the data grid.

The XML file design must consist of the XML child elements, where each element is going to cause an additional iteration during execution. The XML attributes for the elements represent the value to which the UI control's properties bind to. The following XML code represents sample data for the test case based on the **History** tab:

```xml
<TestCases>
        <TestCase Data_ID="1" Date="2/8/2013" RowsNumber="3"/>
        <TestCase Data_ID="2" Date="2/9/2013" RowsNumber="4"/>
</TestCases>
```

The first attribute, called `Data_ID`, stands for test metadata similar to the example we have seen before. The second attribute, called `Date`, provides the date value for the combobox selection at the `Select by index '1' in 'DatesCmbCombobox` step. The third attribute, called `RowsNumber`, represents the number of expected rows after the filtering occurs.

Importing an XML data source

To import an XML file to Test Studio, execute the following steps:

1. Open the Test Studio's **Project** tab.
2. Click on the **Add** button from the **Data Sources** ribbon and choose **XML File** from the list.
3. In the **Create new data source** window, browse for the XML file contained under the `History` folder.
4. Confirm the creation by clicking on **OK**.

Since the test is identical to `Func-4_History_SingleDate_Successful`, copy the file present under `Functional Tests` and paste it under the `Data-Driven Tests` folder. Rename it to `Func-4_History_SingleDate_Successful_DDT` to differentiate it from the old test.

The automated test and the data source configuration are ready. Next, we need to reference the attributes from the test. Firstly, start binding the test to the XML file by right-clicking on the test and choosing **Data Bind** from the context menu. Set the values inside the **Bind test to date source** window, as shown in the following screenshot, and click on **OK**:

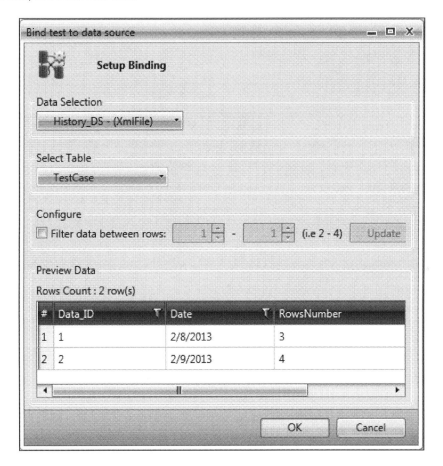

Binding to an XML source

Binding columns to XML attributes

Open the test and select the `Select by index '1' in 'DatesCmbCombobox` step
to preview its properties in the **Properties** pane. Click on the **Bindings** variable
arrow from the **Data Driven** section and bind the `SelectedText` property to `Date`,
as shown in the following screenshot:

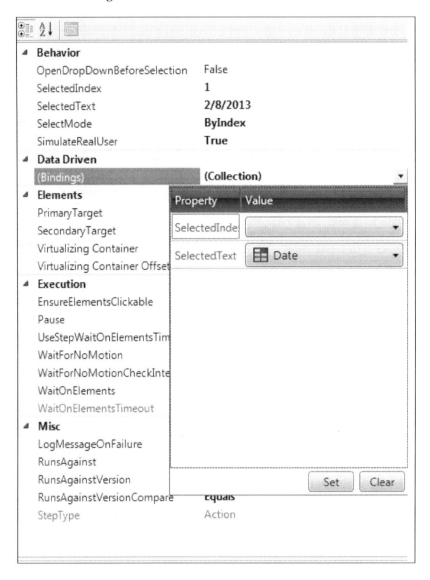

Binding the dates combo box

Expand the properties for this step and change the value of the `SelectMode` combobox to `ByText`.

In order to verify the data grid rows based on to the `RowsNumber` attribute, a verification step needs to be inserted. So execute the following steps:

1. Click on the **Record** button
2. Click on the **Pause** button from the recording toolbar
3. Go to the **History** tab
4. Choose **2/8/2013** for the date
5. Insert the verification step shown in the following screenshot:

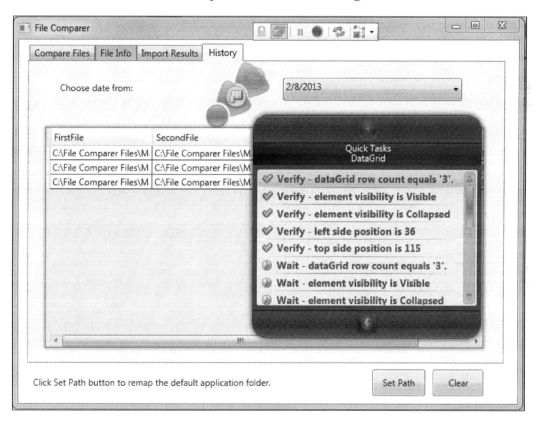

Adding verification on the data grid row number

6. Select the added verification, click on the **Bindings** property from the **Properties** pane and set the value of the verification step to `RowsNumber`.

7. The last step would be to disable the checkbox for the **Loop (3) times** and its child step to avoid executing them.

8. Click on the **Run** button.

Having both iterations passing and knowing that the number of loaded rows differs with each iteration, this means that the RowsNumber XML values were changed when passed at runtime.

Database binding

In this section, we are going to see how to make database tables act as data sources for our tests. The previous examples revolved around one-level tests where none of them involved the **Test as step** feature. In contradiction, we are going to walk through three scenarios that use two-level tests. They will highlight how Test Studio interprets the execution of two embedded tests where at least one of them is data-driven. The cases we are going to tackle are as follows:

- Outer test is a regular test and comprises a data-driven embedded test
- Outer test is data-driven and comprises a regular test
- Outer test is data-driven and comprises also a data-driven test

Each of the preceding approaches is going to be demonstrated in the right context where we will see how to implement them and how they will execute.

A non data-driven test comprising a data-driven test

In this scenario, we want to create a situation where some operations are needed to perform before and after a data-driven test. The outer test will execute once and when the inner test is hit, it will execute for a certain number of iterations and then the outer test will continue again. The execution flow is as depicted in the following diagram:

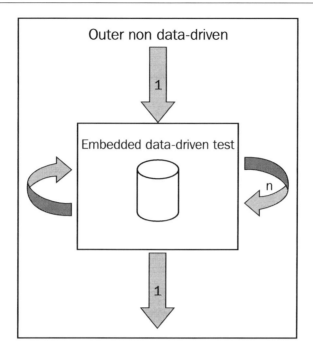

A non data-driven test comprising the data-driven test model

Let us assume that we want to test the acceptance of values in the **File Name** text field of the **File Info** tab. Well, the requirements state more restrictions on the filenames format to avoid the insertion of random data. The input is rejected if any of the following rules are violated:

- Input length must be less than 50 characters
- Empty values or only spaces are not allowed
- Special characters are not allowed

So now we know that values such as: `Testing Design and Implementation Document for File Comparer Application,` `" "`, or `Test Reporting & Assessment` are going to be declined by the application due to the violation of the preceding rules, respectively.

During the creation of the functional test cases, the preceding inputs are generated as part of the test data for the `File Info` data-driven tests. As a tester, running the test cases manually, you would input the preceding invalid values and set all the other UI elements to acceptable values. Otherwise, an error masking situation will emerge where another potential error on the form occurs and hides the error situation induced by the unacceptable input inside the **File Name** text field. So, in short, you don't need to care about the other values on the form as long as they are correct. This scenario exactly necessitates the execution flow depicted in the preceding diagram.

Creating parent and child tests

Technically, the parent test is going to contain some static steps that set the values for all the UI controls on the form except for `File Name`. The word static means that the steps will execute only once for the same hardcoded values. This test will call another data-driven test responsible for typing the text values inside the **File Name** field. To automate the data-driven test we are going to use the built-in data tables inside Test Studio.

Let us record the parent WPF test called `Func-7_FileInfo_FileName_DDT` as follows:

1. Click on the **File Info** tab.
2. Input `Mark Moore` inside the **Creator Name** text field.
3. Select **DOC** from the **File Extension** combobox.
4. Check the **Reviewed** checkbox.
5. Set the slider value to 3 for the **Effort** field.

We stop here without filling any value for the `File Name` parameter. The test steps are as follows:

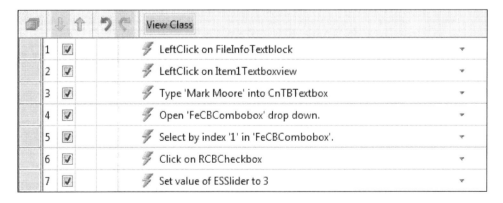

Steps of the Func-7_FileInfo_FileName_DDT test

The child test is also based on the WPF template. Create it under the `Data-Driven Tests` folder and rename it to `Op_FileInfo-FilleName`. The creation and population of the data table is going to take place as we record the test:

1. Click on the **Configure** button in the **Application** ribbon.

2. Browse for the `File Comparer.exe` application.

3. Click on the **Record** button.

4. Click on the **Pause** button from the recorder toolbar to be able to navigate to the **File Info** tab without inserting new recorded steps.

5. Once you are there, enable the recording again by clicking on the **Record** button.

6. Enter `Test Reporting & Assessment` inside the **File Name** text field.

7. Pause the execution again.

8. In Test Studio, click on the **Local Data** button from the **Test Views** ribbon as shown in the following screenshot:

The Local data button

This panel allows us to craft the data table playing the role of the test data source.

Perform the following steps to end up having the table shown in the screenshot:

1. Click on the Create a new data table icon ( ).

2. Update the number of **Columns** to 1.

3. Click on the Update Columns icon ( ) and confirm the removal of the columns.

4. Right-click on the column header and rename it to `FileName`.

5. Enter the **FileName** values as shown in the following screenshot.

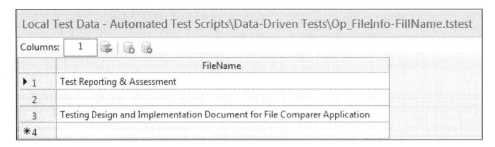

Local data table for the Op_FileInfo-FilleName test

Remember that, according to the preceding submission violation rules, the second value in the preceding table intentionally contains only one space.

Click on **Steps** button from the **Test View** ribbon to go back to the test steps again. To bind the File Name text field, perform the following steps:

1. Select the test step that was lastly added by Test Studio to preview its properties in the **Properties** pane.
2. Click on the arrow of the **Binding** property in the **Data Driven** section.
3. Bind its TypedText property to the FileName column we just created.
4. Click on the **Set** button.

Go to the application's window, enable the recording again, and perform the following steps:

1. Click on the **Create** button.
2. Add a verification step from the **Quick Tasks** element menu of the submission result label to verify that its content contains File Name.
3. Click on the **OK** button in the **File Info** tab.
4. Close the application.

The resulting test steps are as shown in the following screenshot:

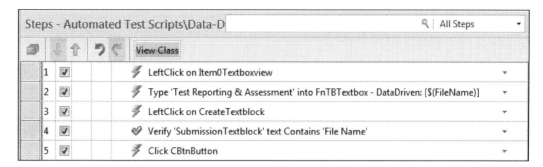

Steps of the Op_FileInfo-FilleName test steps

Go back to the parent test created in this example and click on the **Test as Step** button from the **Add** ribbon. In the **Select Test(s)** window choose Op_FileInfo-FillName and click on **OK**.

Make sure that the added step is the last one to be executed.

Click on the **Run** button and notice how the embedded test has executed three times for each value inside the data table while the outer test has executed only once. The logfile provides details about the verification step inserted inside Op_FileInfo-FillName as follows:

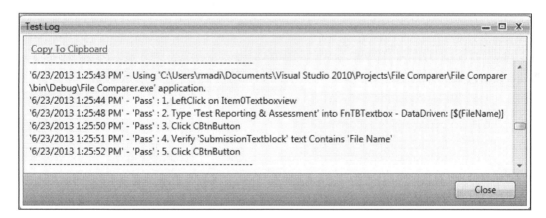

The Func-7_FileInfo_FileName_DDT test execution log

A data-driven test comprising a non data-driven test

In this scenario, we have a regular test residing inside a data-driven test. The outer test executes the number of times it calls the inner test. The latter will perform the UI operations using the data passed from the parent. The execution flow is depicted in the following diagram:

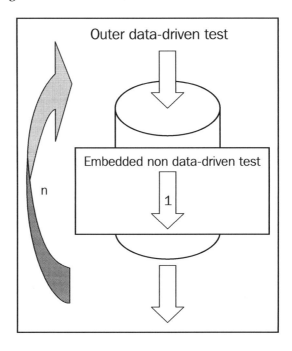

Data-driven test comprising non data-driven test model

The scenario starts where you, as a tester, is responsible for automating the `File Info` feature, were asked to redesign the data-driven test for this tab. The new design consists of separating the subprocedures from the main test flow to enhance long-term component maintainability and reusability.

Subprocedure is a term introduced in *Chapter 2, Automating Functional Tests* to refer to a block inside a test case procedure constituted from UI element verification, operations, and log steps.

So the solution states that you must create an independent WPF test for the subprocedures contained in the parent test. Thus, should you proceed by binding each of the resulting tests to a data source? What if in the future they decide to change the data source type? This will incur changes on all current test data bindings. So was it worth the trouble of dividing the parent test in the first place?

The solution starts with creating a copy of the `Func-6_FileInfo_Create_Successful` test under the `Data-Driven Tests` folder. Rename the newly added test to `Func-6_FileInfo_Create_Successful_DB`.

The copied test still reads from the Excel file, however, this time the data source happens to be a table inside MS SQL. To remove the binding, right-click on the test to open the context menu again and choose **Remove Data Binding** as shown in the following screenshot:

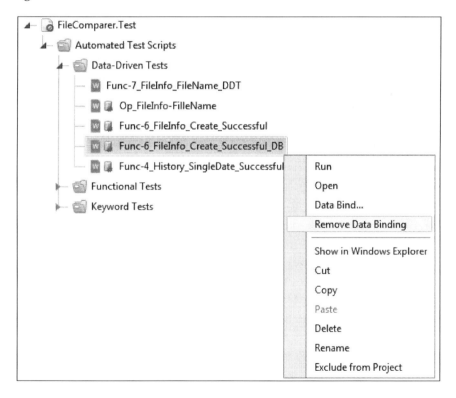

Removing data binding

The SQL table shares the same concept with the `FileInfo_DS.xls` table. The following screenshot depicts a table called `FileInfo`:

	File Name	Creator Name	Reviewed	File Extension	Effort	Data_ID	Result	Filter	CreatedOn
1	Test Case...	Paul Johnson	true	XLS	8	1	Allowed	Run	2013-03-18 14:34:56.610
2	Test Case...	Jack Thomas	False	XML	2	2	Allowed	NULL	2013-03-08 14:49:07.000

The FileInfo SQL table

An additional column appears in the snapshot and is called `Filter`. The value inside this column is going to serve as the filtering criteria for the rows that will be assigned for execution. This notion will get clearer as we create the data source corresponding to the `tblFileInfo` table in the following manner.

In Test Studio, go to the **Project** tab and click on the **Add** button from **Data Sources** and choose **Database Source**. In the **Create new data source** window select **SqlClient Data Provider** from the **Provider** combobox. The **Connection String** text field should hold the data used by Test Studio to establish a connection to the destination database containing the table holding the test data. The communication will happen through a user already created on the database having read rights on it. So, insert the following text in the **Provider** text field:

```
Data Source=localhost;Initial Catalog=FC_DB;Persist Security
Info=True;User ID=FC_DB_USER;Password=po0$wt
```

Click on the **Test** button to verify that the connection string is valid. You will not be able to continue with data binding if the connection is not successful.

Enter `FileComparer_DB` in the **Friendly Name** field and click on **OK** to finalize the creation of the data source.

It is time to bind the test to the database source, so right-click on the `Func-6_FileInfo_Create_Successful_DB` test and choose **Data Bind** from the context menu.

The **Bind test data to data source** window opens, choose `FileComparer_DB` from **Data Selection** combobox and select the **Use T-SQL** checkbox. This checkbox will show the **T-SQL Editor** text field to allow filtering out the unwanted table rows. We are going to input a query, which retrieves only the table rows having `Run` in the `Filter` column. Enter the following text inside the **T-SQL Editor** and click on **Update**:

```
SELECT [File Name],[Creator Name],[Reviewed],[File
Extension],[Effort],[Data_ID],[Result],[Filter]
  FROM [FC_DB].[dbo].[FileInfo]
  WHERE [FC_DB].[dbo].[FileInfo].[Filter] = 'Run'
```

The **Preview Data** section displays only one row where the others were not returned since they failed to satisfy the query condition. The retrieved row is shown in the following screenshot:

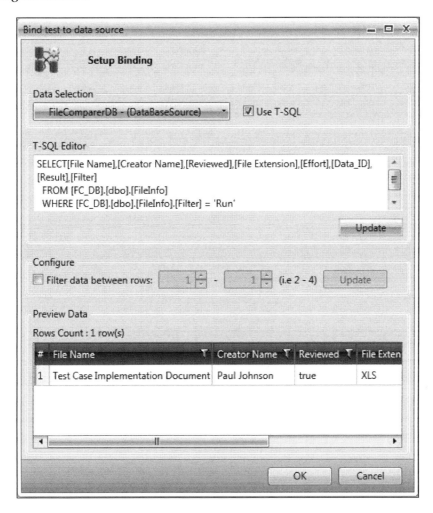

Binding to an SQL data source

Click on **OK** to confirm the data binding.

Creating child tests

The Func-6_FileInfo_Create_Successful_DB test runs successfully without any modifications since the Excel table column header names are exactly the same as those in the database table. The shift to the second data source was almost effortless and is purely dynamic, since each time the test runs, the query of the test data binding is evaluated and the test executes according to the returned rows. So any update on the database table will be reflected the next time you run your test.

Back to our problem, as the data binding part is finished, we now need to separate the subprocedures from the test. Open the Func-6_FileInfo_Create_Successful_DB test and then right-click on the steps of the subprocedure responsible for entering data inside the **Creator Name** field, and choose **Create Test as Step** from the context menu as shown in the following screenshot:

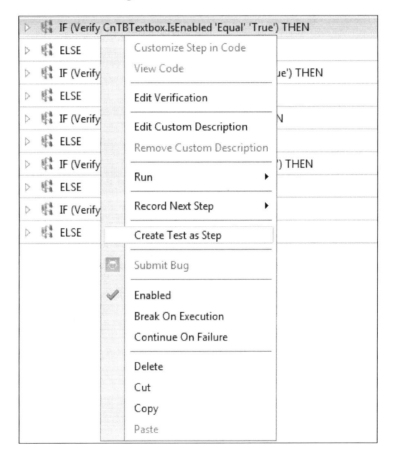

Creating a test as a step

This action will remove the steps and replace them with a call to a new test. The created test inherits the test template and location of its parent, so now it can be found under the `Data-Driven Tests` folder. In the **Create Test as Step** window, rename the test to `Op_FileInfo-FillCreatorName` and click on the **Create** button.

Notice how the steps are removed and replaced with the **Execute test 'Op_FileInfo-FillCreatorName'** step.

So what happened to the data-driven binding of the extracted steps? Go to the **Project Files** pane of the **Project** tab and double-click on the `Op_FileInfo-FillCreatorName` test to open it. Expand the steps and notice how the data entered inside the `File Creator` field still binds to the **Creator Name** value.

This means that the higher level test data is expected to propagate down to the lower level test. In order to instruct Test Studio to deal with the tests as such, go to **Project** tab, and then from **Project Files** panel click on the test to preview its properties in the **Properties** pane. Select the **InheritParentDataSource** option as shown in the following screenshot:

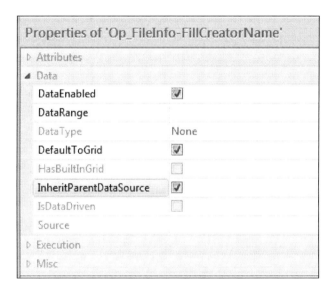

Setting the InheritParentDataSource option

Run the test and notice how the child receives the data from the parent in a transparent way. The test will run for as many rows in the database while calling the child test each time.

Note that the execution will equally work if the inner non data-driven test is created from scratch, because when binding a UI element property to a variable, Test Studio gives you the option to bind to a new nonexistent variable as shown in the following screenshot:

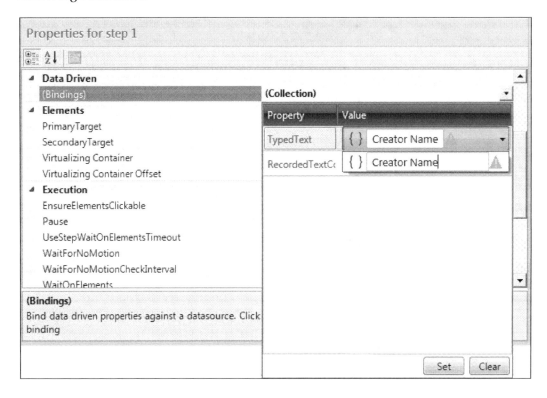

Binding to a new variable

A data-driven test comprising another data-driven test

In this scenario, the outer data-driven test executes a fixed number of times, where for each iteration the inner data-driven test is called to execute its own number of times. In other words, if the parent test has four rows and the child has three, the child will execute 4 x 3 times. The execution flow is depicted in the following diagram:

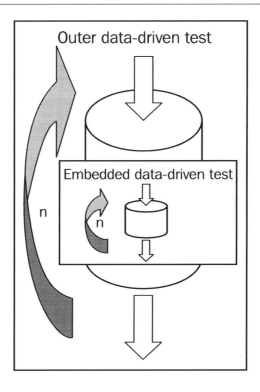

Data-driven test comprising the data-driven test model

As new features are being added into the application, a new rule related to the **File Info** tab is also introduced. It states that some critical testing documents cannot be committed to the database if they are not reviewed. For example, documents created during the test planning phase must be rexamined at least once. Therefore, an additional verification has been introduced to the file creation source code upon submission. An update is also being made to the manual test scripts, where the test cases that involve creating a document belonging to the planning phase are now being doubled. But do you really want to duplicate the corresponding data-driven rows?!

Creating parent and child tests

Let's take for example, `Func-6_FileInfo_Create_Successful`. All the
tests contained in the `FileInfo` table, which has `Rev` in the `Filter` column,
are required to run for both the `Reviewed` values, `true` and `false`.

The solution is going to be handled within Test Studio without having to add any
row to the `tblFileInfo` table. Firstly, create a copy of this test and rename it to
`Func-6_FileInfo_Create_Successful_CN`. Next, change the binding for the test
to make it execute for all the rows having the `Rev` value inside the `Filter` column.
So, right-click on the test and then from the context menu, choose **Data Binding**
and fill the **Bind test to data source** window as follows:

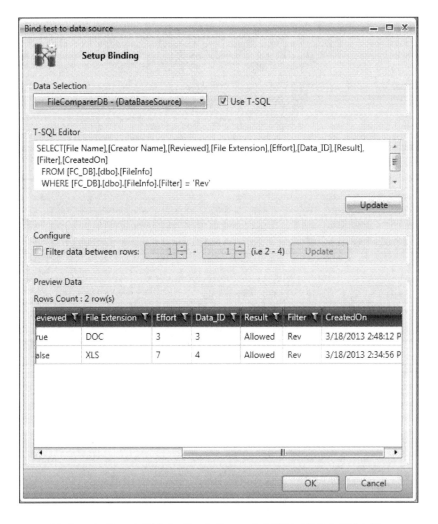

Binding the Func-6_FileInfo_Create_Successful_CN to FileInfo SQL table

Creating parent and child tests

The subprocedure block that deals with setting the **Reviewed** checkbox is still integrated within the `Func-6_FileInfo_Create_Successful_CN` test. However, the solution consists of extracting that block and connecting it to another data table inside the database. This table is called `tblReviewed`, and it contains two rows holding the two possible values for the document review status: `true` or `false`.

Open the test and execute the following steps:

1. Delete the two verification steps.

2. Select the last two subprocedure blocks, which handle actions on the **Reviewed** checkbox, the **Create** button, and the **OK** button.

3. Right-click on it and select **Create Test as Step** from the context menu.

4. Name the new test `Op_FileInfo-SelectReviewed`.

5. Go back to the **Project** tab, and then from `Project Files` select the `Op_FileInfo-SelectReviewed` test, right-click on it, and choose **Data Bind** from its context menu, and then fill the invoked window as follows:

Binding the Op_FileInfo-SelectReviewed to tblReviewed SQL table

6. Click on the **Run** button and notice how for each iteration of the `Func-6_FileInfo_Create_Successful_CN` test, two iterations of the `Op_FileInfo-SelectReviewed` test are made for each value `true` and `false`. So on the whole, the former test will be executed twice whereas the latter will be executed four times.

Summary

In response to the problem raised at the beginning of this chapter and for any similar matters in the future, we have seen how to transition from simple record and playback tests to data-driven architecture by releasing the test from the hardcoded values and binding its input to various types of data sources. On one hand, the binding was demonstrated for simple UI controls which already expose a readymade property, and on the other hand for more complex UI controls where the binding had to be customized in code. This is not all, since binding does not confine only to UI controls where we have learned how to bind data columns to verification steps also. We have also highlighted dynamic filtering on data sources, where the set of the executing rows can be evaluated and retrieved based on automation criteria just before the test executes. A powerful feature inside Test Studio was also explained and illustrated in the examples discussed previously. This happens when one test is nested inside another. Depending on the nature of the tests, whether data-driven or not, the execution flow, and transmission of data varies from one scenario to the other. The three possibilities are calling a data bound test from a regular one, calling a data bound test from another data bound test, and finally calling a regular test from a data bound test. The aforementioned feature list constitutes the solid ingredients to implement data-driven tests to resolve automation needs for the applications under test. With this, we conclude this chapter and present hints and solutions to fit your testing environment.

The next chapter deals with the test scripts building blocks, which are the UI screen elements that the steps interact with. We will discover Test Studio's default generation for element definitions and how we can edit them to improve test reliability.

4
Maintaining Test Elements

One day, as usual you report to work where on your way you were planning the next test to automate. Ideas were flowing in your head now that you are satisfied with all the knowledge you have gained so far in Test Studio automation. You reach work with the invincible QA automation engineer attitude and you get called for the testing team meeting. So just when you expect to be praised for having finished the data-driven tests automation before the targeted date, you disappointedly discover the results of yesterday's overnight execution. Most of the test cases crashed when they were run against the latest application build! "You designed the test logic very carefully so it must have been an element recognition problem after the updates of the developers!", you say to yourself. Surely, testing cannot afford test execution crashes with each build so the element recognition for all tests has to be enhanced. As a solution to this problem, this chapter will teach you how:

- Test Studio understands, interprets, and deals with elements
- How to manually organize UI test elements
- How to build flexible find expressions to locate UI test elements

Automation element recognition

As the proverb says, "A chain is only as strong as its weakest link.". In automation, no matter how smartly you devise your tests the element recognition mechanism can still break test execution. Hence, one of the factors for making automated tests robust is the capability to induce unique element identification at runtime. You will not be able to guarantee stable and reliable test executions unless you build a flexible and valid element repository.

In addition to carefully crafting the element's recognition logic, the long term aim is to have the logic behind these elements centralized in one place. This will boost test maintainability and increase the automation return on investment.

The material in this chapter is the common ground for automating any test using Test Studio. The element recognition topic is going to be tackled from its different sides to enable comprehensive decisions when storing elements.

The element repository

Recorded test steps are composed from two parts: elements and actions. The UI elements constitute the skeleton whereas the UI actions constitute the engine. So the actions are driven against the elements.

As we have seen in the previous chapters, a typical test step looks like: `LeftClick on HistoryTextblock`. The element is `HistoryTextblock` whereas the UI action is `LeftClick`. In the application under test, the way a UI element is identified by Test Studio is through its find expression found in a property called `FindLogic`. This is a property present on the element and it holds the keys for Test Studio to uniquely find its way through the application object hierarchy to identify that element. At runtime, Test Studio evaluates the `FindLogic` expression and executes the UI actions on the yielded element. This expression could enclose evaluation conditions either around element properties such as `Name` or element path in the object hierarchy, for example, `XamlPath`. This is all what is needed by Test Studio to recognize an element and it does not use any outside criteria such as parent element or container. In the preceding test step, the `HistoryTextblock FindLogic` expression is `[TextContent 'Exact' History] AND [XamlTag 'Exact' textblock]`, which means that the target element's apparent text is `History` and is of type `TextBlock`.

Element existence is either tied to a recorded step or to a test by external reference. The `LeftClick on HistoryTextblock` step is an example of an element linked to a recorded step where the `HistoryTextblock` is linked to the mentioned step. When a recorded step is converted to code, the comprised element is said to now exist by external reference. Similarly, the elements used in script steps belong to the external reference element set. The last way to store elements is by adding them manually through DOM explorer or during recording from outside any test step scope. In this case, the element is also said to exist by external reference to the active test.

The element repository contains the elements existing in recorded steps or by external reference after being manually added. It does not have a physical existence on your machine's hard disk, on the contrary, it is assembled when Test Studio launches, and it ceases to exist when Test Studio shuts down. In other words the UI elements neither have a persisted definition in a physical file nor do they get loaded from that file at startup, rather, they are consolidated from all test steps when Test Studio starts.

During the element repository consolidation process, which consists of creating an entry inside the element repository for each UI element partaking in the definition of a test step, any other element that is evaluated and found to already have an existing definition is disregarded. Thus, only one entry will exist for any element appearing more than once in the test steps and this is due to the find expression which is used at startup to filter out duplicate elements. The consolidation covers test steps for all the tests residing under a project and does not limit its scope per test. Thus, the element repository is centralized where at runtime Test Studio will have one place to fetch the elements from.

Test repository elements have a certain life span. As long as a recorded test step carries a certain element in its definition, that element will have to exist in the element repository when Test Studio is running. When the last test step is removed the last definition having reference to that element is also removed, so the element dies and is deleted from the element repository. The manually added elements will always appear in the element repository whether or not it is used by any test step.

The subsequent examples will demonstrate how to tune some options related to consolidating elements inside the element repository. This along with understanding Test Studio's strategies for finding elements covers the automatic building of the element repository where manually adding elements is going to be addressed as well. The examples also demonstrate how to build the logic of the find expression around the test elements through recorded and coded steps. In conclusion, this chapter lets you discover how Test Studio deals with elements and finds them to make an optimal decision when defining your next element's Find logic.

Adding elements

Building the element repository for your project does not confine to the automatic recording process of Test Studio. You can contribute to this task by firstly intercepting the element either through the application UI during recording or through the DOM explorer. The DOM explorer, a language-neutral interface, displays a tree formed of all elements in a page in case of a web application, or in a window in case of a WPF application. This explorer uses the **DOM** (**Document Object Model**) language in order to translate the content and structure of application elements. After intercepting the element and depending on the means of interception, some operations can be reachable through its element menu or context menu out of which we list adding the element to the element repository.

The recorder toolbar DOM Explorer

The element repository is displayed inside the **Elements** pane whenever you are on the **Test** tab, as follows:

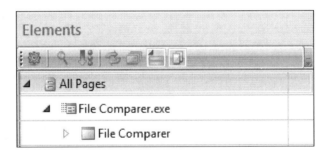

The Elements pane

After the initial elements consolidation at Test Studio startup, the repository is augmented as you are crafting your tests during recording, when Test Studio adds new test steps for the UI interactions that you are making on the screen. By default, Test Studio creates names for these elements. This name is called FriendlyName and is shown in the **Properties** pane when selecting an element inside the element repository. The following screenshot shows the friendly name for the **Dates** combobox in the **History** tab of the File Comparer application:

Properties for Element 'DatesCmbCombobox'

▷ **Find Logic**

◢ **FriendlyName**

   FriendlyName   **DatesCmbCombobox**

▷ **Misc**

FriendlyName

Friendly name to easily identify this node. This name will also be used for code generation as a variable name or a collection indexer.

Element friendly name

Generally, the WPF UI element friendly name generated by Test Studio is a concatenation of the element's `Name` property value and `Type`. This strategy is applicable whenever Test Studio uses the predefined UI element, `Name`, to locate that element in the application under test. In some situations, static names cannot be assigned to UI elements, for example, with dynamic rows in data grids. In this case, Test Studio will not use the `Name` property but rather the hierarchy path.

The **Dates** combobox of the **History** tab is named `DatesCmb` and is of type `Combobox`. The concatenation of the aforementioned values results in Test Studio's naming convention and therefore the friendly name is `DatesCmbCombobox`.

As mentioned, it is not always the case that developers assign names to UI elements during design phase especially to containers such as frames and grids, which are given random names at runtime. Therefore, handing over the complete responsibility to Test Studio to create friendly names for your application elements will not always end up very friendly. Luckily, you can make interventions to rename elements or add them with customized names from outside the recording scope.

In this example, we are going see how to save and name application elements but firstly we start by enabling this option from the project configuration:

1. Go to the **Project** tab.

2. Click on the **Show** button from the **Settings** tab.

3. In the ensuing dialog, choose the **General accordion** tab.

4. Make sure the **Prompt for element name before adding** checkbox of the **Element repository** section is selected.

5. Click on **OK**.

The **File Info** tab of the `File Comparer` application gives the option to export the file's metadata in case if the submission is not going to be made on the spot. This feature is achievable by clicking on the **Export** button of that tab. So we will first automate the test procedures by recording the steps and then before performing any action on the **Export** button, we will add it to the element repository with our own custom friendly name using the DOM Explorer.

From the **Project** tab, create a test based on the WPF template under the `Functional Tests` folder and rename it to `Func-8_FileInfo_Export_Successful`. Record the following steps for the created test:

1. Click on the **File Info** tab.
2. Enter `Project Risk Document` inside the **File Name** field.
3. Enter `Pamela Clark` inside the **Creator Name** field.
4. Choose **DOC** from the **File Extension** combobox.
5. Set **Effort** slider to **9**.
6. Select **Reviewed**.
7. Click on the Pause button from the recorder toolbar to temporarily stop the recording and let's access the DOM hierarchy of the application by clicking on the DOM Explorer button highlighted in the following screenshot:

The DOM explorer button

The **DOM Explorer** window is invoked and the controls currently displayed on the screen are resolved in a tree. Our aim now is to locate the **Export** button tag inside the hierarchy and add it to the repository and then perform the following steps:

1. Enable the surface highlighting button.
2. Hover over the **Export** button.
3. Open the button's element menu.
4. Click on **Locate in DOM**, which corresponds to the second button.

Notice how in the DOM explorer window, the tree is expanded and the target element's tag is highlighted.

There exists another way to locate an object in a tree using the **DOM Explorer** window's powerful search feature. Firstly, click on the Hierarchical DOM View icon outlined in the following screenshot in order to fold the tree and then on the Search Tree icon also outlined:

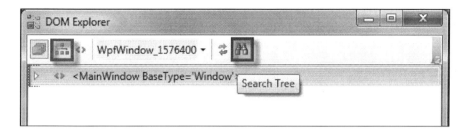

The DOM Explorer tree toolbar

This will enable a **Search** text field to receive the text criteria we want to search against. As simple as it may look, this feature is very powerful in helping us to find our way through a complex DOM tree. This field accepts either keywords or rich expressions that are understood by the Test Studio search engine. On the left side of the expression comes the attribute, where the search value will occupy the right side separated by a comparison operator.

On the **DOM Explorer** window, enable the advanced search using find expressions by clicking on the outlined button preceding the **Search** label, as shown in the following screenshot:

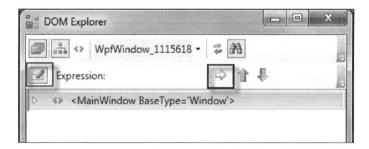

The DOM Explorer search toolbar

Our knowledge of the **Export** button is limited to the apparent text on the screen and in such cases we need to query the `TextContext` attribute to find the element by this criterion. The **Export** label is found on a button and since the WPF `Button` class inherits from the `ContentControl` class, it has a property called `Content` to which a string parameter can be passed to display on the UI as `<Button Content="Export"/>`. The `Content` property can be queried with the `TextContent` operator. `ComboBoxItem` and `Label` are also examples of classes that inherit from the `ContentControl` class.

Therefore, type `TextContent=Export` inside the field and execute the search by clicking on the yellow arrow outlined in the preceding screenshot. The DOM tree will be expanded to show the occurrence of the clicked result entry. Nevertheless, we are aware of the fact that we want to add the button itself and not the button label, so this is why we want to drill up in the hierarchy to find the targeted button.

In order to track our navigation in the object hierarchy tree, Test Studio has the highlighting feature embedded in the **DOM explorer** window as well. In this case, this feature will box the UI element with a red rectangle as we dwell on its corresponding tag in the hierarchy. So make sure to activate the highlighting feature by toggling on the **Enable highlighting on recording surface** button in the **DOM explorer** window. From the **DOM explorer** window, click on the first **Button** tag shown above the currently selected tag and notice how the **Export** button is highlighted on the screen, as shown in the following screenshot:

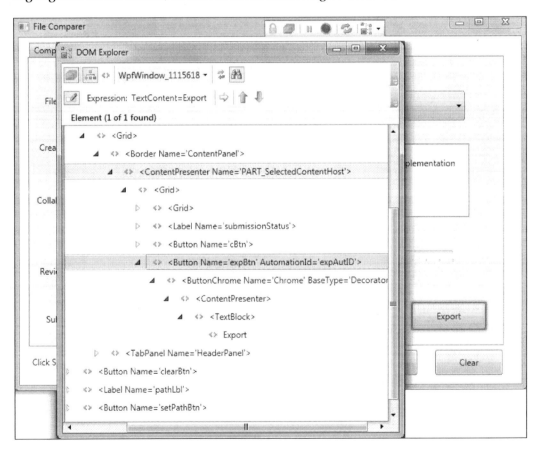

Highlighting surface feature inside DOM explorer

Right-click on the **Button** tag and choose **Add to Project Elements** from the context menu, as shown in the following screenshot:

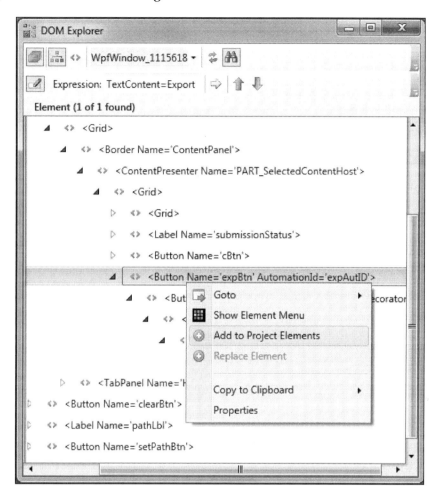

Adding elements to project elements from DOM Explorer

Now, Test Studio prompts you with the custom name while still displaying its suggested friendly name in the **Element Friendly Name** dialog. Enter `Export Button` in the text field and click on **Add Element** as shown in the following screenshot:

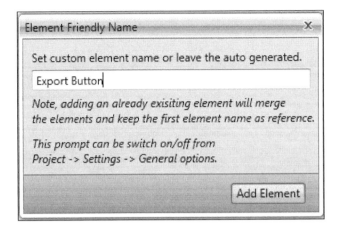

Editing friendly names

In order to finish the test recording, perform the following steps:

1. Click on the **Record** button from the recorder toolbar.

2. Click on the **Export** button.

3. In **Export Dialog**, enter `Exported File Metadata` inside the **File Name** field.

4. Click on **OK**.

5. Close the application.

Notice how the added step responsible for clicking on the **Export** button now holds the friendly name which was manually added: **Click Export Button.**

The search expressions in WPF applications can also be based on other element properties. WPF supports the `AutomationProperties` class, which is dedicated for the UI accessibility support. The values for the `AutomationProperties` class' attached properties can be set in the XAML markup in the corresponding element declaration. These properties are powerful because they preserve their values when other properties of the same element change during the development of the application. Hence, during automation, the first property that should be sought is `AutomationProperties.AutomationId`. For example, based on the following **Export** button XAML declaration, you can locate the **Export** button by its automation ID property: `AutomationID=expAutID`:

```
<Button Content="Export" Height="37" HorizontalAlignment="Right"
Margin="0,167,21,0" Name="expBtn" VerticalAlignment="Top" Width="104"
Click="expBtn_Click" AutomationProperties.AutomationId="expAutID"
Grid.Row="1" />
```

Furthermore, we can also use other search attributes such as the type of the UI element to search for it inside the DOM Explorer. For example, the search expression involving the XamlTag type of the **Export** button is XamlTag=Button. However, other buttons are also present in this window, so performing the search on this criterion would result in all the button tags being displayed in the interface. Therefore, we can add further criteria as the value of the Name attribute of the element to narrow down the search. In complex expressions, the search criteria are appended with a comma as: XamlTag=Button,Name=expBtn.

Forming the element repository

Test Studio structures the WPF application's element repository at **Applications | Windows | Elements**

This hierarchy can be viewed in the screenshot provided in the *The recorder toolbar DOM Explorer* section. The element repository flattens the hierarchical nature of the WPF elements found in the XAML design. Although any tab item declaration encloses those of the UI elements appearing inside it, this is not the case in the element repository. The tab item node and the elements underneath it are contained in one level.

In the **Elements** pane, the entire hierarchy under the File Comparer.exe element, which represents the executable file of the application is organized under three nodes. These subtree root nodes stand for the three windows that we have seen while using the application: File Comparer, Set Application Path, and Export Dialog. The underlying list of elements, under each of these nodes corresponds to the UI elements found in each window when the application runs. Despite this visual categorization of the element repository, Test Studio does not need parent elements to locate UI objects at runtime.

The following exercise will explain how this translates in reality when Test Studio consolidates the element repository and runs the tests.

We will again add an element by external reference, which is the **Cancel** button of the **Export Dialog** window by performing the following steps:

1. Click on the **Record** button.
2. Pause the execution to navigate to the **Export Dialog** window without actually recording the actions.

3.   Click on the **File Info** tab.

4.   Click on the **Export** button.

5.   Again stop the recording on the invoked dialog by clicking on the Pause
     button from the attached recorder toolbar.

6.   Toggle the hover over highlighting feature button.

7.   Point the mouse over the target button until the blue nub appears and
     click inside it.

8.   Select the first button in the element menu to add the element to the
     repository, as shown in the following screenshot:

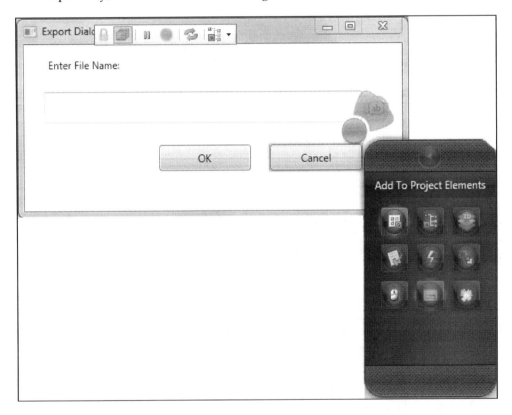

Adding elements to element repository from the element menu

9.   Rename the button to Cancel Button and then click on the **Add Element**
     button. Close both the application windows to exit the recording mode.

In the **Elements** pane, the **Export Dialog** node now has two children: OKBtnButton
and CancelButton, which correspond to the **OK** and **Cancel** buttons of the **Export
Dialog** window respectively.

Filtering options

Let's adjust a bit. How does Test Studio evaluate elements when constructing the element repository and precisely how it clears the duplicates:

1. Go to the **Project** tab.
2. Click on the **Show** button from the **Settings** ribbon
3. In the **Project Settings** window, choose the **Recording Options** from the left accordion.
4. Then choose **Title** from the combobox corresponding to the **Elements Page Compare Mode** settings.
5. Click on **OK**.

Following this step, any two project elements sharing the same captions will be considered identical, therefore, one of them will have to be omitted from the element repository. Go back to the **Test** tab, and click on the **Export Dialog** node from the **Elements** pane to view its properties. In the **Properties** pane edit the `Caption` element's property to `File Comparer`, as shown in the following screenshot:

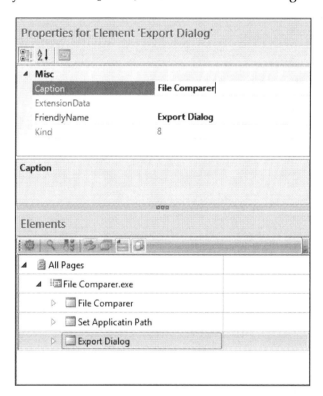

Renaming elements from the Properties pane

Click on the **Refresh** button of the **Elements** pane in order to force Test Studio to regenerate the element repository. Notice how the two buttons that belong to the **Export Dialog** window UI are now appended to the element list under the **File Comparer** node whereas the former **Export Dialog** node is removed. What happened is that Test Studio got rid of the second entry having a caption already present in the project element's list.

How do you think this has affected the recognition of the **OK** button of the export dialog? As you have perhaps expected the execution should be successful. Why is that? Because Test Studio's recognition is only dependent on the find expression for the element!

Click on the `OkBtnButton` project element and locate its `FindLogic` property from the **Properties** pane. The Find logic underlying this button is `[Name 'Exact' okBtn] AND [XamlTag 'Exact' button]`. These conditions are solely evaluated to retrieve the element during test execution.

3D Viewer Element Adding and Verification

UI object containers such as grids, frames, or panels are hard to be manually intercepted on the screen using the Test Studio highlighting feature, especially when they have transparent borders. As an example, the **File Info** tab contains a label that conveys the file submission result to the user. The border of this label is transparent and does not appear to the eye. So to enable the `TextBlock` element menu, you would have to hover the mouse over the area surrounding the label and play around with the highlighting surface feature to access the targeted element menu. In fact this control was already utilized in one of the previous tests that we have recorded. `Func-6_FileInfo_Create_Successful` builds a verification expression around the content of this label. Now suppose that you want to make sure that the text block exists before you actually verify its content; in that case, you will have to map the label border by performing the following steps:

1. Open the test.
2. Click on the **Record** button.
3. Pause the execution.
4. Click on the **File Info** tab.
5. Click on the hover over highlighting button and hover over the Result Submission Label until you get the blue nub.
6. Click on it.

7. In the element menu, click on the **View 3D** button (which is the third button).

A **3D Viewer** window opens displaying the visual representation of the target element and its parents in the upper section of the window, where the lower section has the element tags as shown in the following screenshot:

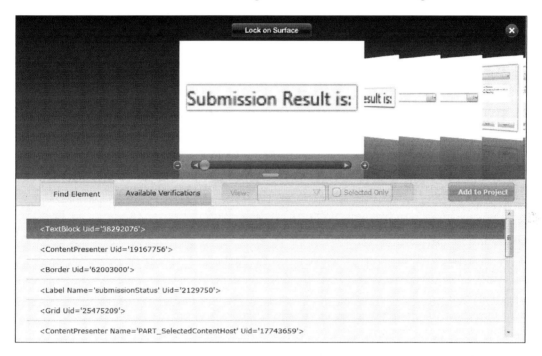

3D Viewer

Currently the text label occupies the window. To bring any of the parent elements to the front, either click on the background elements of the visual part or use the slider, or you can just click on the tag that starts with Label Name='submissionStatus' to directly navigate to the element in question. The text block is now accessible for us to operate on via the **3D Viewer** window or the element menu. The latter is displayed by clicking on the **Lock on Surface** button at the top of the window, which highlights the button on the screen and opens its automation menu. However, it is not necessary to go through the element menu since some operations are already within our reach:

1. Click on the **Available Verifications** button to, for example, add verifications we have seen in the previous chapters.

2. From the list, select **Visibility element is Visible**.

3. Click on the **Add to Project** button.

4. Close the window and then the application's instance.

An entry for the text block label is added to the project's element as `submissionStatusLabel` along with the corresponding test step.

In conclusion, if you want to manually add an element to the repository you can do so using the **DOM Explorer** window, which is accessible through the toolbar recorder or the **Build Verification** window of any element. If any of the element properties is in your disposition, for example, the content label, you can input this criterion into the DOM Explorer's search field to narrow down your search. In addition, if the element is visible on the screen, you can open its element menu and use the first three available buttons to directly add the element to the repository, locate in DOM Explorer, and view in 3D.

Finding locators

As in the case of friendly names, Test Studio also has a default way of finding the application elements, which, as we have seen so far, is saved in the `FindLogic` property. In the case of WPF elements with static names, it consists of the concatenation of the `Name` and `Type` properties. In the HTML case, the priority in which Test Studio uses element properties to build the find expressions is determined from the project settings. To arrange the order of the element properties perform the following actions:

1. Go to the **Project** tab.

2. Click on the **Show** button in the **Settings** ribbon.

3. Click on the **Identification Logic** tab in the **Project Settings** window.

The following screenshot shows the area in the **Project Settings** window, which allows the shuffling of priorities of the element's properties. Also, the screenshot shows the **Add Tag to list** free input field, which can be used to input a preferable property to be used in the element's recognition:

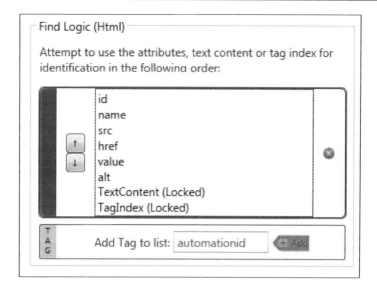

Prioritizing element properties for Find logic

After the element is added to the repository, the Find logic can be edited manually and the neater you define the element's locators the less fragile the tests will turn out to be and the scripts would require less maintenance.

Before mapping any element or changing its find strategy, you would require a few minutes to really isolate the inherent fact of the element, which does not change. If the element is declared with the AutomationId property, this is the first strategy you want to use to store the element irrelevant of its position or any other property susceptible to change over time. Relying on other properties, especially if they are not declared statically is very risky, because the test will likely fail in the future when changes that affect the interface elements occur.

Firstly, we will see how you can change the Find logic of an element inside Test Studio and secondly we will apply the various locator strategies on the elements.

So let us say we want to edit the locator logic for the slider element on the **File Info** tab. We know that the slider contributes to the definition of the step that sets the effort value inside the `Func-8_FileInfo_Export_Successful` test. Open the test and click on this step to let Test Studio guide you to the element in the repository by drawing a yellow arrow before the element name. Right-click on that element and choose **Edit Element** from the context menu. The **Find Element** window opens up and presents the user with three ways to locate the element, as shown in the following screenshot:

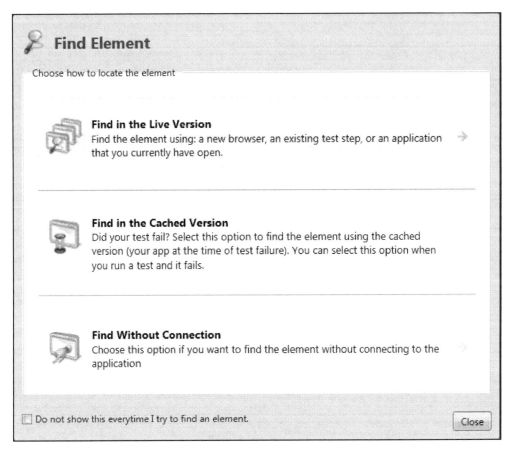

The Find Element window

Choose the first option to edit the find expression of the element and validate it on the spot against a running instance of the application. On the next page, choose the **Existing Test Step** option since **New Browser** can only be launched for web applications, and the last option, which is **Current Page**, requires an instance of the `File Comparer` application to be already running. The second option will open the **Test Step Selector** dialog having all the steps that have the UI operations tied to the slider. Scroll down to this test entry and choose the listed step underneath, and then click on the **Select** button. This will cause Test Studio to run the test up to the slider step and hand over control to the user to operate on the **Find Element** window shown in the following screenshot:

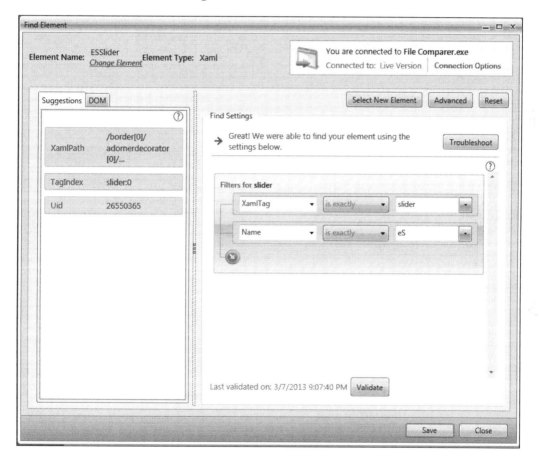

The Find element window

Initially, this window displays the current values to the right based on which the element is located on the screen. Had the element name not been static, the operators would have been changed to evaluate only a substring of the automatically generated element's subname, if applicable. For example, we would have needed to compare the prefix only by using the **starts with** operator from the combobox or suffix only by using the **ends with** operator.

The path of the element in the DOM tree can also be used in the element locator strategy along with some other attributes. This is achievable through the element `XamlPath` attribute. Hover over the find expressions in the **Filters for slider** section of the **Find Element** window until the **Delete** button appears, and then remove both expressions. From the suggestions panel to the left, click on the **XamlPath** box to add it as a criterion in the **Find Settings** section. The `XamlPath` value currently suggested by Test Studio starts with the path from the DOM root as follows:

```
/border[0]/adornerdecorator[0]/contentpresenter[0]/grid[0]/
tabcontrol[name=tabControl1]/grid[0]/border[name=ContentPanel]/
contentpresenter[name=PART_SelectedContentHost]/grid[0]/grid[0]/
slider[name=eS]
```

This is not safe with regards to the changes that could affect the application since you don't want to hardwire all parent element tags in the XAML path of any element. For example, the removal or addition of any element that would impact the XAML path such as grids or panels will preclude Test Studio from locating the slider.

So instead, you can remove all the elements for the `XamlPath` value leaving the slider only as `/slider[name=eS]`. Following this, the operator should be set to **ends with** instead of **equal**.

Click on the **Validate** button to verify whether the locator passes or fails with respect to the slider. As you can see, Test Studio has successfully managed to locate the element, so for now, click on the **Cancel** button.

Using the chained expression

We have seen so far how the element locators can be built on top of attributes or `XamlPath`. There exists a third way to locate an element and this way is especially used when dealing with table like data, for instance, when trying to locate a cell amongst a pool of cells inside a data grid. If you attempt to translate the actions you take into a step-by-step procedure in order to locate a cell you would find yourself first looking for the data grid, then looping over each row, where for each cell inside that row you would compare its content to the value you are looking for. The locator's chained expressions allow you to build such flexible complex expressions to find the element.

Inside the `File Comparer` application's **History** tab, let us say that after choosing a date value from the combo box we want to check the details for the row by doing a right-click on the first cell. Firstly, let us record these steps under a test called `Func-9_History_Details_Successful` based on a WPF template. Create this test under the **Functional Tests** folder. The test procedure is as follows:

1. Start **File Comparer** application.
2. Click on the **History** tab.
3. Choose **2/26/2013** from the combobox.
4. Right-click on the first cell of the first row.
5. Click on **Details** from the context menu.
6. Click on **OK** from **Details Dialog**.
7. Close the **File Comparer** window.

Select the step that does the right-click on the data grid row cell. The underlying element entry for this test step called **CFileTextblock** is marked with a yellow arrow inside the element repository. Click on that entry to explore its Find logic, which is as follows:

```
[name 'Exact' PART_RowsPresenter] AND [XamlTag 'Exact'
  datagridrowspresenter] [XamlPath 'Exact' /datagridrow[0]
  /border[name=DGR_Border]/selectivescrollinggrid[0]/
  datagridcellspresenter[0]/itemspresenter[0]
  /datagridcellspanel[0]/datagridcell[0]
  /border[0]/contentpresenter[0]/textblock[0]]
```

Notice how redundant elements of the hierarchy are hardcoded into the `XamlPath` expression, where the position of the row inside the data grid is also included. This means that if you sort on any column inside the data grid, regardless of where this row might end up, Test Studio would still perform a right-click on the first row because it is not made aware of the cell content. To make the element finding more flexible we will edit the find locators of that element as follows:

1. Right-click on the **CFileTextBlock** element.
2. Choose **Edit Element** from the context menu.
3. In the **Find Element** window, choose **Find in the Live Version**, then choose **Existing Test Step** on the second page by clicking on the **Choose Test Step** button.
4. In the **Test Step Selector**, choose **RightClick on CFileTextBlock**, which is the test step responsible for clicking on the data grid cell.
5. Click on the **Select** button and wait until Test Studio executes the test right until the chosen step.

The **Find element** window currently reflects the **FindLogic** content, as shown in the following screenshot:

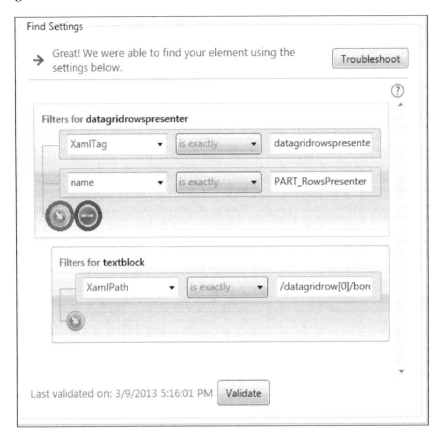

Data grid cell Find settings

The search expression on the **textblock** is embedded under those of **datagridrowspresenter**. This means that at runtime, Test Studio will first execute the filters on the **datagridrowspresenter**; once an object satisfies these criteria, Test Studio will then execute the filters on the collection of its children textblock. This is how the chained expressions work.

Update the filters as shown in the following screenshot. To add or delete any embedded expression click on the buttons highlighted in the previous screenshot.

After editing the expressions or adding a child level, click on the **Validate** button in order to force the **Find Settings** window to update the current object based on the constituting expressions.

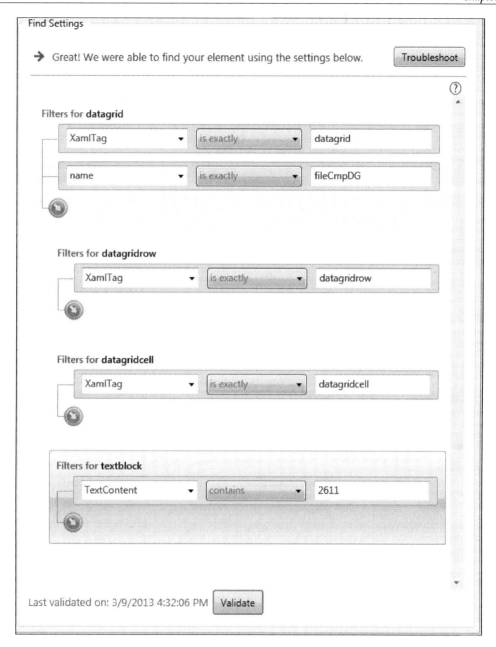

Chained expressions for data grid cells based on the content

Finding the cell in question requires a four-level search. Firstly, it starts by locating the data grid object using its tag type and `name` attribute. Once located, the second-level search would be to find any child object with a tag equal to **DataGridRow**. By default, if we stop here, the first row inside the data grid is returned; this is why we need to provide further attributes for evaluation in order for Test studio to uniquely identify an element mapping to our criteria. This can be understood in depth by clicking on the **Validate** button at this stage. The following diagram shows the object that Test Studio has identified after adding the first two chained expressions only:

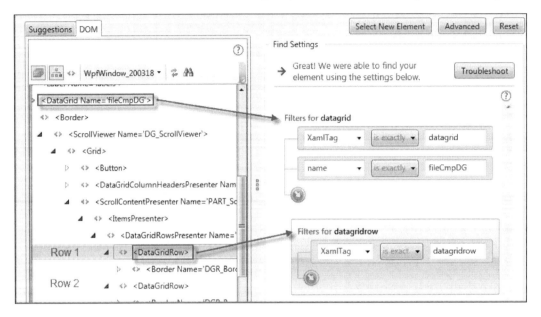

Chained expressions behavior

The third level looks for any data grid cell inside a **datagridrow**. Again if we stop adding filters, the first data grid cell of the first data grid row is returned. The last level queries apparent screen text content of the data grid cells. Hence, we are looking for a cell that contains the value `2611`. By doing that we would have concluded the crafting of a chained find expression yielding to the same cell independent of its position inside the data grid.

Had the content been irrelevant to the test case context, the Find logic of the following screenshot would result in the first cell of the first row inside the file comparison data grid, without having to resort to hard-wiring hierarchy objects in the XamlPath attribute of the cell.

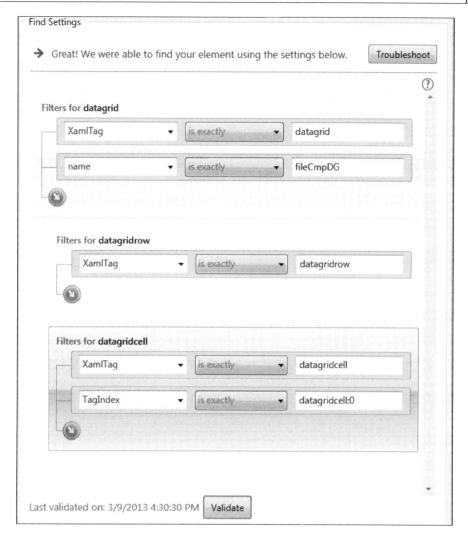

Chained expressions for data grid cells based on position

Lastly, click on the **Save** button to finalize the editing of the locator. You can rename the element-friendly name to `File2611` to make it more informative. Run your test to verify that the updates did not interfere with the test execution.

The Find class

The capabilities for Test Studio UI locators are founded in the ArtOfTest automation library. This means whatever was done through the Test Studio IDE is also doable from the code. All the search methods for locating an element are wrapped inside the Find class. In a WPF application, this class is accessible from any container. In our case, each window will hold a reference for this class through which we can exert our search expressions.

This has two applications in real life. The first one is when accessing an element that is not yet defined in the element repository. Hence, accessing the element becomes allowable through the dynamic evaluation of search expressions fed to the various find methods of the Find class. The accessed element can then be interacted with by applying different UI operations. The other area of application is in automating tests for UI and that is verifying properties for UI elements, and the hierarchical relation with respect to their surrounding elements. For example, making sure whether an element exists, validating its width, layout, content, and so on.

Suppose that in the previous example, we want to verify that there exists a cell with content 2611 before actually clicking on it.

In the `Func-9_History_Details_Successful` test, add a script step by clicking on the **Script Step** button of the **Add** ribbon. Edit the description to the added step as follows:

```
this.ActiveApplication.GetWindow("File Comparer").
  RefreshVisualTrees();
XamlFindExpression xamlFindExpression = new
  XamlFindExpression("XamlTag=datagrid","name=fileCmpDG","|",
  "XamlTag=datagridrow","|","XamlTag=datagridcell","|",
  "TextContent=~2611");
Assert.IsNotNull(Applications.File_Comparerexe.File_Comparer.Find.
  ByExpression(xamlFindExpression));
```

The first statement of the code refreshes the DOM tree for the **File Comparer** window, in order to force Test Studio to rebuild the hierarchy element in the event of selecting a value from the dates combobox. Once the DOM is updated, it is safe to search for the newly appeared data grid item.

The second statement is responsible for building the filter expressions, where, by convention, the pipe sign (|) is used to introduce a chained expression. The chained expressions consist of sequentially finding the data grid, data grid row, data grid cell, and then cell content as we have seen in the **Find Settings** window of the previous example.

The third statement uses the `Assert.IsNotNull` method, which serves in verifying that the search execution did actually result in an element. The outcome of this statement will affect the test result. The search is invoked through a call to the `ByExpression` method of the `Find` class. The tilde sign (~) implies that search value `2611` has to be contained inside the cell text. The remaining comparison operators are represented as follows:

- `!` = NotContain
- `^` = StartsWith
- `?` = EndsWith
- `#` = RegEx
- `-` = Missing
- `+` = Exists

After you finish editing the method, place the coded step before the one which performs the action of clicking on the cell, then run the test and verify that the assertion was successful in Test Studio execution log.

The `Find.ByExpression` method is just one way of building your expression criteria. The powerful thing about it is that it allows you to build complex filters just as we have seen with chained expression. Other methods are available, for example, to search by name using the `Find.ByName` method or automation ID using the `Find.ByAutomationId` method, where their parameters correspond respectively to the element name and automation ID.

The Element factory

Test Studio surely enables a powerful and flexible mechanism to locate UI elements without having the need to hardcode values. Despite this flexibility, remember that the elements defined by external reference are scattered among the test scripts and in the normal case the same logic for the find expression is replicated inside those tests' coded steps. Eventually, you might encounter a change to the application UI, which will cause a change to all those find expressions and that is a maintainability deficiency in your tests. As an attempt to find a solution, you strive to abstract out the element's definitions from your test's steps and centralize them at one place. Hence, any change in an inevitable UI element that falls upon your application will engender editing the find expression of that element in only one place. The solution consists of storing the different Find logic for the application elements in one physical file on your disk, and then upon any test startup a coded step is inserted to load the elements and their find expressions in a dictionary, which will be accessible throughout all the test steps. The physical file resembles a factory providing element ingredients to produce test elements at runtime.

To implement the solution:

1. Place the `ElementRepository.xml` file in the `root` directory of the `C:` of your machine.

2. To process XML files, add reference to the `System.XML.dll` and `System.XML.Linq.dll` libraries through the **Show** button in the **Project** tab **Settings** ribbon.

3. Create a WPF test under the `Functional Tests` folder.

4. Open it for editing and record one test step to perform a click on the **File Info** tab.

5. Add a script step.

6. Click on the **View Class** button to show the underlying class code.

7. Add the two `using` statements to enable accessing the XML file through the coded steps as follows:

```
using System.Xml;
using System.Xml.Linq;
```

8. Add to the beginning of the class, the following statement to instantiate the `Dictionary` structure that is going to hold the elements with their respective `findExpressions`:

```
Dictionary<string, string> findExpressions = new
Dictionary<string, string>();
```

9. Update the coded step body with the following code whose purpose is to read the XML file and populate the dictionary with its content:

```
string pathToXmlFile = @"C:\ElementRepository.xml";
XElement elementRep = XElement.Load(pathToXmlFile);
foreach (XElement element in elementRep.Elements("add"))
{
    findExpressions.Add(element.Attribute("element").Value,
        element.Attribute("expression").Value);
}
```

10. Add another coded step that will be used to simulate typing certain text inside the **File Name** text field:

```
this.ActiveApplication.GetWindow("File
    Comparer").RefreshVisualTrees();
Applications.File_Comparerexe.File_Comparer.Find.
    ByExpression(new XamlFindExpression(findExpressions
    ["FileName"])).User.TypeText("Testing File", 1000, true);
```

The first statement refreshes the DOM element tree in the event of clicking the **File Info** tab. The second statement uses the retrieved find expression of the **File Name** text field defined in the element repository file, and calls the `TypeText` method to imitate writing a text inside it.

Run your test and notice how the `Testing File` expression is entered inside the **File Name** field.

Summary

This chapter has dealt with issues related to constructing and locating UI elements constituting the automated tests. Firstly, we saw how elements are on one hand added automatically by Test Studio and on the other hand added manually with custom-friendly names. Secondly, the mechanism by which Test Studio forms the `Element` repository at startup was explained and demonstrated by tackling those element's properties. Thirdly, the element's find expressions were described while also exhibiting the options available to constructing filter expressions based on the controls' properties. Finally, the last section dealt with a way to provide a flexible, centralized, and maintainable element repository by saving the element's Find logic in a unified physical file.

By that we would have tackled from different sides, the element recognition and reliability problem raised at the beginning of the chapter. The material in this chapter wraps up the learning of functional automated testing started in the first chapter and continued in the second. Next, we will see how to create manual test scripts inside Test Studio and automate their execution process.

5
Manual Testing

On an ordinary day, you report to work where you run into your boss down the office coridoor. And there you go! Thirty minutes later, your fine day is struck by the fact that your boss is expecting a list of test cases not automated, yet to be automated, and already automated. All kinds of problems start popping inside your head: "Test workbooks are dispersed all over testers' machines, so how can I possibly get the count of all these test cases? There is a weak traceability between automated and manual scripts, so how can I tell which test case is automated and which one is not?"

If this is your typical testing work environment, you are probably familiar with the trouble you've put into compiling a list of all the tests and producing statistics around certain criteria. In reality, if the manual scripts were saved in Excel workbooks, we would most likely utilize the sheet columns to fill them with values referring perhaps to the automated test ID, incident report ID, feature ID, and so on. We would also use the folders in the filesystem to mimic the hierarchy of projects and their corresponding releases.

This is what the era looks like prior to automating the test management process. With the automation of the manual testing process, the difficulty for maintaining an orderly repository phases out and gets substituted with a smart mechanism capable of promptly responding to testing-specific queries.

This chapter uses features from Test Studio to cope with the preceding problems. It contains examples illustrating:

- A manual test creation
- A manual test integration with MS Excel
- The automated setup and teardown routines for preparing and restoring system states
- A manual test execution
- How to manage manual test case attributes

Manual Testing

During the process of converting a manual test into automated scripts, a decision needs to be made concerning which tasks and tests are to be conserved in their manual states, which test cases are suitable for automation, and when would you gain more by keeping a test in its manual state.

There are some assessments that you need to reflect on concerning a test's nature and worth with respect to the project's lifetime before choosing to develop an automated test.

Hence, when a test case is intended for automation, you want to firstly ask yourself, "What is the value behind automating it?"

First of all, you would want to consider the test development effort with respect to the test's lifetime. The prevalence of one of the preceding factors tilts the equation of ROI (return on investment) to one side or another. Ultimately, the less the effort and the longer the usage of the test is, the greater the ROI. For example, to create an automated test involving a user interface surely requires more work than a test calling a web service, given that the former needs to firstly overcome the challenges related to capturing screen objects. If the user interface test will run only once or will deprecate with the next interface remodeling, the durable value for the test is poor and therefore the automation cost is negatively affected this way.

Moreover, consider the test's worth also with regards to its lifetime. As you know, the applications under test gain immunity as fixes are introduced following each test suite execution. So during the early phases, you need to primarily focus on tests that are able to ascertain the appropriateness of a certain functionality and postpone tests in which the underlying bug is fixed and is not likely to recur. For instance, favor automating tests related to the successful submission of a form over a field's input limit. If the field input limit was buggy at some point in time, it is improbable that a developer will deliberately revert it; whereas, in the form submission case, any change elsewhere in the application could create an unforeseen negative impact. Hence, ask yourself, is the test in question adding value for my regression suite?

Secondly, consider the point at which the automation has started with respect to the project's timeline. How far is the project towards its completion? Proper time needs to be accounted for automation, especially if the knowledge in the automation tool is not present yet. For this reason, squeezing in additional tasks in the project schedule could result in delaying feedback on the application's quality state, where this feedback becomes ineffective if not processed in the needed time. This also brings up the question of what to automate versus when to automate? Therefore, you should consider looking at test maintenance effects and start automating those tests with the lowest maintenance cost where updating them is affordable as changes are introduced into the application.

Thirdly, think about the degree of intervention required by the tester. Tests necessitating less human analysis and interference in response to the system events are favored, since more complex the scenarios are, higher is the complexity of the scripts. Eventually, the tests lose their credibility when lots of reported bugs are traced back to the automation code rather than the source code. These situations are called false positives.

All of the preceding points are arguments that support why you should sometimes stick to manual testing. Nevertheless, manually carrying out all the tasks related to manual testing is tedious and devalues its advantages. Common problems with the manual execution process are repository maintenance, subjectivity in test interpretation that requires a prior consent to the extent of procedures' details, reporting results, performing repetitive time-consuming tasks, and others.

Test Studio embeds a solution that starts with creating manual tests and then gradually transitioning them into automated ones. It also provides the possibility to automate fractions of these tests to deliver the tester from the manual handling of tedious tasks. As we will also see, Test Studio's integration with third-party solutions offers versioning and collaboration control over tests.

Manual tests

Let's store the steps for creating a file metadata through `File Comparer` inside a manual test. The folder that is going to contain the entire set of manual tests is called `Manual Test Scripts`; therefore, right-click on the `FileComparer.Test` project node, choose **Create Folder** from the context menu and rename it.

Test Studio has a dedicated template for manual testing, having its specialized toolkit and runner. The template will appear among the list of available templates when attempting to create a new test as follows:

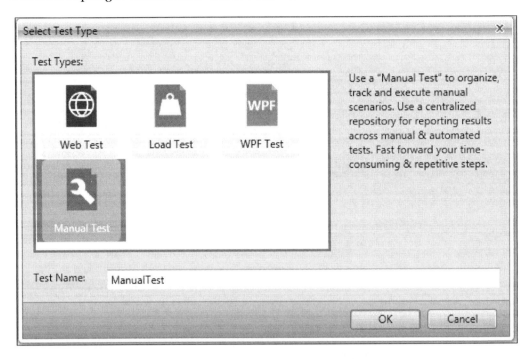

Creating a manual test

Create a manual test under the recently added test. Enter `Func-6_FileInfo_Create_Successful_Manual` in the **Test Name** field and then click on **OK**. Enter the test edit mode by double-clicking on the test entry. The test initially looks as follows:

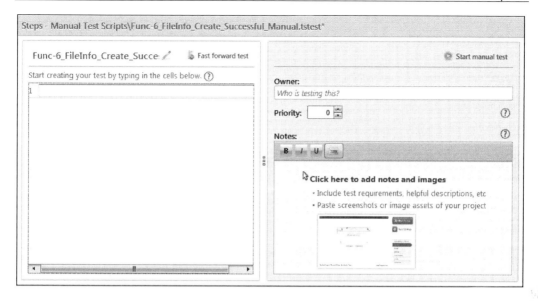

The manual test workspace

The pane to the left is the workspace for creating and editing the manual steps. It currently has the mouse focus. We will input the manual steps starting with launching the application, so enter `Start File Comparer` and press *Enter*. Repeat the same steps to add the subsequent test steps as follows:

1. Map the default path to: `C:\File Comparer Files`.
2. Go to the **File Info** tab.
3. Enter `Incident Report` in **File Name**.
4. Enter `Jack Thomas` in **Creator Name**.
5. Set **File Extension** to **DOC**.
6. Set **Effort** to **2**.
7. Click on the **Create** button.
8. Verify that the result contains the word, **allowed**.

This is all that is required to create manual test steps. Let's pass this test for *Bill Tester* to run. Conveniently, he is the new tester in the team and seems very excited to start with his testing tasks.

The right pane shown in the preceding screenshot captures metadata for the test. Enter `Bill Tester` in the field allocated to enter the name of the owner. Since a failure in this test could signify a blocked feature, let's set the test priority to `9` where `10` refers to the highest priority.

Now Bill opens his assigned test to run it and finds himself wondering about the way to execute certain steps. He thinks that this difficulty is due to his lack of experience, where in fact it is due to the inadequate precision of the manual steps' instructions. This sheds light on one disadvantage of manual testing, that is, high-level procedures are well suited only for experienced testers, especially knowledgeable in the application under test. For new testers, some application-specific vocabulary such as the map default folder can be ambiguous. On the other hand, providing too many details during a test case generation can be time consuming. Test Studio resolves this conflict by offering a rich text editor that allows attaching additional description and snapshots in order to decrease chances of step misinterpretations only when they are needed. Hence, in the **Notes** section, inside the right panel, we can leave the following message:

To map the application folder click on the Set Path button as depicted in this snapshot:

Excel integration

Test Studio alleviates the repetitive nature of the manual test step creation through its integration with MS Excel. If you already have your tests stored in Excel workbooks, converting them into manual tests is effortless as you will see.

The `File Comparer - Manual Test Scripts.xlsx` workbook has the manual test cases generated by applying various testing techniques on the `File Comparer` application. In this example, we will see how to import a test case from the `Concrete Tests` sheet. Before we get into this, we will create a manual test called `Func-10_ FileInfo_Create_Failing_Manual` and place it under the `Manual Test Scripts` folder. Double-click on it to enter its edit mode and then locate the **Excel Import** option from the Excel ribbon highlighted in the following screenshot:

The Excel Import button

An **Import Manual Step...** window is launched. This window allows you to specify the location from which Test Studio will retrieve the test description. Browse for the Excel workbook location by clicking on the ellipsis button of the **Select Excel File** field. Select **Concrete Tests$** and **Description** for **Select Table** and **Select Column** comboboxes respectively.

Upon setting the window parameters, the **Preview Data** section of the **Import Manual Step...** window shown in the following screenshot retrieves the filled rows of the `Description` column.

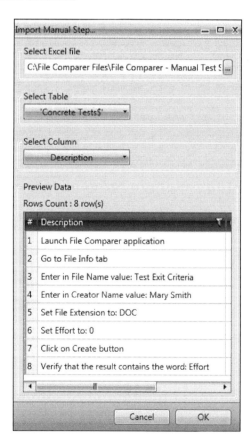

Importing manual steps

After clicking on **OK**, the steps for importing manual tests are concluded and the manual test steps are inserted into the newly created test. This test covers the equivalence partitions highlighted in dark red in the Design sheet. Equivalence partitioning is a testing technique used to divide the system input or output into sets such that any value belonging to the same input set will result in the same system output behavior, and vice versa. Any value belonging to the output set will be induced by applying the equivalent input. Finally, the test should look as follows:

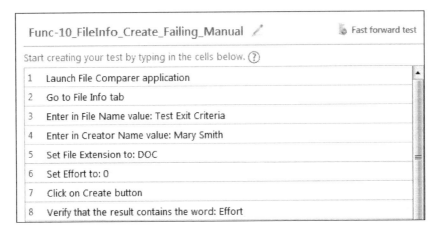

Steps of the Func-10_FileInfo_Create_Failing_Manual test

The Excel integration inside Test Studio is a two-way process. We have seen how to import test cases, and now we will see the reversed process, which is exporting. This means that if you had your manual tests initially created directly inside Test Studio, you have a way to extract the contained steps and save them in an Excel workbook.

To do so, from the **Export** ribbon, click on the **Excel Export** option. The **Save As** dialog is invoked which allows you to specify the destination directory.

Adding existing tests

So far we have seen how to create raw tests by entering the underlying steps and how to create tests by importing the underlying steps. Test Studio offers more flexibility while creating tests, such as adding an existing one. This feature applies on all the test types.

Right-click on the `Manual Test Scripts` folder and choose **Add Existing Test** from the context menu. Browse for the `Func-13_Login_Failing_Hybrid.ts` test and then click on **OK**. Following this action, a new entry for the existing test is added to the `Manual Test Scripts` folder.

Hybrid tests

Manual and automated tests coexist in a compatible way inside Test Studio where, as a side effect, the transition between them is smooth. At any point during the lifetime of the test, the test resides on an automation scale beginning with a fully manual test up to a fully automated one. Between the two boundaries, a test is called hybrid. This test is a blend between the two extreme types, and it profits from both of their powerful particularities.

A hybrid test is a manual test made convenient for execution. Its convenience is derived from the fact that it mitigates mechanical repetitive tasks that challenge the tester with time and continuous focus. Let's take an example of a login dialog that appears during an application's start-up. Firstly, this operation is repeated in the same manner for all test cases that make up a test suite designated for execution. Secondly, it is mechanical and can even be performed almost unconsciously by a tester. Thirdly, this step is only a bridge to get to the test core, where the inability to achieve it is sufficient to bring the test execution to an end and assert its failure. As you can see in this context, this operation has no reason for it to be carried out manually. On the contrary, all the arguments mentioned previously call for an automation.

In Test Studio, the feature that makes the preceding flexibility available is called fast forward. This feature allows advance operations, similar to the preceding login example, at any point inside the test. Fast forward is mostly useful in the setup and tear down procedures, which are normally used to put the system in a certain state and restore it back after execution.

In the coming test, we will demonstrate the usage of the fast forward feature to automatically simulate operations at the beginning and at the end of a manual test. Create a test called `Func-6_FileInfo_Create_Failing_Hybrid` under the `Manual Test Scripts` folder and add the following manual steps to it:

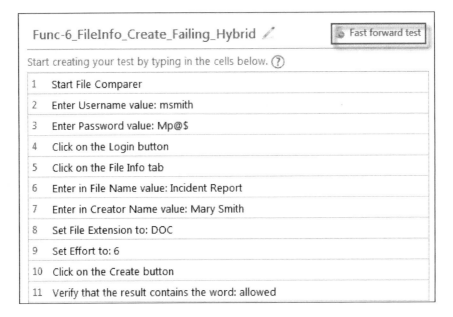

Steps of the Func-6_FileInfo_Create_Failing_Hybrid manual test

 Note that although this test title contains the word `Failing`, this test is not failing yet.

Steps 1 to 4 seem to be recurring for all tests and hence they fit the criteria for an automated setup routine. Consequently, let's apply the fast forward feature to them.

Firstly, we need to enable authorization for the `File Comparer` application so that a login dialog is launched to ask the user for their login credentials before the main application window is displayed. So open the `settings.xml` file from the application's `Bin` folder and edit the authorization tag to `<authorization>True</authorization>`.

Back to the test inside Test Studio, click on the **Fast forward test** button outlined in the preceding screenshot.

The first step of the **Fast Forward Manual Test** dialog is to choose whether you want to use the forward feature with a WPF Test or a Web Test as shown in the following screenshot. Click on the **WPF Test** option:

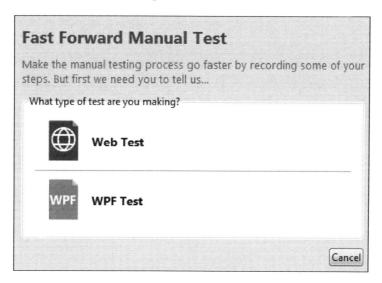

The Fast forward test button

The second step consists of examining further information about the fast forwarding feature. To finish enabling this feature, click on the **Close** button.

Notice how the ribbon for the test now holds the automation toolkit seen in the previous chapters. For instance, to continue adding manual test steps, you have to use the same procedures for an automated WPF test and that is by clicking on the **More** button of the **Add** tab.

If the **More** button is not visible, first click on the **Advanced** button of the **Workspace** tab.

The **Application** tab is available again, so click on the **Record** button to capture the steps that we want to fast forward when executing the test manually. As usual, map the application executable by clicking on the **Configure** button of the **Application** tab and start recording. The `File Comparer` application is now started and the **Login** window is invoked before we could use the remaining application functionalities. Enter the username and password found in the preceding procedure steps and then click on the **Login** button.

Move the recorded steps to the very beginning of the test and disable their matching manual steps as follows:

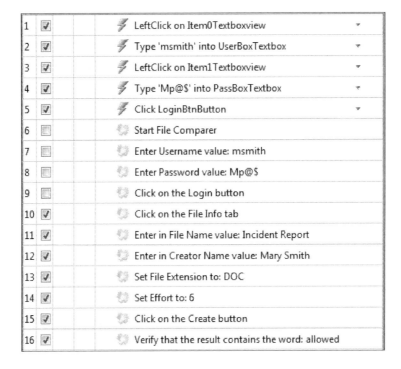

1	✔		⚡ LeftClick on Item0Textboxview	▾
2	✔		⚡ Type 'msmith' into UserBoxTextbox	▾
3	✔		⚡ LeftClick on Item1Textboxview	▾
4	✔		⚡ Type 'Mp@$' into PassBoxTextbox	▾
5	✔		⚡ Click LoginBtnButton	▾
6	☐		Start File Comparer	
7	☐		Enter Username value: msmith	
8	☐		Enter Password value: Mp@$	
9	☐		Click on the Login button	
10	✔		Click on the File Info tab	
11	✔		Enter in File Name value: Incident Report	
12	✔		Enter in Creator Name value: Mary Smith	
13	✔		Set File Extension to: DOC	
14	✔		Set Effort to: 6	
15	✔		Click on the Create button	
16	✔		Verify that the result contains the word: allowed	

The Func-6_FileInfo_Create_Failing_Hybrid test in the hybrid mode

After this test is successfully executed, an entry for the file is added to the database. The next time the test runs, the submission will be rejected since the file cannot be committed to the database due to uniqueness constraint on the filename. Therefore, the created entry should be cleared from the database right after the first execution before the test ends.

Since our test has now become hybrid, we can add scripted steps similar to tests based on the automated WPF template. In the **Add** tab, click on the **Script Test** button. Move this method to the last step and then edit its signature and body as follows:

1. Update the method name to `Func6_FileInfo_Create_Failing_Hybrid_ DeleteFile`.

2. Update description to `Deletes database entry for the file name`.

3. Add the `using` block to the class:

   ```
   using System.Data.SqlClient;
   ```

4. Update the body to:

   ```
   string query = "DELETE FROM [dbo].[FileInfo] WHERE [File Name] =
   'Incident Report'";

   using (SqlConnection hrCon = new SqlConnection("Data
   Source=localhost;Initial Catalog=FC_DB;Persist Security
   Info=True;User ID=FC_DB_USER;Password=po0$wt;Connection
   Timeout=30"))
               {
           hrCon.Open();

           SqlCommand hrCommand = null;
           hrCommand = new SqlCommand(query, hrCon);
           hrCommand.CommandType = System.Data.CommandType.
             Text;
           SqlDataReader sqlDR =  hrCommand.ExecuteReader();
           sqlDR.Close();
           hrCon.Close();
       }
   ```

5. Add a reference to the `System.Data.dll` library by clicking on the **Show** button in the **Settings** option in the **Project** tab.

This method is supposed to firstly establish a connection to the database, which the application interacts with, and then delete the created row. The connection to the database is specified in the connection string of the `using` block. As for the query, it is defined as the first line in a T-SQL statement. The query firstly searches for an entry inside the destination table with a filename identical to that entered in the manual steps and then deletes it.

 In the code for the preceding step 4, remember to update the data source parameter for the `Sqlconnection` constructor with the connection string to your database.

With that we would have guaranteed that neither the repetitive execution of this manual test will be invalidated as a result of filename duplicity, nor the generation of a new filename value is needed upon each execution instance.

Refactor tests

The setup and tear down procedures for the case we have just covered are operations that are likely to be common to other manual tests. Basically, many test cases will involve application login and database restoration and would therefore need some automated steps to accomplish them on behalf of the tester. So, it would be beneficial to find a way that unifies these operations and save the tester's time and maintenance effort in the long run. In general, if you notice such deficiency in your tests or any room for improvement, it is time to pause and shift your automation efforts towards some refactoring. The refactoring that we are going to apply consists of abstracting the definition of the coded steps inside the test and raising it up to a higher level.

As a start, we will extract the automated steps concerned with the application login. So select the first five steps, then right-click anywhere inside the selection, and choose **Create Test as Step** from the context menu as shown in the following screenshot:

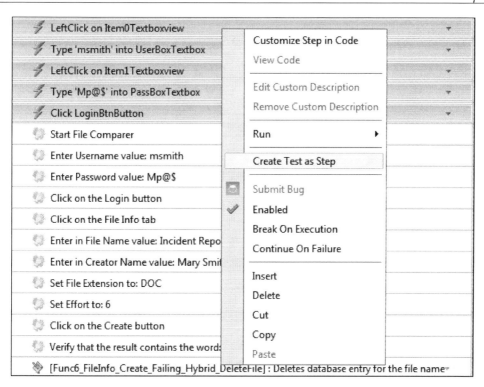

Exporting steps to a new test

In the invoked dialog, rename the test as 'Op_Login'.

The outcome consists of removing the steps and replacing them with a call to an external test that we called Op_Login. Further on in the project, whenever a manual test calls for login procedures, the manual steps can be replaced by Op_Login, which is now accessible and shareable between other manual tests.

We will apply the same concept to the last scripted step responsible for deleting the created record from the database table. However, first we need to update its definition to comply with its targeted purpose. Currently, the query that gets executed in the database deletes the record having the filename, Incident Report. Since not all testing documents are called incident reports, this query is ought to be generalized. We will update it so that it sorts the table in a descending order based on the date the file was created on to pull the last inserted entry to the first row.

Afterwards, we will delete the top first row that, given the preceding information, corresponds with the lastly created file. Consequently, double-click on the coded method and update its implementation to the following code snippet that caters for the provided preceding description:

```
string query = "DELETE  fn from (SELECT TOP(1) [File Name], CreatedOn
FROM [dbo].[FileInfo] ORDER BY CreatedOn DESC) fn";

using (SqlConnection hrCon = new SqlConnection("Data
Source=localhost;Initial Catalog=FC_DB;Persist Security Info=True;User
ID=FC_DB_USER;Password=po0$wt;Connection Timeout=30"))
        {
            hrCon.Open();

            SqlCommand hrCommand = null;
            hrCommand = new SqlCommand(query, hrCon);
            hrCommand.CommandType = System.Data.CommandType.Text;
            SqlDataReader sqlDR =  hrCommand.ExecuteReader();
            sqlDR.Close();
            hrCon.Close();
        }
```

The query has now become general enough to handle any type of file, so right-click on the coded step and again choose the **Create Test as Step** option. Rename it as `Op_DeleteFileInfo`. Open the `Op_DeleteFileInfo` test, and add the following line to the code behind the `using` block:

```
using System.Data.SqlClient;
```

Lastly, delete the disabled manual steps for the `Func-6_FileInfo_Create_Failing_Hybrid` test. The resulting test is shown in the following screenshot:

1	☑		⚡ Execute test 'Op_Login'	▾
2	☑		Click on the File Info tab	
3	☑		Enter in File Name value: Incident Report	
4	☑		Enter in Creator Name value: Mary Smith	
5	☑		Set File Extension to: DOC	
6	☑		Set Effort to: 6	
7	☑		Click on the Create button	
8	☑		Verify that the result contains the word: allowed	
9	☑		⚡ Execute test 'Op_DeleteFileInfo'	▾

Steps of the Func-6_FileInfo_Create_Failing_Hybrid test

Repository maintenance

With the intention of organizing the test repository inside Test Studio and allowing easy navigation inside it in the future, reorganize your tests as shown in the following screenshot by wrapping the newly created tests in descriptive folder names:

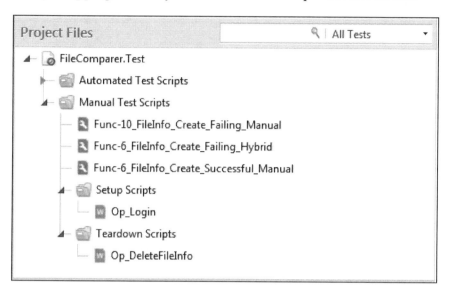

Organizing the test project

Test execution

Test Studio not only gives you the possibility to store manual tests and keep them manageable in a neat repository, but it also guides their execution process. Generally, problems in manual test execution are raised at many levels. The first problem is the lack of relevant critical proofs on the system state, interactions, and responses during execution, especially for test steps marked as failing. In such cases, the difficulty in tracking back and reproducing failures particularly related to intermittent bugs increases. The second problem is complementary to the first one where even if these helpers do exist, accessing them can be a challenging task in a scattered environment. The third problem is the increased complexity in monitoring and verifying the test execution process when the reporting granularity does not start at a test step level.

Test Studio dedicates a special runner for tests based on manual templates that functions differently from that of automated tests. This runner frees manual testing from the preceding difficulties by guiding the execution in a step-by-step manner. In addition, it integrates the process of gathering and saving visual aids, which makes capturing the system state an eeasy and a straightforward task.

Enter the `Func-6_FileInfo_Create_Failing_Hybrid` test, and click on the **Run** button from the **Quick Execution** tab to start the manual test runner.

A window is launched comprising of two steps as shown in the following screenshot:

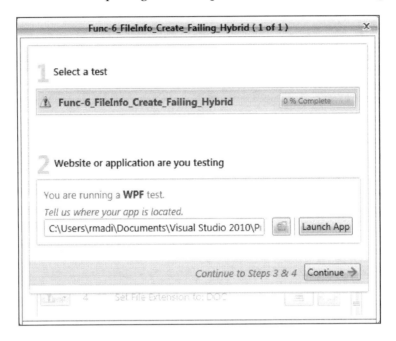

Test runner for manual tests

The first step represents the percentage of execution completion. Upon test startup, zero percent of the test is completed. This number is updated as the test runs and can be sought at any point in the test's execution. The second step prompts the tester whether Test Studio should launch the application before the manual execution starts where changing an executable application is still allowed by browsing the filesystem after clicking on the button showing the folder icon.

Click on the **Launch App** button to start the `File Comparer` application against which the automated tests will execute. After the **File Comparer Login** window appears, click on the **Continue** button to bring the test steps into view.

The runner now displays step 3 of the process which is a test step for execution, assessment, and annotation. At the bottom of the window, step 4 is also displayed, which holds the overall test status. The following screenshot shows the invoked window with the created manual and automated steps:

Executing and annotating test steps

The uppermost set of outlined buttons is used to change the result status for manual steps in the batch mode. The second set of outlined buttons is used for steps' annotation. Finally, the last outlined button and all subsequent similar ones denote the individual step result.

As it was intended during the test design, the `Op_Login` test is supposed to execute automatically. Therefore, select this step by simply clicking on it, and then click on the **Selected** button following the **Fast Forward** label. The runner will execute the UI operations against the **Login** window by populating its **Username** and **Password** fields and then clicking on the **Login** button.

Notice how the test result button icon for this automated step is changed to a green tick symbol representing the automatic result of the test. This button is disabled for automated steps and therefore cannot be manually updated. Click on the **Notes** button corresponding to the button located in the right side of the set highlighted in orange. A rich text editor is expanded to receive custom notes that can contain any relevant details. Enter the line `Pre-Conditions have successfully executed` and click on the **Done** button.

The next set of steps is the manual ones. Manually execute the instructions of the next step and update the result depending on whether you were able to execute it successfully or not. Repeat the same procedure and stop at step 9.

The outcome of step 8 dictates the overall test end result, hence it is worth attaching to it a snapshot of the current system state. Click on **Capture**, which is the left button of the set highlighted in orange. In the **Capture image** window, click on the **Capture** button on the upper-left corner to take a snapshot of the desktop. Then you can use the **Annotate** buttons to draw a rectangle around the result in order to make it remarkable as shown in the following screenshot:

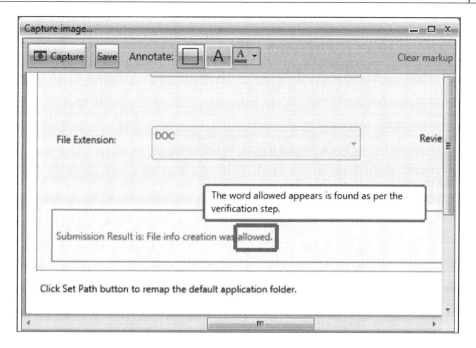

Capturing images during manual steps execution

This wraps up manual steps for this test. Step 9 is supposed to clean up the created data. This is an automatic operation, hence select it and click on the **Selected** button. Again the underlying test is executed by Test Studio, and the result is set right upon completion.

We have now reached step 4 where we have either the option to save the result or to reset it and start over. Click on the **Save & Close** button to stop the manual runner and end the execution.

The manual test execution process that used to bear the load underneath the tedious tasks of creating, organizing, maintaining, running, and reporting test results of manual tests has now become simpler as we have seen. Test Studio shares the load by taking over the mechanical tasks to leave your focus on the analysis and usage of its annotation abilities to capture significant data.

Data binding

Suppose that you want to associate the manual test to the input values different from those that are hardcoded inside its definition, then there are normally two options, either create a duplicate test for each set of input or store these inputs in an Excel workbook and come up with a way to associate it with the test. The disadvantages of the preceding suggested strategies are redundancy and deficiency in having all the test data centralized in one repository and accessible through one portal. Consequently, both the strategies lead to a less maintainable and manageable solution. Here again, the situation calls for the need to convert the test definition to a data-driven one.

Therefore, go to the **Project** tab and then right-click on the `Func-6_FileInfo_Create_Failing_Hybrid` test under the `Manual Test Scripts` folder. Choose the **Data Bind** option from the context menu and set the values for the **Bind test to data source** window as follows:

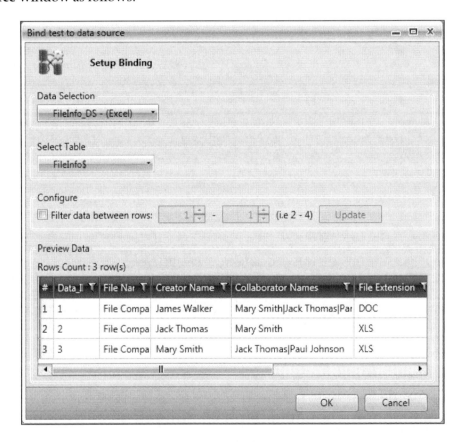

Binding a manual test to a data source

This data source is of the type Excel and was used previously for the fully automated version of this test with the purpose of automating a data-driven execution.

The properties of the test are updated by Test Studio, as shown in the following screenshot:

The DataEnabled property for data-driven manual tests

The test property for `DataEnabled` is set to true where the **Source** now refers to the data source belonging and residing within the whole project solution. Notice how this feature facilitates the finding and accessing of input data to be fed into the manual test where it makes Test Studio a unique gateway for gathering all the information needed to execute a test.

Transitioning to automated tests

As automation becomes integrated in the company testing strategy, little by little, the manual test cases that are well suited for automation will eventually all finish by becoming fully automated. The previous sections have demonstrated how Test Studio allows a congruent storage for automated and manual tests. We have also seen how these extreme types can be merged by adding automatic steps to manual tests and vice versa. Now we will see how Test Studio supports the complete transition of a test case from its manual to automated state through its built-in features.

For instance, after automating all the manual steps for `Func-6_FileInfo_Create_ Failing_Hybrid` and removing the data binding source, it will change to something similar to the following screenshot:

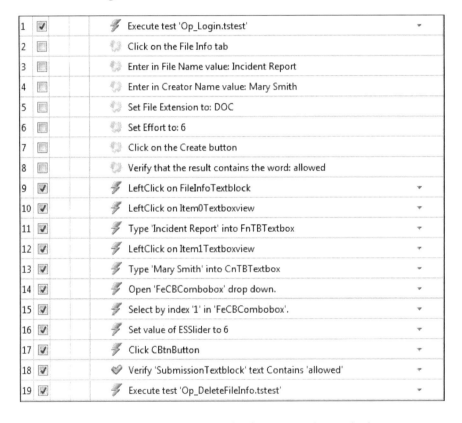

1	☑		⚡ Execute test 'Op_Login.tstest'	▾
2	☐		Click on the File Info tab	
3	☐		Enter in File Name value: Incident Report	
4	☐		Enter in Creator Name value: Mary Smith	
5	☐		Set File Extension to: DOC	
6	☐		Set Effort to: 6	
7	☐		Click on the Create button	
8	☐		Verify that the result contains the word: allowed	
9	☑		⚡ LeftClick on FileInfoTextblock	▾
10	☑		⚡ LeftClick on Item0Textboxview	▾
11	☑		⚡ Type 'Incident Report' into FnTBTextbox	▾
12	☑		⚡ LeftClick on Item1Textboxview	▾
13	☑		⚡ Type 'Mary Smith' into CnTBTextbox	▾
14	☑		⚡ Open 'FeCBCombobox' drop down.	▾
15	☑		⚡ Select by index '1' in 'FeCBCombobox'.	▾
16	☑		⚡ Set value of ESSlider to 6	▾
17	☑		⚡ Click CBtnButton	▾
18	☑		♥ Verify 'SubmissionTextblock' text Contains 'allowed'	▾
19	☑		⚡ Execute test 'Op_DeleteFileInfo.tstest'	▾

Automated steps for the Func-6_FileInfo_Create_Failing_Hybrid test

This test no longer needs a manual runner to execute. Hence, to change the associated runner, go to the **Project** tab, and select the test to display its properties in the **Properties** pane. From the **Misc** section, uncheck the `IsManual` property as shown in the following screenshot:

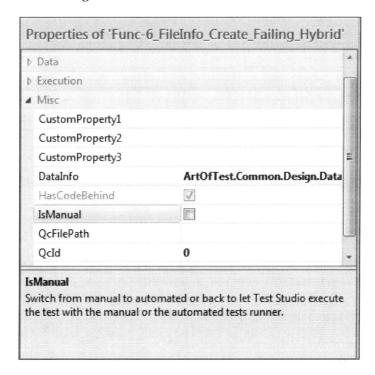

Editing the IsManual property for manual tests

In the **Project Files** pane, notice how the test icon changes to that of a WPF template. The test will now use the automation runner to execute, which (as we have seen in the previous chapters) will start off by automatically executing the steps in contrast with the manual runner. Whenever a manual step is encountered within the test, the execution will pause until the step is manually executed and verified.

Versioning

So far you have been working alone on designing and crafting the tests. The same process will get complicated when many persons are collaborating on the same file instance, or even worse when creating updated instances of that file. Problems such as overwriting each other's versions or losing track of the correct order of the file versions may arise—not to mention other risks such as completely losing the accomplished work following the unexpected event of a machine failure.

Source control systems are created to resolve the aforementioned conflicts by offering a centralized monitored repository where all files are backed up. Each change on these files is audited, starting from check out until check in, where at that point, the discrepancies between the local and the server versions are resolved by choosing which change to overwrite with what. Alternatively, some source control systems give you the option to forbid operations on a file from the beginning unless that file is not checked out by any other party. Changes are usually submitted in incrementing versions, where the ability to revert back to a previous version is allowed. In addition to that, it is possible for all parties working on the document to retrieve each other's work to alter or append it.

Source controls could have additional benefits; however, in this section, we will be concerned only with working around the preceding problems in Test Studio through its integration with **TFS (Team Foundation Server)**. In addition to TFS, Test Studio offers integration with other source controls such as SVN, Git, and Vault.

In order to bind your project to TFS, you need to start by connecting Test Studio to it. To define the connection, go to the **Project** tab, and click on the **Connect** button from the **TFS** section. The **Bind to Source Control** window shown in the following screenshot is invoked:

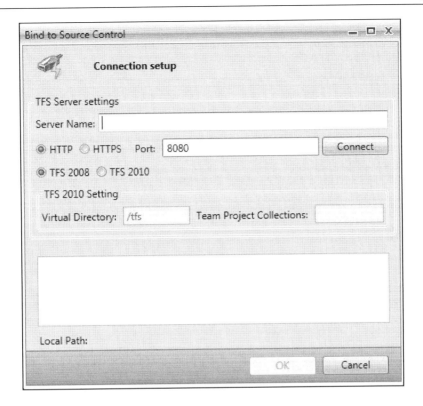

Binding to TFS

Enter the values for **Server Name**, **Port**, and **TFS version** depending on the deployed instance of your TFS and then click on the **Connect** button.

If the connection is successful, TFS projects are retrieved and listed in the blank area allowing you to pick the one that is going to hold the `File Comparer` automated solution. Select a project node and then click on the **OK** button.

Subsequently, you can start committing the project items. Note that the icons marking any node of the project tree are important in indicating the state of the Test Studio item with respect to TFS; their significance will be explained with each source control operation. Currently, all the nodes are marked with a yellow plus sign, which means that they are still only bound to a source control. They will maintain this sign until they are committed. The following screenshot shows the `File Comparer` solution after binding it to TFS:

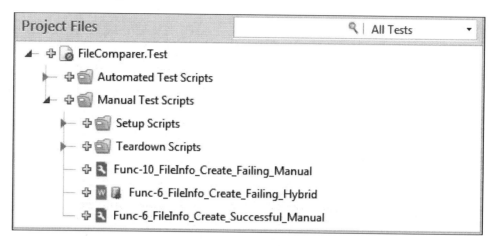

The FileComparer.Test project bound to TFS

The context menu for any source-control-bound test contains in its last section the operations that are specific to source management. Right-click on the `Func-10_ FileInfo_Create_Failing_Manual` test and choose **Check In to Source Control** as shown in the following screenshot:

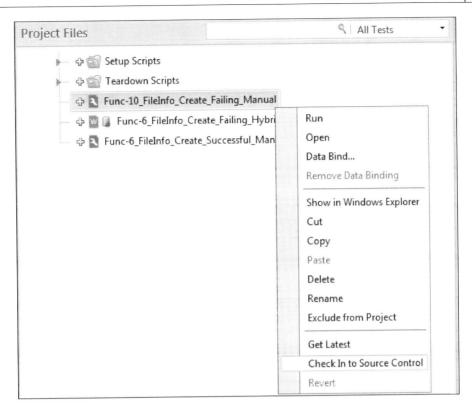

Checking in a test to a source control

A dialog is invoked requesting a confirmation on the set of tests to be committed and a comment on these versions of the tests. If you notice, this window displays two entries. The file with the `.tstest` extension contains the test definitions for the steps of Test Studio, whereas the file with the `.resx` extension contains the images for the storyboard, and both files can be committed to TFS. Enter the comment `Checking in version 0 for Func-10_FileInfo_Create_Failing_Manual` and then click on **OK**.

The Storyboard is the visual representation of the steps defined in the test. Each step is represented by a snapshot taken at the time of recording. Tests can be viewed in the storyboard mode by clicking the corresponding button from the **Test Views** tab. The storyboard view also allows you to export the steps into HTML documents.

The test icon is changed to a lock symbol, as shown in the following screenshot, signifying that the test is now locked to TFS and that no local changes are present:

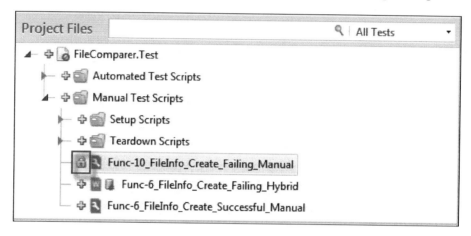

Test checked in to TFS

Double-click on the test and add any manual step; go back to the **Project** pane and notice how the icon has changed to a green tick signifying that there are local uncommitted changes:

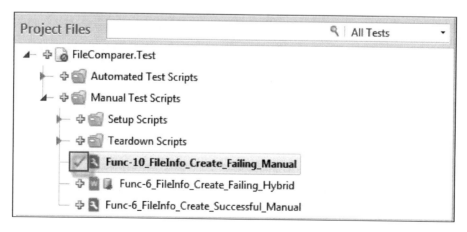

A test with local uncommitted changes

This summarizes the states a test can be found in with respect to a source control. Next you will see, the three source-control-specific operations that will alternate the test between these states.

Right-click on the `Func-10_FileInfo_Create_Failing_Manual` test and choose **Check in to Source Control** again. This will send the applied changes locally and commit them to the server.

Open the test and add another manual step. From the **Project** pane, choose **Get Latest** from the context menu. This option is responsible for pulling the latest test version from the TFS committed by you or any other party working on the file, and then merging it with the local test without overwriting them. This means that the step that was lastly added will not be removed.

Go to the **Project** tab again and, this time, choose the **Revert** option from the context menu. A dialog prompts you to choose whether you want to abandon the local changes and overwrite them with the latest version present on the server. Click on the **Yes** button and notice how the last added step is now deleted.

Integration with Visual Studio

Since Test Studio projects are fully portable into Visual Studio and can in fact be developed within it, versioning is also an induced benefit. As a result, Test Studio tests can be controlled with TFS through Visual Studio as well.

At any point after creation of the testing project inside Test Studio, this project is migratable using the export to Visual Studio feature. From the Test Studio main menu, select the **Export to Visual Studio** option as shown in the following screenshot:

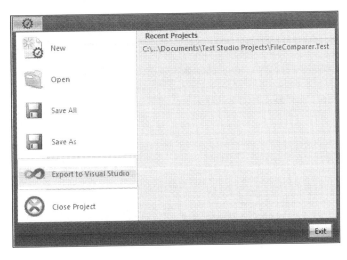

Exporting a test project to Visual Studio

The **Select Visual Studio Selector** window prompts you for the Visual Studio version to which the solution is going to be exported. Choose the latest available version on your machine and click on **OK**.

Open the exported solution in Visual Studio, and after configuring TFS from the **Team** menu, perform the following steps:

1. Right-click on the solution node from the **Solution Explorer** window, and then select the **Add Solution to Source Control** option from the context menu.
2. Once completed, click on the node again, and this time, choose the **Check In** option.
3. In the ensuing window, choose the items you want to check in and click on the **Check In** button.

The project is now committed to TFS; right-click on the project node to view the available source control operations that are depicted in the context menu of the following screenshot:

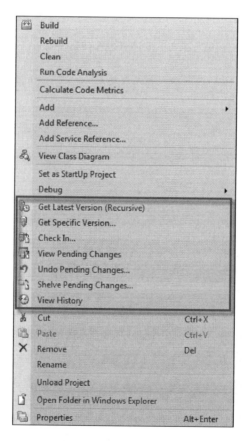

TFS source control operations

The two options available for retrieving the changes from the server are: **Get Latest Version** and **Get Specific Version**. The former gets the last committed version, whereas the latter allows retrieval of a history version based on some criteria, for example, date. To commit the changes, use the **Check In** option. Finally, the **Undo Pending Changes** option reverts the local changes to the version present on the server.

Tailor tests in Test Studio

So far we have learned how to integrate Test Studio within test management and execute activities of the manual testing process. This section inspires you on how you can style tests by using what Test Studio intrinsically offers to easily locate, filter, and group tests together based on their common features.

What do we get to deal with during manual tests' generation and implementation? Test design documents, test cases documents, test data stores, and what not. Earlier, Test Studio had presented a built-in solution to inherently combine a test with its test data, thus solving the problem of storing and maintaining them alongside. This time it will provide another solution to link test cases to their test design documents and from that achieve a more complete solution towards a consolidated test repository.

The following will briefly illustrate some of the functional testing techniques applied against the `File Comparer` application features to generate sample test cases, which will be later inserted into Test Studio.

Decision tables

Decision table is a functional design technique used for testing the application's behavior resulting from a combination of business rules. This technique is used to filter down to the smallest set that safely covers all the testing for a feature without having to exhaustively test all combinations.

While automating data-driven tests for the `File Info` application, we have encountered certain rules that manage the submission of the file's metadata. The decision table for the `File Info` application can be found in the `Decision Table` sheet of the `File Comparer - Manual Test Scripts.xlsx` workbook. The upper section of the table contains the conditions that are listed vertically. The lower section contains the actions that correspond to the system feedback and are also listed vertically. The system feedback is dependent on the conditions and varies based on their combinations. A test case is extracted by vertically reading a column from the table.

Using the Excel import feature, construct a manual test having `Test Case 1 - Description` for its procedures by performing the following steps:

1. Create a manual test under the `Manual Test Scripts` folder and rename it to `Func-11_DT-1_FileInfo_Create_Successful`.

2. In the **Import** ribbon of the test, click on the **Excel Import** button.

3. Browse for the Excel workbook and specify the sheet and table for the **Import Manual Step** window.

Upon clicking on **OK**, the manual steps are added to the tests. Firstly, we will build the link to the test design; afterwards, we will adjust the manual test attributes to provide more information suitable for classifying the test based on its type.

Therefore, take a snapshot of the decision table and save it on your local machine drive. Then using the **Attach image** button of the **Notes** section in the manual test work area, browse for the decision table snapshot, and enter a descriptive text as depicted in the following screenshot:

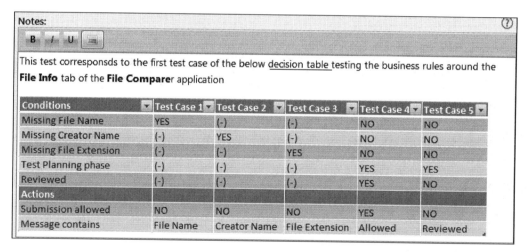

Notes:

B I U

This test corresponsds to the first test case of the below decision table testing the business rules around the **File Info** tab of the **File Comparer** application

Conditions	Test Case 1	Test Case 2	Test Case 3	Test Case 4	Test Case 5
Missing File Name	YES	(-)	(-)	NO	NO
Missing Creator Name	(-)	YES	(-)	NO	NO
Missing File Extension	(-)	(-)	YES	NO	NO
Test Planning phase	(-)	(-)	(-)	YES	YES
Reviewed	(-)	(-)	(-)	YES	NO
Actions					
Submission allowed	NO	NO	NO	YES	NO
Message contains	File Name	Creator Name	File Extension	Allowed	Reviewed

Adding a decision table design to a manual test

Go back to the **Project** tab, and select the test in order to edit its properties. The **Misc** section of the test has three custom properties as shown in the following screenshot:

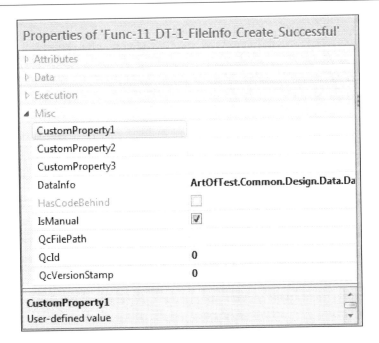

Custom properties for manual tests

These properties are made available to conventionally classify and categorize tests based on their values. Depending on the testing automation environment in your company, you might decide to map these properties to a certain test criteria. In this example, CustomProperty1 will stand for the test design technique that was used to generate the test. CustomProperty2 will be used to denote the feature under the test, whereas CustomProperty3 will refer to the test state of completion. A True value stands for a completed test ready for execution, whereas False means that the test is still under development.

Accordingly, enter the values for these properties as Decision Table, File Info Submission, and True respectively.

State transition diagrams

State transition diagrams are directed graphs used to draw system transitions between different finite states. They have the ability to predict the next state based on the previous state of the system in addition to a certain condition.

State transition diagrams also reveal the system events that translate feedback to the user in case they are present. The state tests sheet of File Comparer, which is the Manual Test Scripts.xlsx workbook, has the state transition diagram for the various system functionalities.

Using the Excel import feature, construct a manual test having Use Case 1 - Description for its procedures by performing the following steps:

1. Create a manual test under the Manual Test Scripts folder and name it as Func-12_SD-1_FileInfo_Create_Successful.

2. In the **Import** ribbon of the test, click on the **Excel Import** button.

3. Browse for the Excel workbook and specify the sheet and table for the **Import Manual Step** window and then click on **OK**.

4. Save a snapshot of the state transition diagram on your local machine. Next, import it into the notes of the manual test by providing a descriptive text as depicted in the following screenshot:

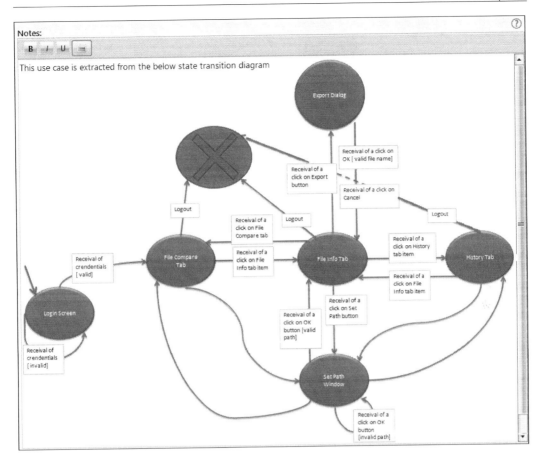

Adding a state transition diagram design to a manual test

Go to the **Project** tab, select this test, and update its custom property values as follows:

- CustomProperty1: State Transition Diagram
- CustomProperty2: File Comparer full set of operations
- CustomProperty3: True

Summary

Out of the various tasks which make up manual testing, this chapter has approached storage and the execution of manual tests while dealing with the problems that arise around them.

The chapter started with demonstrating the inner tools of Test Studio for creating tests and annotating them; alternatively, it showed how this process can be simplified, thanks to the integration with MS Excel.

The chapter continued to talk about the setup and teardown procedures that are usually inherent to manual tests but inconveniently repeated among them. Next, it showed how this repetitiveness can be treated in hybrid tests by utilizing the fast forward feature exemplified in two real-world cases.

Manual test execution was addressed afterwards along with the vulnerabilities that are bound to it. These vulnerabilities were overcome by Test Studio's guided execution and annotation process.

The precedent features have prepared for the fully integrated transition from a manual to an automated test, where together with the manipulation of the test, runner type can enable a previous manual test to run in a purely automated mode.

Having demonstrated the needed features for creating tests, the chapter then deals with source versioning and control through Test Studio integration with TFS, which resolves problems related to file backup and collaboration.

As you know, test cases are usually grouped into test suites. These test suites typically exist to serve an execution purpose. For instance, some are used as smoke test suites, others as regression test suites, and so on. The next chapter approaches this requirement through Test Studio test lists and demonstrates their various advanced capabilities.

6

Test Lists and Reports

Today is the progress meeting where news regarding the testing progress is communicated to the team. While you were thinking how adequately you are prepared to answer testing status questions, your turn comes to present how far the testing efforts have led to, with respect to the execution timeline, and are there any risks interfering with the estimated plan.

Do these questions frustrate you? It is surely the case when concrete testing figures are missing, and your answers are instantly calculated based on the following equation:

$$\text{Any Metric} = \frac{\textit{subjective expectation on future efforts}}{\textit{flashbacks on previous testing efforts}}$$

This chapter helps you remove the abstract factors when relaying testing information to the stakeholders. This is done by grouping tests and reporting numbers based on them through the acquirement of knowledge in:

- Creating automated and manual test suites
- Executing test suites
- Exploring test suite results and analyzing them
- Creating customized reports

Test suites

A test suite is a subset of tests grouped together for a specific testing purpose at a specific time. The execution result of this group of tests delivers data and figures around a certain testing attribute significant in its time context. The composing tests can be either manual or automated.

Test suites come in variations depending on the type and size of the system. The following list shows common test suite examples along with their targeted purpose:

- **Code-coverage test suites**: They are used to measure the extent of code branches covered by a set of tests, where a higher coverage ensures a clearer vision of the system quality. Code coverage percentage is context dependent where a safety-critical system enforces a higher coverage than, for example, a bookstore application.

- **Regression test suites**: They are run after the modifications affecting the source code or design of the application under test. These test suites are mainly used to ascertain that the previously working features did not get affected by the additions of new application features or changes subsequent to bug fixing.

- **Smoke test suites**: They contain test cases verifying the high-level functionality of the system. They could also represent the entrance criteria to system acceptance in the testing process after each build.

Test suite development is not a one-time process; on the contrary, it is continuously maintained through the addition of new test cases and data as issues are discovered within the application even after the release.

Inside Test Studio, test suites are labelled as test lists. Their availability offers a great flexibility in assigning the previously developed automated tests to user-defined test suites. The following sections create and execute test lists based on the `File Comparer` application's features and tests.

Creating test lists

The `File Comparer - Reports.xlsx` workbook contains a sheet called `Summary`. This sheet holds three test suites designed for the `File Comparer` application, where their titles describe the underlying purpose. The tests suites are generated using a chosen set of tests previously created, and they constitute our prospective test lists for this chapter.

To create a test list inside Test Studio, go to the **Test Lists** tab. As shown in the following screenshot, this tab has two read-only panes in which it displays information about the test lists present in the project. The left pane has the created test lists while the right one shows the test entries associated with each of these lists:

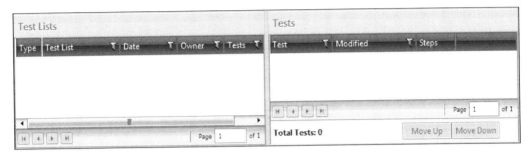

The Test lists tab

Test Studio offers two sorts of test lists accessible from the **Add** tab as shown in the following screenshot. Lists are static test suites that can have their definition changed only through direct manual update. Therefore, if you create a manual list with two tests, it will always have these tests unless it is directly edited. Dynamic lists, on the other hand, are smart, self-updating test suites. They offer greater flexibility and less maintenance cost. The following two sections further discuss the nature of the two lists and demonstrate how to create and manipulate them.

The Test list types

Lists

As briefly mentioned before, regular lists are not automatically updated. They are mainly defined by a set of tests manually assigned upon creation, which can be changed in the future. We will map the smoke testing suite showing in the `Summary` sheet of the `File Comparer - Reports.xlsx` workbook to a static list by first clicking on the **List** button of the **Add** tab. The **Create a New Test List** window shown in the following screenshot is invoked:

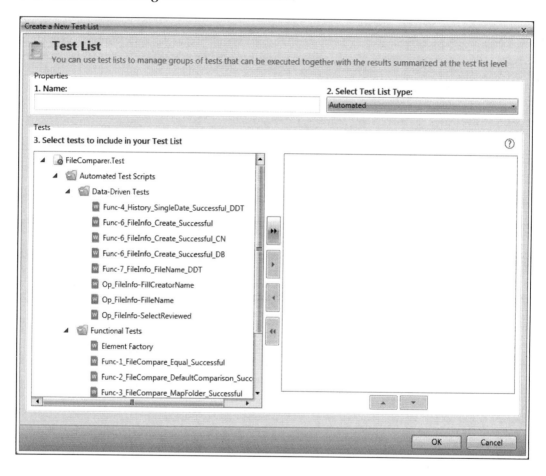

Creating lists

Three types of information need to be supplied in order to complete the creation of the list. Firstly, it receives the title for the test suite in its free input **Name** field, which is `Smoke Testing` in our case. Secondly, it allows the specification of the test type that can be any of the following values:

- **Automated**: This value permits the addition of only the automated tests
- **Manual**: This value permits either manual or hybrid tests but not the automated ones
- **Performance**: This value permits only performance tests

Since the smoke testing suite contains automated tests, choose **Automated** from the **Select Test List Type** combobox. Thirdly, it contains a section that allows the addition of the tests that will contribute to the definition of this static list. The project hierarchy is entirely displayed in the left pane called **Tests**. However, notice how only the tests based on the WPF template are enabled and can therefore be moved from left to right. This is in fact not a problem with the test selection feature but, as discussed before, it is a restriction on the type of tests that can be added under a list with an automated type. Had there been web tests in the project, those tests would also appear in the **Tests** pane. As identified in the `Summary` sheet, select the following four tests, add them to the right pane, and then click on **OK**:

- `Func-1_FileCompare_Equal_Successful`
- `Func-2_FileCompare_DefaultComparison_Successful`
- `Func-3_FileCompare_MapFolder_Successful`
- `Func-4_History_SingleDate_Successful`

Notice how an entry for the list is added to the **Test Lists** pane with the corresponding tests shown under the **Tests** pane.

Dynamic lists

Dynamic lists offer flexibility because they are smart enough to update their own definitions each time they are invoked for execution. Instead of accepting a predefined set of tests, dynamic lists are rather defined using a combination of criteria. The evaluation of these criteria will result in the actual tests that are going to run under the scope of the list. The gained advantage is that knowing how automation and maintainability should be an inseparable pair, and keeping the test lists up-to-date, no longer requires maintenance effort upon the creation of a new test. The newly added test will be automatically appended to the suitable dynamic list whenever its attributes pass the verification. There are many criteria based on which we can filter the tests as we will see shortly.

The `Summary` sheet contains a test suite called `File Info Upload Feature`. This suite is supposed to hold the tests responsible for verifying the functionality of the `File Info` feature. As you may have noticed, `File Info Upload` suggests changeability in its constituent tests based on the following levels:

- **Feature test case generation**: The process of generating functional tests for a feature expands in time to some extent. This process contains generation of test cases based on the various test techniques. Hence, tests will keep on emerging until the entire generation activity is completed. Accordingly, each created test needs to be added to the appropriate feature test list.

- **Bug identification**: The generated test cases for a feature will most likely uncover only a part of the residing bugs. As other bugs are revealed during the application's lifetime, matching tests need to be added to the automated project and therefore to the corresponding feature test list.

- **Feature change**: As changes are introduced to the feature, new test cases are going to emerge during the regression testing cycles and those need to be added to the feature test list as well.

- **Pesticide paradox**: This testing principle states that as a test suite is run over and over again, its capacity in finding new bugs will gradually decrease. This is due to the fact that bugs that were already uncovered got fixed by the developers. In order to avoid this situation, test cases are regularly reviewed and could perhaps have their inputs altered. Additionally, new tests can be added, which also need to be appended to the feature test lists.

The preceding four reasons apply to the `File Info Upload` feature and incur maintenance cost that is alleviated by dynamic lists. This test suite is therefore recommended to be created as a dynamic list.

The criterion we are going to use in order to identify the characterizing tests for this dynamic test list is the `CustomProperty1` variable, which we have seen in the previous chapter. Remember that we conventionally mapped this property to the feature under test. Since the importance of these custom properties is further highlighted in this section, this conventional mapping can now be more particularly adapted to each testing environment. Let's edit the value of `CustomProperty1` of the following tests to `File Info`:

- `Func-6_FileInfo_Create_Successful`
- `Func-8_FileInfo_Export_Successful`

The `CustomProperty1` is accessed after selecting the test from the **Project File** pane of the **Project** tab and displaying its properties in the **Properties** pane.

Now that the conditions are satisfied, go back to the **Test Lists** tab and click on the **Dynamic List** button of the **Add** tab. The **Add Dynamic Test List** window shown in the following screenshot is invoked:

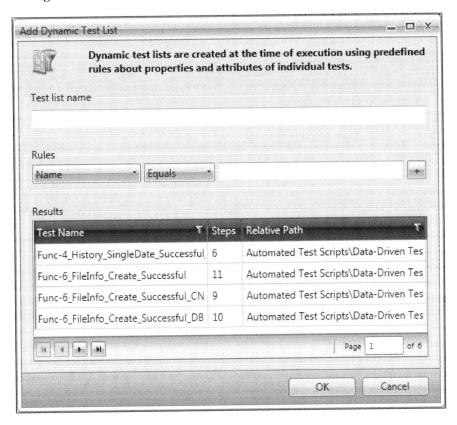

Creating dynamic test lists

As in the regular lists case, we firstly need to fill in the dynamic list title. So, enter `File Info Upload` inside the **Test List Name** field.

The second section contains the options for crafting the rules based on which the tests will be filtered. Initially, the **Results** section displays all the tests present in the project since no rules are added yet. To retrieve only the preceding listed tests, add the rule shown in the following screenshot and then click on the plus button:

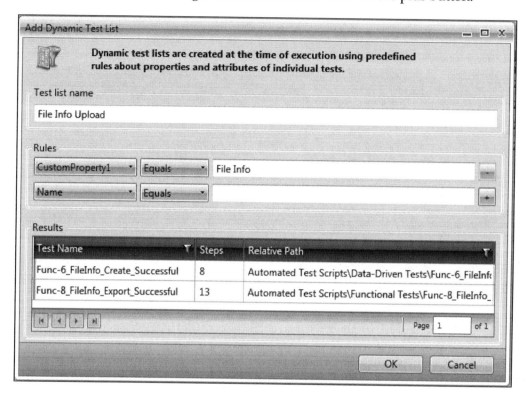

Adding dynamic lists rules

More complex rules can be constructed by adding further criteria that will be joined with an AND operator. The additional criteria can be a combination of one or all the following:

- `CustomProperty1`, `CustomProperty2`, `CustomProperty3`: They are found and are editable in the **Misc** section of the test's **Properties** pane

- `Name`: They are found in the **Attribute** section of the test's **Properties** pane and are editable in the **Project Files** pane

- `Owner`: They are found and are editable in the **Attribute** section of the test's **Properties** pane

- `Path`: They are found in the **Attribute** section of the test's **Properties** pane and are editable in the **Project Files** pane
- `Priority`: They are found in the **Attribute** section of the test's **Properties** pane and are editable in the **Attribute** section of the test's **Properties** pane

Click on **OK** to finish the creation of the dynamic list.

Lastly, we will create a test list of manual type for the security test suite. Click on the **List** button and create a list similar to the one depicted in the following screenshot:

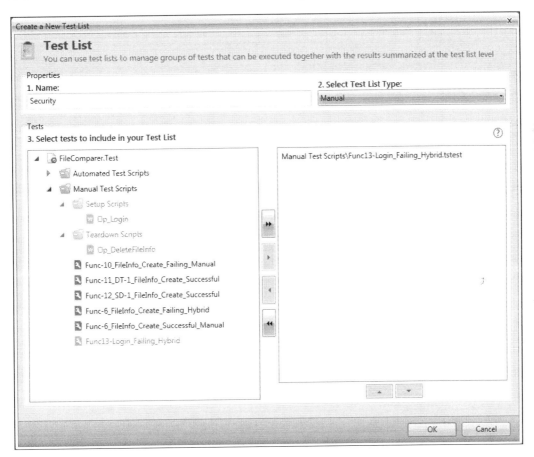

Creating a security test list

Executing test lists

Test lists group tests having a special common purpose and run them in a sequential manner without the tester's intervention. Hence, in the case of a smoke testing list or any other one with similar type, the tests will be invoked and executed one after the other.

Before we attempt to run the smoke testing list, we need to firstly disable the authentication window since these tests were not developed to cater for it. From the application's `bin` folder, edit the `authorization` tag inside the `Settings.xml` file as follows:

```
<authorization>False</authorization>
```

In the **Test Lists** pane, select the **Smoke Testing** entry and click on the **Run List** button from the **Execution** tab, as shown in the following screenshot:

The Run list button

After the tests finish execution, Test Studio opens the **Results** tab to display the execution results. The following screenshot shows three execution runs for the smoke testing list:

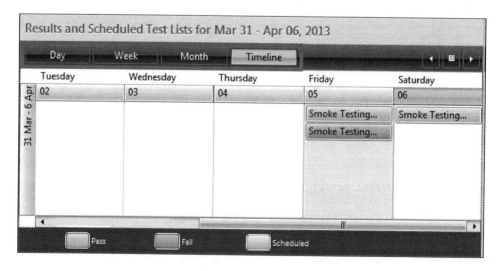

Test execution results

The **Smoke Testing** entry colored in green and executed on **Friday** affirms that all comprising tests have been successfully executed, whereas the one beneath it, which is colored in red, denotes that errors were encountered.

Since the test runs are shown in a calendar, the buttons boxed in a rectangle allow you to navigate between a daily, weekly, or monthly view for a broader analysis.

Suppose now that you want to inquire more about the reason of failure, which is usually the first action after identifying a failed execution. Firstly, you need to reproduce the error depicted in the preceding screenshot, so run the test list again. When the manual step for the first test is encountered, press on the **Fail** button and then wait until all the tests finish execution. From the calendar, double-click on the **Smoke Testing** entry colored in red. A **Test Results** pane is enabled in order to summarize the execution result for each test as shown in the following screenshot:

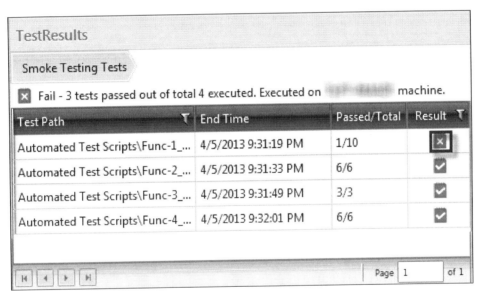

Summary for failed execution of the test list

The error now is easily spotted. It is the first test that is marked by the red and white cross outlined in the preceding screenshot. Double-click on the cross to drill down into the error details as shown in the following screenshot:

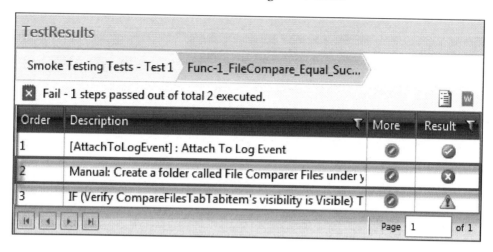

Viewing failing steps in test list execution summary

It is now apparent that the problem resides in the second manual step highlighted in the preceding screenshot. Double-click on the cross button again to further inspect about the error. The **Step Failure Details** window seen in the first chapter is invoked.

Manual test list execution similarly invokes all the underlying tests in a row but with a slight difference. In order to demonstrate this, perform the following steps first:

1. Revert the `authorization` tag of the settings file to `True`.
2. Create a manual test called `Func-14_Login_Successful` under the `Manual Test Scripts` folder defined with these steps:
3. Start the `File Comparer` application.
4. Input `msmith` in the **Username** field.
5. Input `Mp@$` in the **Password** field.
6. Click on the **Login** button.
7. Verify that the login was successful.
8. Close the application.
9. Go to the **Test Lists** tab.
10. Edit the `Security` test list definition by selecting the list and then clicking on the **Edit List** button of the **Edit** tab, as shown in the following screenshot:

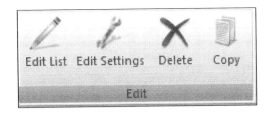

Test lists edit ribbon

11. Move the created test to the right pane and click on **OK**.

Select the `Security` test list and click on the **Run List** button of the **Execution** tab. The execution window is invoked where in the first section, all the underlying tests' names are listed as shown in the following screenshot. Unlike the automated list, you are not forced to abide by a certain execution order for the tests. On the contrary, you can alternate between them by selecting the target test.

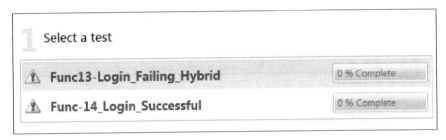

Display of tests during test lists manual execution

Click on the **Launch App** button to start the application which is going to invoke the **Login** window at first. Click on the **Continue** button to proceed with manual testing. The page contains additional navigation buttons to control the test execution order. These buttons are depicted in the following screenshot:

Navigation buttons during test lists manual execution

After executing the `Func13-Login_Failing_Hybrid` test, click on the **Next Test** button to move forward to the next test. At this stage, the previous button is enabled which can be clicked in order to go back to the first test and edit its corresponding steps' annotations and results. After the manual execution is completed, click on the **Save Results** button.

Dynamic list automatic update

At this point, we can detect the behavior of a dynamic list. Go to the **Test List** tab and select the `File Info Upload` list from the **Test Lists** section. The right pane currently displays two tests. Set the value of `CustomProperty1` of the `Func-7_FileInfo_FileName_DDT` test to `File Info`, and then go back to the **Test List** tab and select the `File Info Upload` list again. Notice how the tests in the right pane are incremented by one where `Func-7_FileInfo_FileName_DDT` is now included.

This demonstrates the behavior of dynamic lists where the set of tests is updated each time the list is invoked.

Test list settings

In addition to the list, results are automatically displayed by Test Studio at the end of a test list execution, logfiles still remain an important resource in accessing information about the tests' execution. Therefore, their availability in test lists is also an added value. We previously saw how to manage logfiles at a test level. We will now see how these files are also manageable at this level through the test list settings.

From the **Test Lists** pane, select the **Smoke Testing** entry, and click on the **Edit Settings** button from the **Edit** ribbon. The **Edit Test List Settings** window opens as shown in the following screenshot:

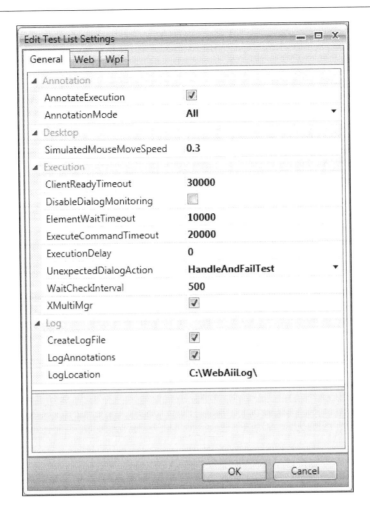

The Edit Test List Settings window

The last section titled **Log** has settings for the logging mechanism. Enable the **CreateLogFile** and **LogAnnotations** checkboxes, if not already enabled.

Annotations are descriptive texts generated by Test Studio when a test is executing. They contain the target element and the actions that are being executed against. The following screenshot contains an annotation example:

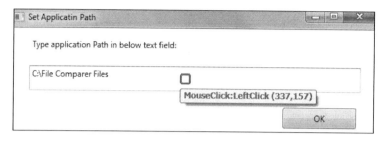

Annotation text during test execution

Annotations are enabled from the **Annotation** section of the same window, therefore, select the **AnnotationExecution** checkbox from that section if not already selected. With these options, the logfile will now contain a summary of the steps that are executed and any additional custom logging inside the tests. Logfiles will be available after execution under the directory specified in the `LogLocation` property of the **Log** section. For example, running the `Smoke Testing` list will result in the following log for the `Func-1_FileCompare_Equal_Successful` test:

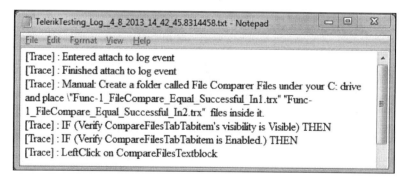

The test list logfile

Other settings are also available in the settings window, and they are concerned with the dialog handling. For example, `DisableDialogMonitoring` will stop Test Studio from handling dialogs, whereas `UnexpectedDialogAction` will specify the way of handling dialogs that weren't expected in the tests' definition. The following three options are available for the unexpected dialog action setting:

- `HandleAndFailTest`

- `HandleAndContinue`

- `DoNotHandle`

Test lists also have options to allow you to customize time settings, for example, the maximum default time to wait for element availability through `ElementWaitProperty`, the maximum time to wait for a command to execute through `ExecuteCommandTimeout`, and the time to insert between the consecutive steps' execution through `ExecutionDelay`.

Specialized test list settings

The preceding settings are common to WPF and web tests. Test lists offer more specialized settings based on the application type. The following screenshot shows the **Web** tab of the **Edit Test List Settings** window:

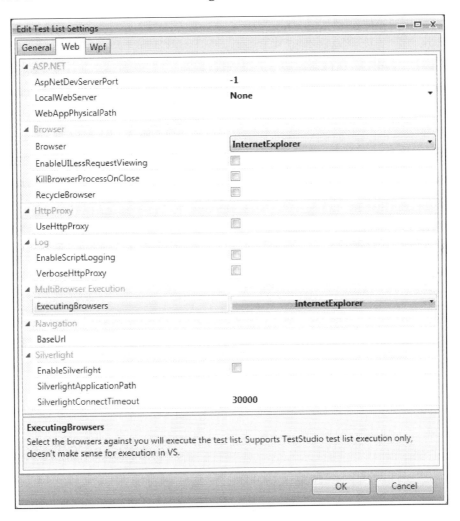

Test list settings for web tests

Some application-specific settings can be specified in the **ASP.NET** section. Hence, the ASP.NET development server port, the local web server, and the path to the application on the development server can be defined in the first three parameters appearing in the preceding screenshot. The value -1 indicates that a random port value will be used.

Other global handy features can also be defined as follows:

- **Browser** corresponds to the default browser to be launched for a web test execution
- The **HTTPProxy** checkbox whose state indicates whether or not to use the proxy browser during a test execution
- The **ExecutingBrowser** listbox, where you can select the list of browsers for which the test list will sequentially run
- The **BaseUrl** field that corresponds to the URL of the application against which the tests will execute

The **WPF** tab of the test list settings also allows you to specify the default path of the application against which the test will run.

Reporting

Sometimes projects fail, and they do not get released on time or if they are released, they do not meet the planned quality. With all this pressure during testing, many activities could be carried out successively or even concurrently. For instance, the manual test case generation and implementation, the automated scripts' development and validation, test lists crafting, and perhaps some execution also could overlap in time. Such diverse tasks distributed among team members, or even teams, require management and monitoring. Charts are an effective way that helps in achieving these purposes. Every testing task that yields a number can participate in building visual, informative report charts. They can help in various domains briefly described in the following list:

- Explain how testing is going and relay discrete numbers to the management instead of speculative assessments.

- Give visibility on testing results by also transmitting numbers related to the result of the executed tests.

- Present the progress of testing, especially for critical areas either containing coding challenges or with high impact on user satisfaction.

- Draw future trends since they not only hold a meaningful evaluation of the present, but are furthermore very important in predicting efforts and quality with respect to time constraints.

Before chart generation takes place, a goal must be identified. For example, developing a testing plan that will address high-risk areas first. That identified, you need to secondly list down the questions that address the perspective of your goal. For example, can test case generation and implementation be calculated? Can the actual test case number be estimated against risky areas? Can test case automation and execution be quantified? Thirdly, you extract the helpful metrics. The suggested metrics for this example are as follows:

- Manual test case count with respect to risk areas

- Actual test case count with respect to planned test cases based on risk areas

- Automated test case count with respect to risk areas

- Actual count of passing and failed tests

The preceding described example follows the **GQM (Goal Question, Metric)** paradigm. More material on the GQM paradigm can be found in this paper, `http://www.cs.umd.edu/~basili/publications/technical/T78.pdf`.

Before you totally decide on the list of metrics, you need to first confirm that they are measurable. This means that there is a clear data type in question, and its corresponding data is available. Once, this is achieved, the implementation phase comprises of making the data available, collecting it, communicating it, and finally analyzing and taking the needed measurements.

In addition to displaying test results with respect to time, Test Studio also has ready-made reports that can be extended, thanks to its integration with outside tools. Switch to the **Report** tab to view the automatic reports generated by Test Studio. A typical report is shown in the following screenshot:

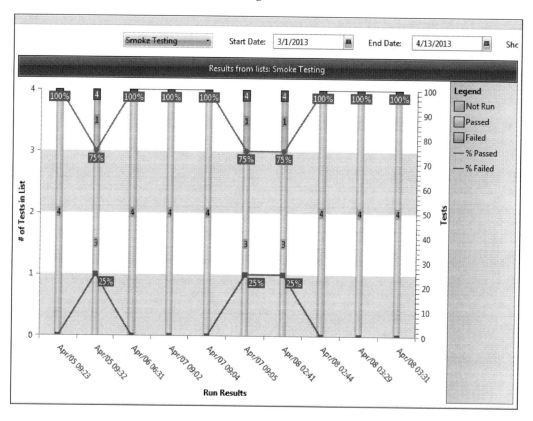

Test list execution summary report

The chart depicts the execution status with respect to time. In our case, the Smoke Testing list was executed several times from April 5 until April 8. On the first day, the list was executed with four tests that were run at 9:23 a.m and yielded a successful result for all. The second execution resulted in a failing test out of the four, and thus, the line denoting the **Passed** metric fell from 100 percent to 75 percent. On the other hand, the line denoting the **Failed** metric increased from zero percent to 25 percent, which complements the behavior noticed with the **Passed** line. The last three executions for the list resulted in a fully successful end result that gives us some assurance for the rest of the day. The report is customizable through some parameters on top, where switching between the test list's parameters, Start Date and End Date, is possible.

So, you are probably thinking that the result of the second run on April 5 is interesting, especially that the bug was directly fixed on the second day. What was the bug? All you have to do is double-click on the column from where you need to gather more information. The report will drill down one level to display the following chart on the left, which allows you to easily navigate back and forth between tests by clicking on the links of the list results pointed by red arrows:

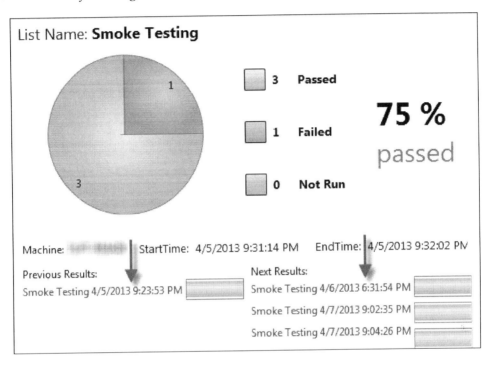

The test list execution report

To the left, details about the currently displayed test are shown similar to the previous screenshot.

Result integration

While on the **Results** tab, the upper ribbon shows further capabilities that comes within Test Studio, and that is its integration with external tools, which is close to what we have seen during a regular automation and source control. The **Export** tab depicted in the following screenshot lists these possibilities:

The Export tab

Click on the **Excel** button and save the file on your local machine. The following is the report table automatically generated by Test Studio:

Test Path	End Time	Passed /Time	Result	Failure info
Automated Test Scripts\Func-1_FileCompare_Equal _Successful.tstest	4/5/2013 9:31:19PM	"1/10"	Fail	Manual step 'Create a folder called File Computer Files under your C: drive and place \"Func-1_FileCompare_Equal_Successful_In1.trx" "Func-1_FIleCompare_Equal_successful_In2.trx" files inside it.' failed. Failure Comment:
Automated Test Scripts\Func-2_FileCompare_ DefaultComparison_ Successful.tstest	4/5/2013 9:31:33PM	"6/6"	Pass	
Automated Test Scripts\Func-3_FileCompare_ MapFolder_ Successful.tstest	4/5/2013 9:31:49PM	"3/3"	Pass	
Automated Test Scripts\Func-4_History_SingleDate _Successful.tstest	4/5/2013 9:32:01PM	"6/6"	Pass	

The report table

The description for each of the table columns is as follows:

- **Test Path**: It is the relative path of the test
- **End Time**: It is the time at which the test has finished execution

- **Passed/Total**: It gives the total number of passing test steps over the total number of steps
- **Failure Info**: It provides more information about the step at which the test has failed

Visual Studio report integration

Test Studio has the capability of generating files with the `.trx` extension, which can be viewed from Visual Studio. Hence, click on the **VS Result File** button and save the resulting file on your machine. This file can be previewed in Visual Studio as shown in the following screenshot:

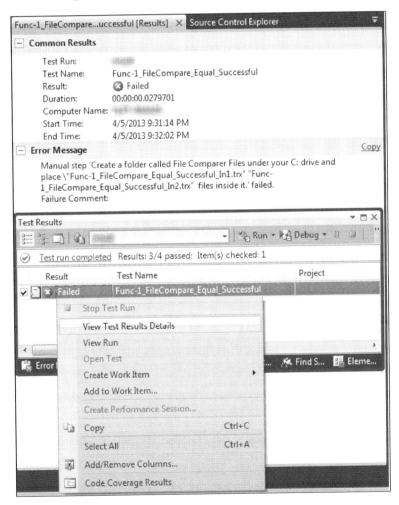

Viewing reports in Visual Studio

SQL integration

So far in this chapter, we have seen how Test Studio offers the standard built-in reports. However, knowing how much reporting is critical for making comprehensive decisions, your organization may need more specialized reports. So, this section takes the VS result file generated by Test Studio and suggests methods to create customized advanced reporting. These reports are going to be the result of the following processes:

1. Submitting the contents of VS result file to an SQL database
2. Creating queries based on this database table
3. Using MS Excel to import data returned by these queries
4. Creating charts based on this data

First, let's examine the content of these files. Open the result file of the preceding example in a text editor to view its content. As mentioned before, it contains XML data where some of its significance is described in the following elements:

- The `TestRun` element holds:
    - A unique identifier referring to the test list's execution ID in its `id` attribute
    - The name of the person (tester) who actually executed the test in its `runUser` attribute

- The `TestRunConfiguration` element holds:
    - The configuration ID for the test run in its `id` attribute, which varies based on whether the test was run locally or, say, remotely
    - A `Description` node containing the test list name in its inner text

- The `ResultSummary` element holds important attributes in its `Counters` child that refers to the number of executed and non-executed tests that fall under one or more criterion such as failing, passing, aborted, completed, and so on. Each of the aforementioned criteria is represented by a corresponding attribute and will be referred to in the next section by a basic metric.

- The `Times` element out of the available dates contains:
    - The start date of the test list in its `startTime` attribute
    - The end date of all the tests inside the list in its `endTime` attribute

- The `Results` element contains:
    - An entry for each test comprised in the test list with details about the test's unique identifier, the name contained in the `testId`, and the `testName` attributes respectively
    - The execution's unique identifier that provides uniqueness to the test ID within the execution context of all the test list runs, and it is contained in the `executionId` attribute
    - The test outcome contained in its `outcome` attribute
    - The start date of the test in its `startTime` attribute
    - The end date of all the tests in their `endTime` attribute

After getting familiar with the structure of the test file and its significance, we can now draw a relation between its different components that allows building further customizable reports. In the following sections, we are going to create these reports by firstly submitting data to SQL tables and then charting them via Excel pivot tables.

Submitting to SQL

The FC_DB database introduced in the previous chapters contains tables that could suggest an underlying storage design for the XML architecture. The following diagram depicts the relationship between the various tables:

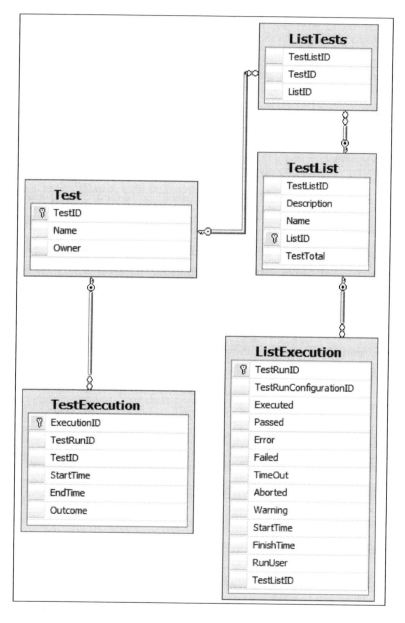

Design of the FC_DB database

The `File Comparer` application has a tab called **Import Results**, which serves as the tool for submitting the file results into the SQL tables. The database is already populated with some sample data coming from the execution of the created test lists in this chapter. To upload other files, the following steps are to be performed:

1. Start the `File Comparer` application.
2. Enter the complete path in the upper field, and click on the **Add Files** button.
3. Repeat the preceding step for any number of files.
4. Click on the **Import** button.

Excel Charts

Submitting the data to SQL has now granted us more flexibility in crafting the reports based on metrics that were extracted from any GQM paradigm activity. The forthcoming charts are examples of reports that could contribute to test reporting in your environment now or perhaps after slight variations. The charts can be found in the `File Comparer - Reports.xlsx` workbook.

> In order to update the properties of any chart or refresh its content through the Excel's **Data** tab, you need to provide these user database credentials, username: `FC_DB_USER` and password: `po0$wt`.

Execution metrics for last run

- **Goal**: This metric represents each basic metric extracted from the last run of all the test lists. Its goal can be to identify problems in the system under test and hint at the areas of improvements. It also serves to reflect a concrete picture about the testing progress and system quality, for example, in terms of how far are we from achieving the required user satisfaction.

- **Data**: This metric represents the actual test lists' execution of the basic metrics and their test list names.

- **Influences**: This metric will help in notifying and alerting stakeholders, supporting conclusions related to the exit criteria, presenting the cost of delaying the release, and determining the level of confidence.

- **Query**: The query is as follows:

```
SELECT [Executed]
, [Passed]
, [Error]
, [Failed]
, [TimeOut]
, [Aborted]
, [Warning]
, [StartTime]
, tl.[Description]
FROM [ListExecution] AS le
INNER JOIN(SELECT TestListID, MAX(StartTime) as LastExecution
FROM [ListExecution]
GROUP BY TestListID) AS lae
ON le.TestListID = lae.TestListID AND le.StartTime = lae.
LastExecution
INNER JOIN [TestList] AS tl
ON le.TestListID = tl.ListID
```

- **Summary table**: The following is the data table returned by the preceding query. The test lists are displayed under the **Row Labels** heading, whereas the remaining columns hold the number of tests that satisfy the condition stated in the headers:

Row Labels	Sum of Failed	Sum of Error	Sum of Executed	Sum of Passed	Sum of TimeOut	Sum of Warning	Sum of Aborted
Test Results for Smoke Testing	1	0	4	3	0	0	0
Test Results for File Info Upload	1	0	3	2	0	0	0
Test Results for Security	2	0	2	0	0	0	0
Grand Total	4	0	9	5	0	0	0

Data table for the execution metrics of the last run

- **Chart**: The following figure shows the data returned by the query in a column chart:

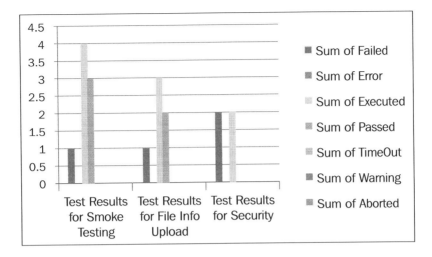

Column chart for the execution metrics of the last run

- **Description**: The chart has three types of columns repeated for each test list. The columns in green represent the number of executed test cases, whereas the purple and blue columns represent the tests that have passed and failed respectively. The pivot table for this metric can be further customized using the field list panel contained in the **Execution Metrics for Last Run** sheet of the `File Comparer - Reports.xlsx` workbook.

Test case defect density

- **Goal**: This metric represents the percentage of failing test cases with respect to the total number of tests that were developed and executed. Its goal can be to determine the test case, the effort spent, and how efficient it is.

- **Data**: This metric represents the total number of executed test cases and the total number of failed tests during their last execution.

- **Influences**: This metric helps in making decisions related to the adopted testing techniques and whether the spent effort is effective in improving the quality.

- **Query**: The query is as follows:

```
SELECT (COUNT(te.TestID) * 100)/(SELECT COUNT(distinct TestID)
FROM [TestExecution]) AS [Defect Density]
FROM (SELECT MAX(StartTime) AS startTime, TestID
FROM [TestExecution]
WHERE Outcome = 'Failed'
GROUP BY TestID) AS te
```

- **Equation**: This metric represents that the total number of failed test cases divided by the total number of executed test c the total number of executed test cases is equal to 33 percent.

- **Description**: This metric suggests that 33 percent of the total executed test cases have resulted in errors.

Execution metrics over time

- **Goal**: This metric represents the changes of a specific test suite's results with respect to time. Its goal can be to view bug-fixing activities over time. It helps in trending bug fixing from one run to the other. In addition, it can help in assessing the regression effect on the component in question following bug fixing on the system.

- **Data**: This metric represents the actual test list execution results.

- **Influences**: This metric could suggest taking actions, having a purpose to decrease the regression effect, such as enforcing quality starting from the developer through an application. An example of this is test-driven development.

- **Query**: The query is as follows:

```
SELECT [Executed],
[Passed],
[Error],
[Failed],
[TimeOut],
[Aborted],
[Warning],
[StartTime],
tl.[Description]
FROM [ListExecution] AS le INNER JOIN [TestList] AS tl
ON le.TestListID = tl.ListID
WHERE le.TestListID = 3
```

- **Table**: The data table returned by this query is shown in the following table. The first column in the table has the execution start time for the smoke testing suite. The remaining table columns contain summations of the basic metrics:

Row Labels	Sum of Aborted	Sum of Error	Sum of Failed	Sum of Executed	Sum of Passed	Sum of TimeOut	Sum of Warning
⊟ Test Results for Smoke Testing	0	0	2	20	18	0	0
4/5/2013 21:22	0	0	0	4	4	0	0
4/5/2013 21:31	0	0	1	4	3	0	0
4/7/2013 21:01	0	0	0	4	4	0	0
4/7/2013 21:03	0	0	0	4	4	0	0
4/7/2013 21:04	0	0	1	4	3	0	0
Grand Total	0	0	2	20	18	0	0

Data table for the execution metrics over time

- **Chart**: The following chart displays the data returned by the query:

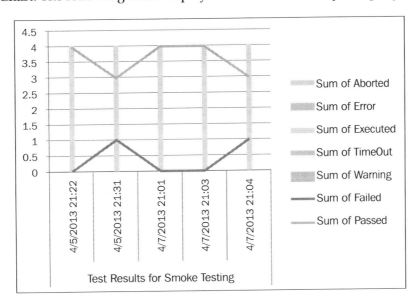

Chart for the execution metrics over time

- **Description**: This chart represents results for five runs of the smoke testing test list. The line in blue draws the changes in the number of passed tests over time, whereas the one in green draws the same change but in the number of failed tests. The pivot table for this metric can be further customized using the field list panel contained in the **Execution Metrics over Time** sheet of the File Comparer - Reports.xlsx workbook.

Feature Coverage

- **Goal**: This metric is a summary that holds information about feature coverage related to, firstly, the generated test cases for a specific feature versus the planned ones, and secondly, the executed test cases belonging to this feature. Its goal is to assess the actual testing progress with respect to the plan. It can also help in the calculation of risk coverage in case the risk residing in the various features is already identified. These types of metrics play an important role in determining the status against the testing exit criteria.

- **Data**: This includes the complete system feature list, the number of planned tests, the number of actual tests, the number of executed tests, and the last execution outcome for each test.

- **Influences**: These metrics affect decisions regarding release dates with respect to the quality confidence in the system. They help in evaluating the trade-offs between system quality, release time, and cost. It answers questions such as:

  - The amount of risk residing in a feature based on the number of nonexecuted and failed test cases

  - The cost of fixing the failing tests versus the cost of delaying the release

  - The cost of releasing tests on time versus client dissatisfaction

- **Query**: The query is as follows:

```
SELECT a.FeatureName, a.ListID, a.TestTotal, a.Outcome, a.Name,
CASE
WHEN a.Outcome = 'NotRun'  THEN '0'
WHEN a.Outcome is NULL THEN '0'
ELSE '1'
END AS Executed
FROM (SELECT t.FeatureName,
        t.ListID,
        t.TestTotal,
        lts.TestID,
        test.Name,
        (SELECT TOP(1) outcome FROM [TestExecution] AS te WHERE
exists (SELECT * FROM [TestExecution] WHERE te.TestID = lts.
TestID)
```

```
      ORDER BY StartTime DESC) AS Outcome
      FROM (
       SELECT FeatureName, lt.ListID, lt.TestTotal
         FROM [FeatureList] AS fl left join [TestList] AS lt
         ON lt.[Description] LIKE '%' + FeatureName
       ) AS t
    LEFT JOIN [ListTests] AS lts ON t.ListID = lts.ListID
    LEFT JOIN [Test] AS test ON lts.TestID = test.TestID
    GROUP BY t.FeatureName, t.ListID, t.TestTotal, lts.TestID,
test.Name
  ) AS a
```

- **Table**: The following table shows the data returned by this query. The first column holds the list of features contained in the [FeatureList] table. The ListID column has the ID of the test list that covers the feature appearing to its left. The TestTotal column has the total number of tests under this test list, where the Name column lists these test names. The Outcome column shows the last execution result for the test appearing in the Name column. The Planned Tests column has the estimated number of tests entered manually:

FeatureName	ListID	TestTotal	Planned Tests	Name	Outcome	Executed
File Comparison	(-)	0	3	(-)	(-)	0
File History	(-)	0	4	(-)	(-)	0
File Info Upload	1	3	5	Func-8_FileInfo_Export_Successful	Passed	1
File Info Upload	1	3	5	Func-10_FileInfo_VerifyTestingActivityOrga	NotRun	0
File Info Upload	1	3	5	Func-6_FileInfo_Create_Successful	Passed	1
Security	2	2	2	Func13-Login_Failing_Hybrid	Failed	1
Security	2	2	2	Func-14_Login_Successful	Failed	1

Data table for feature coverage

- **Description**: This summary table displays in its first column to the left the list of all the features of an application. The columns highlighted in green display the difference between the number of planned tests and the actual developed tests. The columns highlighted in red list the tests corresponding to each feature with their execution outcome if available. This table can be found in the **Feature Coverage** sheet of the File Comparer - Reports. xlsx workbook.

Test Execution Duration

- **Goal**: This metric reflects the execution duration of a specific test over multiple executions. Its goal could be to assess how the execution time of a specific test is influenced by improving the efforts such as script refactoring or redesigning. To be able to accurately calculate the test duration, some factors should be stabilized, such as the system against which the specific improved test script should be repeatedly run or the connection speed. These measurements are for minimizing the external factors that could interfere with the execution duration of that test.

- **Data**: The start and end time duration of the repetitive test executions.

- **Influences**: This metric helps in assessing the automated development and improvement efforts adopted on the scripts and whether the time spent is justified by the amount of improved efficiency.

- **Query**: The query is as follows:

```
SELECT [ExecutionID]
, [TestRunID]
, [TestID]
, [StartTime]
, [EndTime]
, [Outcome]
,DATEDIFF(SECOND, StartTime, EndTime) AS duration, 'Func-1_
FileCompare_Equal_Successful' AS Name
FROM [TestExecution]
WHERE TestID = (SELECT  TestID FROM [Test] WHERE Name = 'Func-1_
FileCompare_Equal_Successful')
AND Outcome = 'Passed'
```

- **Table**: The following table contains the data returned by this query. The Row Labels column has the execution times for the Func-1_FileCompare_Equal_Successful test. The Test Execution Duration column contains the amount of time taken by the test to finish execution:

Name	Func-1_FileCompare_Equal_Successful
Row Labels	**Test Execution Duration**
2013-04-05 21:22:22.0000000	91
2013-04-07 21:01:32.0000000	63
2013-04-07 21:03:10.0000000	76
Grand Total	**230**

Data table for the test execution duration over time

- **Chart**: The following figure shows the data returned by the query in a pie chart:

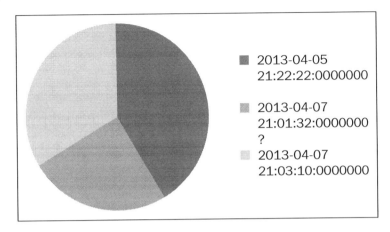

2013-04-05
21:22:22:0000000

2013-04-07
21:01:32:0000000
?

2013-04-07
21:03:10:0000000

Pie chart for test execution duration over time

- **Description**: This pie chart represents the different durations for executing the `Func-1_FileCompare_Equal_Successful` test in its sections multiple times. The pivot table for this metric can be further customized using the field list panel contained in the **Test Execution Duration** sheet of the `File Comparer - Reports.xlsx` workbook.

List result comparison

The VS Result file has further benefits that allow you to come up with a customized way of comparing test execution results. The **File Compare** tab of the `File Comparer` application, that we have previously automated, actually accepts these types of files generated by Test Studio and calculates the comparison scores based on the following formula:

Test Execution Score = Total number of executed test - (number of errors – number of failed – number of timed out – number of aborted – number of inconclusive – number of not executed – number of disconnected – number of warnings / 2).

Summary

This chapter has demonstrated the need for creating test suites that map to lists. Test lists inside Test Studio can be of static or dynamic nature where the criteria ensuring this dynamicity can range from fixed test attributes to custom properties. The execution of test lists produced built-in results and reports which were further extended by Test Studio's integration with MS Excel and Visual Studio.

After setting the grounds for single test case automation, followed by the automated batch execution of tests, we are able to take automation to the next level by looking at the nonfunctional characteristics of a system through performance testing. The next chapter explains the process of preparing performance testing scripts, gathering and analyzing data around critical end user scenarios.

7
Performance Testing

So far the discussions about the nonfunctional specifications have been dormant during testing progress meetings. On the other hand, the development of the system components is still going on and these components have reached a stable state along with the automated test scripts. Consequently, at this point, the automation vision can be enlarged, and of course what follows is a meeting to discuss the action plans, such as:

- How are the developed components performing?
- Are there any improvement key points to be targeted?
- What are the hardware and network capacity requirements?
- What are the numbers around resource utilization?

Obviously, you were expecting to hear about performance testing. So where do you start and how do you execute this in Test Studio?

This chapter takes you through a step-by-step performance plan for a web application, and it demonstrates the following activities:

1. Configuring Test Studio for performance testing
2. Creating web application tests
3. Assigning performance counters
4. Running web tests in the performance mode
5. Viewing and analyzing the test results

Performance testing

This chapter is a portal to the nonfunctional aspect of an application where it uses the Test Studio features for nonfunctional testing. In the general performance testing process, which is delimited by the successive activities of putting performance objectives, expectations, test execution, and results capturing and analysis, Test Studio automates the latter three activities.

So what are the variables that underlie this performance process and which of these do we want to address in this chapter?

For answering this question, let us first establish the criteria for a well-performing application. We are not seeking general principles in response to this question since it is highly bound to the application's contextual factors, such as the criticality of the operation carried out by the user, the potential financial loss, the amount of information that needs to be kept in the user memory until the next operation, and the operation type (whether it is two-sided, such as conversations) However, we could always say that a well-performing application is an application that offers timely, consistent, and efficient service to its clients. It provides user satisfaction and improves the users' productivity with respect to the manual services or processes they are seeking to automate. In addition, this application can maintain a level of competitiveness in the market, and will not cause its users to rush to the next competing application! For this reason, the expectation around application performance variables is not solely the decision of the product managers. It is a collaborative decision involving the product owners, company marketing department, and the clients.

Hence, back to our variables, despite the differences in the application types, the two terms mentioned earlier, timely and efficient, suggest the operation response time and resource utilization parameters respectively. The operation response time determines how fast the application is returning the operation results to the user whereas resource utilization determines how well the application is making use of the available hardware and software resources.

The next sections revolve around how to set up and go about performance testing in Test Studio to eventually extract response times and utilization for your web applications.

Performance time measurements

Knowing how time was highlighted as an important factor that governs user satisfaction, high priority must be assigned to improve unacceptable client wait time. However, this statement holds enough ambiguity making it hardly solvable from the application development perspective. Hence, performance testing is applied to help break down this wait time in order to identify the portion that is outside the range of an allowed delay and subsequently the components that are causing it.

While testing the performance of an application, three main architectural components play a role in delimiting the different partitions of an operation time. The three components are the client, server, and network. So, the overall time needed for an operation to execute is actually a summation of smaller time portions as the request progresses from the client to the server and back to the client. Therefore, we are going to define a common glossary of the terms to utilize when we speak about the application time performance.

The following diagram depicts the different stages of a request as it propagates between different web application components:

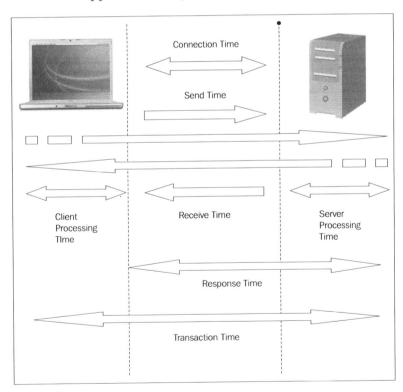

Performance testing time notions

During a transaction, the time spent at the client side, which comprises the request generation time (for example, establishing a connection with the server or handling server data), parsing a query result to draw the corresponding user chart, or any other type of processing related to generating or reading web application requests, is known as **client-side latency time**, and we will refer to it as **client processing time**.

The time spent at the server side to process client requests, such as the time taken by the backend library to analyze the requests based on the application business rule or to execute the command on the database, is known as **server-side latency time**, and we will refer to it as **server processing time**.

The time spend on the network when transferring data between various workstations is known as **network latency time**. First of all, it comprises **connection time**, which is the time spend on the network when the client and the server are trying to establish a connection. **Send time** is the time spend on the network while the request circulates from the client to the server. The other way around is called **receive time**.

Other important time notions are **response time** and **transaction time**. The response time is known as the time which starts from the moment the user submits a request till the first byte of the result is received. It is calculated as follows:

Response time = send time + server processing time + receive time

The transaction time is the total time needed for a transaction to complete. A transaction is one unit of work and can contain various activities at different application architecture components, such as building the client request to establish a connection, sending the request over the network, parsing the request at the server side and validating credentials, sending the authentication result to the client over the network, and processing the result at the client side.

Now that we have seen the details of transaction time, it is clear how performance testing divides down operations to identify the specific portion that is causing time latencies greater than expected. Following this, the components that are causing performance degradation are identified as bottlenecks and later on targeted for transaction time improvement.

Performance testing in Test Studio

Since *Chapter 2*, *Automating Functional Tests*, Test Studio has been used to test the behavioral quality aspects of an application. In addition to manual and automated functional testing, it is also one of the test automation tools that incorporate nonfunctional testing without causing any overhead on the test scripts developed in the functional phase. So here again, Test Studio enables an instant seamless transition enabling a test to run in the performance mode while capturing data related to time and resource efficiency. In this section, we will start translating the discussed performance testing notions on a web application that we are going to test using Test Studio.

How it works

Test Studio allows capturing the web functional scenarios through the web test template. These tests can be run either in the regular mode by using direct execution and test lists or in the performance testing mode. The only difference between the two modes is that in the latter, the default execution performance data are recorded down to a test step level, and you can optionally specify additional performance counters related to resource utilization at the different application tiers.

In order to set up the environment for the web test template to run in the performance mode, another Test Studio version must be installed on the machine that is going to act as a server. This version can be either the full or runtime edition. The reason is that when a web test template is executing, Test Studio connects to the target server machine in order to gather performance metrics. Hence, the server machine needs to have the **Test Studio Profiling** service running.

After a Test Studio version is installed on the server, validate the following requirements:

1. To check whether the required services are running, perform the steps as follows:
    1. From the Windows start menu, access **Telerik**, and then the **Test Execution** folder.

2. Under this folder, click on the **Configure Load Test Services** entry, which will launch the configuration manager window for various services as shown in the following screenshot:

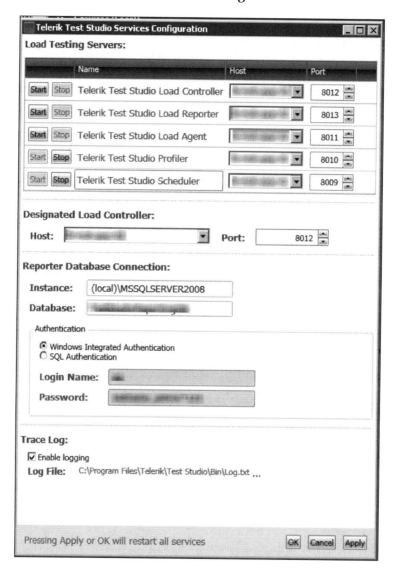

The Test Studio services configuration manager

3. Click on the **Start** button for **Test Studio Scheduler Service** and **Test Studio Profiler Service** if it is not already enabled, which will cause the corresponding services to start.

2. Open port `8010` on the server by creating inbound and outbound firewall rules for it. For more details, you can access the Telerik online documentation available at `http://www.telerik.com/automated-testing-tools/support/documentation/user-guide/performance.aspx`.

Performance test planning and execution

The introduction section described performance testing from its business requirements and its influence on the business of a company. This section starts by drawing the mutual relationship between the business and the technical world in a web application performance to establish the test plan that is to be executed.

Business requirements and marketing targets clearly contribute to the expected response time, while the actual response time contributes to the business of a company. They have a mutual impact on each other and while acting in different realms, they both share the same language described as follows:

- Business world refers to client, while IT world refers to users
- Business world refers to business operations, while IT world refers to transactions
- Business world refers to operation time, while IT world refers to transaction time

Combined together, the preceding three elements help in designing **workloads**. Workloads are the classification of users in groups based on the typical transactions that they perform against the web application and the estimation of the percentage of these users in various groups based on real-life distribution.

Designing proper workloads that are nearly similar to real life is one step towards achieving good performance testing. This also applies to the test environment and estimated response times.

These are the ingredients to start web performance testing for this chapter, and we will see how to implement them by walking through the performance test plan and implementation, execution, and analysis of a web application called BugNet. BugNet is an open source bug tracking system that manages the process of submitting bugs and administering them during their life cycle. The project is publically available on Codeplex at this URL: `http://bugnet.codeplex.com/`.

The planning phase

The planning phase sets up the overall plan and it comprises the following activities:

1. Defining the objectives and expectations.
2. Identifying the test environment.
3. Classifying the users into groups.
4. Classifying their corresponding activities.
5. Selecting performance metrics.
6. Identifying baseline tests.

The following is the plan produced after exercising the preceding activities on BugNet:

Defining the objectives and expectations

The application performance objective can possibly be similar to the following list, which we are going to adopt:

- Improving the testing process by certain productivity percentage
- Having realistic response times
- Knowing whether additional performance tuning is needed
- Ensuring competitiveness with other bug tracking applications

Baseline test environment

While designing the test environment, the following aspects are addressed:

- The different application tiers
- The number and specifications of the servers
- Network specification and infrastructure
- Size of the database with respect to the live operational environment

BugNet user classification

We can identify the three main types of users as follows:

- Administrators
- Testers
- Developers

BugNet user activities

The following list breaks down the types of users with their corresponding typical types of bug management activities:

- Administrators: The following are the activities of an administrator:
  - Configuring BugNet settings
  - Creating and editing projects
  - Creating user accounts

- Testers: The following are the activities of a tester:
  - Posting incidents
  - Commenting on an incident
  - Updating incident details
  - Performing queries

- Developers: The following are the activities of a developer:
  - Commenting on incidents
  - Performing queries

Performance metrics selection

The metrics are delineated from the application topology where the performance counters are chosen based on the application tiers described as follows:

- The response time of major transactions.
  - ASP.NET request execution time
  - ASP.NET request wait time
  - Disk time
  - Total processor time

- Throughput of the major transactions.
  - Total disk operations per second
  - Total processor transactions per second
  - Database transactions per second
  - Various segments operated per second on the network

- Resource utilization of the major components of the system.
  - ○ Average disk operation byte transfers
  - ○ Memory usage

Baseline tests

For the purpose of case study, we will choose one baseline test for each type of user. The following list of tests will be created:

- Creating a BugNet user account by an administrator
- Posting an incident by an authenticated tester
- Performing a query by an authenticated developer

The implementation phase

The implementation phase will start putting the plan into action by acquiring the testing resources related to the environment, configuring the hardware and software, and creating the baseline tests.

In the first step, preparing the environment, you need to have a Test Studio version running locally on your machine with another runtime version running on the server, as mentioned earlier, for which you want to capture the performance metrics. For simplicity, we will have BugNet hosted with the BugNet application and the database database both on one server.

For the second step, configuring the hardware and software, you need to make sure that the machine is connected to the server and the requirements for Test Studio configuration are met.

Even for configuring the software, a project should be created on BugNet to host all the resources that are going to be used by our test cases. To create the BugNet project, refer to *Appendix, Setup Reference*.

Finally, in the third step, creating the baseline tests we will start seeing things in Test Studio. For this purpose, create a new project called `BugNet.Load` to hold all our web tests. Then, create a folder and rename it to `Performance Tests`. Add a new test based on the **Web Test** template and call it `Perf-1_NewAccount` as shown in the following screenshot:

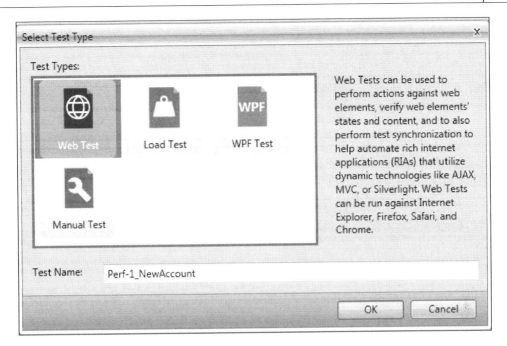

Creating web tests

For this test and subsequent ones, we are going to record our actions in the Internet Explorer browser. Test Studio tests are cross-browser tests, which means that you can record them using Internet Explorer and replay them in any other supported browser without having to make any particular changes to the test configuration.

The **Test** tab now has an additional section called **Quick Execution**, which is responsible for selecting the browser in which the test will execute, as shown in the following screenshot:

The Quick execution ribbon

The `Perf-1_NewAccount` test is going to automate the operations underlined by the following steps:

1. Open the BugNet application.
2. Log in with the username as `admin` and password as `password`.
3. Click on **Admin** from the toolbar.
4. Click on **User Accounts**.
5. Click on the **Create New User** link.
6. Enter **Username** as `projectadmin`.
7. Enter **First Name** as `Jane`.
8. Enter **Last Name** as `Smith`.
9. Enter **Display Name** as `jsmith`.
10. Enter **Email** as `janesmith@bugnet.com`.
11. Enter **Password** as `1234567`.
12. Enter **Confirm Password** as `1234567`.
13. Click on the **Add New User** link.
14. Log out.

Thereafter, from the **Recorder** ribbon, click on the **Record** button. An instance of Internet Explorer will be launched automatically, and Test Studio will attach its recording toolbar to it. Perform the preceding steps in BugNet and close the browser.

As we got used to, Test Studio was adding the test steps as the actions were executed against the browser.

The second baseline test is for posting an incident by a tester. It consists of the following steps:

1. Open the BugNet application.
2. Log in with the username as `tester` and password as `1234567`.
3. Click on **New Issue** from **Quick Links/Filter** of **Load Project**.
4. Enter **Title** as `Load-1: Test`.
5. Choose **Status** as **Open**.
6. Choose **Priority** as **Blocker**.
7. Choose **Assigned To** as **kford**.
8. Unselect the **Notify** checkbox.
9. Choose **Category** as **Response Time**.

10. Select **Type** as **Bug**.

11. Select **Milestone** as **1.0**.

12. Select **Resolution** as **Fixed**.

13. Unselect the **Notify** checkbox

14. Select **Affected Milestone** as **1.0**.

15. Enter **Description** as `Bug Description`.

16. Click on the **Save** button.

Create a web test and call it `Perf-2_NewIssue`. Repeat the preceding steps. Before we move to create the subsequent baseline tests, we will make the test more maintainable.

Since the login steps are going to be used by the subsequent tests, we will extract them to a standalone test by selecting them, then selecting the **Create Test as Step** option from the context menu. Call this test as `Perf_Login`. Switch to the data view by clicking on the **Local Data** button in the **Test Views** ribbon, and create the table as shown in the following figure:

URL	Username	Password
http://localhost/bugnet	tester	1234567

Perf-2_NewIssue data table

Make sure to update the server name of the URL shown in the first column.

In the Perf-Login test, repeat the same steps for local data creation and bind the steps to the columns as shown in the following screenshot:

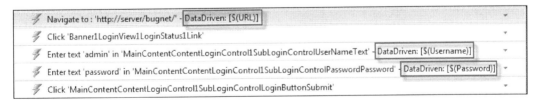

Perf-Login test steps

Finally, enable the **InheritParentDataSource** property check box of the `Perf-Login` test to `true` from the test properties pane.

Run the `Perf-2_NewIssue` test. Surprisingly, although the title field is filled, the following error is thrown by BugNet on submission:

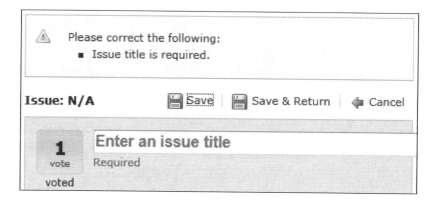

BugNet results after Perf-2_NewIssue execution

In web applications, some JavaScript events are triggered upon interaction with UI items. On the other hand, Test Studio, while replaying the recorded steps, uses by default the underlying object properties to set their values; for example, in the case of incident title field, the **Title** element's **Text** property is directly set to `Load-1: Test` in the DOM without simulating a real-user click inside the field and typing. Hence, from the BugNet perspective, the field is not filled yet and fails the business rules for submission. In order to avoid such situations, expand the step properties and select the **SimulateRealTyping** option as shown in the following screenshot:

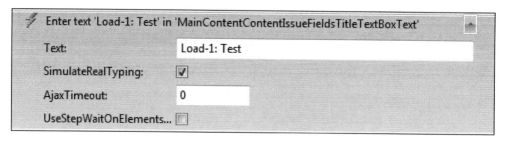

Setting the SimulateRealTyping property

This option's default settings can be changed by accessing the **Project Settings** window from the **Project** tab. The **Show** button of the **Settings** ribbon will invoke the window. Click on **Recording Options** and enable the options highlighted in red as shown in the following screenshot:

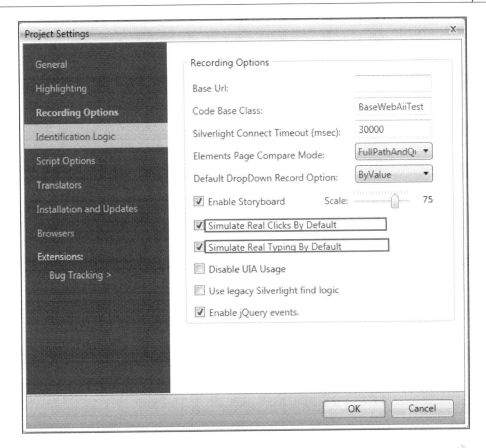

Simulate real typing default settings

The third baseline test is to simulate the performance of a query with developer credentials. The test consists of the following steps:

1. Open a BugNet application.
2. Log in with username as `dev` and password as `1234567`.
3. Click on **Queries** from the **Quick Links/Filter**.
4. Click on the **Add Query** link.
5. From the **Select field** combobox, select **Assigned**.
6. From the combobox corresponding to the value, select **kford**.
7. Click on the **Perform Query** link.

Create a third web test and call it `Perf-3_PerformQuery`. Record steps 3 to 7 listed previously. Insert the `Perf-Login` extracted test and create a local data source with the credentials appearing in this test case as seen in the `Perf-2: NewIssue` test. However, before finalizing the test, we still have one thing to worry about.

After choosing the query criteria, as represented in the first combobox, we need to wait until the last combobox gets populated with the possible list of values. This list is filled with the results fetched from the database after a request is initiated to execute the right query corresponding to the chosen criteria. Accordingly, insert the verification step depicted in the advanced verification builder of the following screenshot:

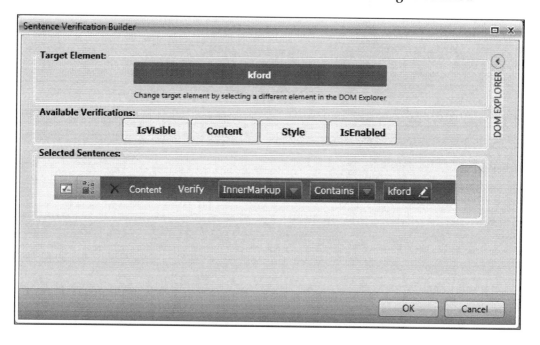

Waiting for a value to appear inside the combobox content

This verification step is created based on the combobox holding the values corresponding to the **Assigned** operator. It verifies that the value `kford` is contained in its text content. This step should be placed just before the action that sets the value `kford` for the combobox. Once added, perform the following steps:

1. Right-click on the **Verification** step.
2. Select **Change Role** from the context menu.
3. Click on **Set as Wait**.

This will convert the verification to a wait step that will delay the execution for 10 seconds until `kford` appears in the combobox items. To change the default wait time, edit the **Timeout** property for this step as follows:

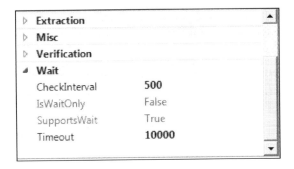

Changing default wait time for a wait step

The execution and analysis phase

The creation of baseline tests is complete, so it is time to run them and gather the performance metrics. Click on the `Perf-1_NewAccount` test, and then click on the **Performance** tab.

How do we specify the server for which we want to collect the metrics? How do we specify the metrics that we want to collect?

The answers to these questions are obtained from the **Set Up** ribbon after clicking on the **Configure** button. The **Configure Performance Settings** dialog box appears as follows:

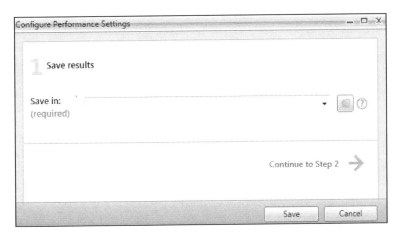

Configuring performance settings

On the first page, you can optionally change the folder in which the results will be stored as shown in the preceeding screenshot. The execution runs are saved to allow a history view and comparisons of various results. These features are handy for the test results analysis that we are going to see.

Click on the **Continue to Step 2** button to continue with the selection of performance metrics present on the **Gather Computer Performance Data** window of the wizard. The steps are as follows:

1. Select the **Gather performance data** checkbox, which if left unchecked will give only a summary of metrics gathered that are related to time, HTTP errors, and data size.

2. Click on the **Add a computer** button.

3. A section is now enabled to specify the server details; the first free input field allows the specification of a friendly name for the server to be monitored, so enter `Application Server`.

4. In the free input field available on the computer, specify the server name of the IP address and click on the **Connect** button, since without a successful connection you will not be able to proceed to the next step.

5. Once the connection is made, a panel containing the performance metrics is expanded. Choose the metrics from the list, as listed earlier, in the **Performance Metrics Selection** section of the test plan, which can be found under these nodes: **ASP.NET, MSSQL$MSSQLSERVER[VERSION]:DATA BASES, Logical Disk, Physical Disk, Memory, TCPv4,** and **Processor.**

6. Click on the **Save as New Template** button to store the current template in order to use it in the further tests.

7. Fill the template name with `BugNet Template` in the pop-up dialog box.

8. Click on the **Save** button.

Our example gathers performance metrics from one server; however, you can click on the **Add a Computer** button to map all the servers in your application topology, and therefore collect the specialized metrics around each of them.

The overview mode

Now we are back to the **Performance** tab. This tab contains the same **Quick Execution Run** ribbon seen in the single test tab. We can optionally change the execution to run in any of the available browsers. Click on the **Run** button and wait until the execution terminates. Make sure that the **Overview** option is selected in the **Views** ribbon. The results are displayed in the overview mode as follows:

Description	Time	Total Time	Server	Client	Size	Errors
IF (Verify element 'Banner1LoginView1LoginSta'.		2.117 sec	0.134 sec	1.983 sec	228 bytes	0
Click 'Banner1LoginView1LoginStatus1Link'		1.170 sec	0.621 sec	0.549 sec	36.8 KB	8
Wait for element 'YouCanLoginDiv' 'is' visible.		0.511 sec	0.511 sec	0.000 sec	0 bytes	0
IF (Verify element 'MainContentContentLoginC.		1.531 sec	1.531 sec	0.000 sec	0 bytes	0
Enter text 'admin' in 'MainContentContentLogi'.		0.688 sec	0.688 sec	0.000 sec	0 bytes	0
IF (Verify element 'MainContentContentLoginC.		0.778 sec	0.778 sec	0.000 sec	0 bytes	0
Enter text 'password' in 'MainContentContentL'.		0.492 sec	0.492 sec	0.000 sec	0 bytes	0
IF (Verify element 'MainContentContentLoginC.		0.791 sec	0.791 sec	0.000 sec	0 bytes	0
Click 'MainContentContentLoginControl1SubLo.		1.618 sec	1.618 sec	0.000 sec	67.6 KB	6
IF (Verify element 'AdminLink' 'is' visible.) THEN		0.947 sec	0.947 sec	0.000 sec	0 bytes	0
Click 'ListItem'		0.498 sec	0.498 sec	0.000 sec	0 bytes	0
Click 'UserAccountsLink'		1.116 sec	1.116 sec	0.000 sec	21.2 KB	4
Wait for element 'ManageUserH1Tag' 'is' visible.		0.809 sec	0.809 sec	0.000 sec	0 bytes	0

Performance test results in the overview mode

This screenshot contains a grid showing the time measurements of the test. The **Description** column has all the steps that form the test. The **Server** time is colored in light orange while the **Client** time in light pink. Notice how some steps involve only client time such as logical steps whereas the others are a combination of both.

Certain metrics map to time notions that we have seen earlier in the chapter, while others are additional custom metrics that are built using the former basic metrics. Therefore, Test Studio does not record all time metrics during the test execution, and only some of them are calculated. The following table represents the different time notions and their translation in Test Studio:

Test Studio terms	Performance time metrics	Type
Server time	Server processing time	Recorded
Client time	Client processing time + network latency	Calculated
Total time	Client time + server time + network time + time to fetch the object for the next step	Recorded

Other useful measurements are also displayed in the overview mode grid. The **Size** column has the amount of bytes processed at the server side whereas the **Error** column has the number of HTTP errors.

Finally, the **Time** column has a symbolic way of denoting the component that has consumed the maximum amount of time indicated in the **Total Time** column. Accordingly, the following can be deducted by simply traversing the test steps in the **Time** column:

- The largest **Total Time**
- The side that is causing the largest **Total Time**
- The largest **Server Time**

The following the identification of the largest time delays, the bottlenecks that are degrading the application performance can be highlighted.

The details view

We haven't seen yet the performance metrics that we assigned for gathering. For this purpose, Test Studio has another view mode called **Details view**. Double-click on any step from the **Overview** mode. The following screenshot is a sample detailed view of the `Perf-1_NewAccount` test:

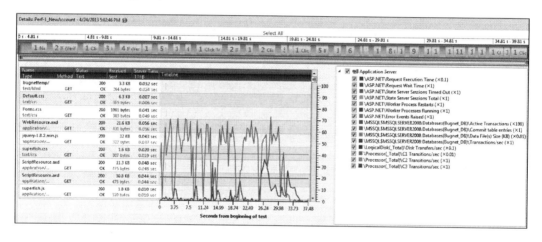

Performance test results in the details mode

The upper horizontal navigation bar highlighted in the preceding screenshot contains all the test steps. It allows you to switch among them in order to display the performance metric around one step at a time. Alternatively, any step range or even a global view can also be achieved by expanding the selection area to enclose as many desired steps. The **Select All** link has a direct alternative way of showing the performance metrics around all test steps.

The panel to the right lists the performance counters that were assigned during the performance test configuration. You can optionally check the set of metrics that you wish to draw on the performance chart.

Finally, the panel to the left contains all requests and responses under the scope of the selection area of the upper navigation bar. It has a detailed view of the HTTP request result, the total byte size sent and received, and the time to first byte or the response time, which is displayed in the **Server Time** column.

All the previously mentioned criteria are represented in the middle area in a chart.

The compare view

After running automated tests on the web application, you might want to compare various runs against each other. This is useful after identifying the bottleneck and tuning the corresponding parameters in an attempt to improve the performance; for example, by increasing the available memory and CPU processors. Hence, at this stage you are seeking to have a closer detailed view of the collection of results.

Open the `Perf-3_PerformQuery` test and make two performance executions using `BugNet Template` created earlier. While on the **Performance** tab, click on the **Compare** button in the **Views** ribbon. We have now entered Test Studio built-in performance test comparisons. This is a powerful feature and it especially allows us to assess executions at a step level.

The first step shown in the following screenshot consists of choosing the execution runs and assigning them labels **A** and **B** correspondingly.

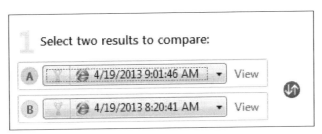

Selecting execution results for comparison

In order to allow Test Studio to quickly perform the calculations for unaccepted metric differences, step two allows the configuration of the thresholds for time, size, and error values. The following screenshot shows an example of the threshold values:

Setting thresholds

Here we are instructing Test Studio to warn us with an error whenever one of the following conditions is met:

- Total Time B - Total Time A >= 3 seconds
- Server Time B - Server Time A >= 2.5 seconds
- Client Time B - Client Time A >= 1 second
- Data Size B - Data Size A >= 3,000 bytes
- Errors B - Errors A >= 4 HTTP errors

The following screenshot shows how Test Studio has calculated the metric differences and applied the rules stated earlier:

Thresholds applied in the comparison mode

The fourth step marked with a red and white cross has failed the client time rule whereas all the remaining steps marked with a green and white tick have passed all the rules.

The history view

The last view mode available in Test Studio is the **history view**. In this mode, all test runs for a specific test are displayed in a grid-like view and then reported in a line chart. Here again, the data in the chart provides a fast way to directly discover the test with the best performance. The following chart is generated after running `Perf-3_NewIssue` four times:

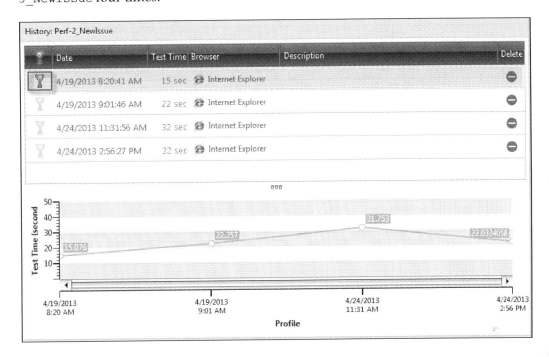

The history view

In performance testing, this test plays an important role in benchmarking other tests against it. Hence, as regression tests are being executed and performance improvements are being carried out on the web application, you may want to compare all the subsequent runs of this test to the one assigned as the benchmark. In Test Studio, you can tag this test by using the baseline feature. Among the list of executed test runs, search for the test with the best performance and click on the corresponding trophy icon to enable it as highlighted in the preceding screenshot.

In this way, we have selected the baseline test which is going to act as our performance reference point later.

Summary

This chapter explained performance testing in Test Studio. We saw how to configure the environment for performance testing. After having chosen the baseline tests, they were recorded using the web test template. Afterwards, with a few configuration amendments at the test level to identify the server and performance counters to be collected, the tests were executed against in the performance mode. Finally, the chapter ended by going through the different test result view modes. The overview mode offers a high-level summary of the performance metrics, where we can delve more into each step level by enabling the detail view mode. The compare view allows a close comparison of the different execution runs of a test whereas the history view allows a global view of all the execution instances of a test to enable a clear and quick analysis for the baseline test.

This chapter ends by demonstrating the performance metric gathering for executing a test in a simple mode. The next chapter revolves around load testing, where you can create more complex execution modes to simulate real-life loads on your web applications using the Test Studio load test template.

8
Load Testing

Performance testing was only half the story! In fact, it was the preparation for studying the application response under user load, which was exactly how you felt during the testing team's meeting. The numbers that were constantly used in the interchanged discussions had their impact.

How will the application perform with hundreds of thousands of users? How will the application perform when consolidating millions of user records? How will the application continue to be reliable without damaging thousands of user benefits and safety? How will the application support and ensure the company's profit?

So, how will Test Studio help you respond to the technical concerns lying behind these questions? This chapter walks you through a step-by-step load plan executed against a web application. It exhibits the following features inside Test Studio:

- Configuring Test Studio for load testing
- Designing and creating load tests
- Tuning and running load tests
- Measuring default performance metrics
- Viewing and analyzing test results

Load testing

There are some scenarios that you face when operating on an application that lacks efficiency. These scenarios can be one or many of the following:

- You decide you are better off without the application service than waiting the amount of time it requires
- You feel your machine is lingering to keep the application running
- You start receiving inaccurate responses after having used the application for so long
- Out-of-memory exceptions start popping up on the screen

Efficiency is a nonfunctional attribute that characterizes the system. It is demonstrated by the latter's consumption for time and resources when subjected to an increasing load. Therefore, an efficient system is one that provides responses while abiding by the predefined limits for time and resource usage.

Testing efficiency is not achieved by applying an arbitrary simultaneous weight of users over the system; neither is it confined to varying their numbers. Actually, lots of other factors play a role in many variations of efficiency testing. Among these variations, we will see **load testing**.

Load testing is a type of nonfunctional testing that studies application performance against a preplanned increasing load of users and their typical activities. It is done to measure the response time and throughput, while parallel operating users are injected to perform on system resources that are designed to be as close as possible to real-life specifications.

Other types of nonfunctional performance testing are listed as follows:

- **Stress testing**: This is load testing taken to the next level. As briefly mentioned, load testing operates the system under the anticipated user and resource specifications that are going to take place in real life after product release. Stress testing is when it pushes these variables beyond their specified limits; for example, by minimizing available resources. The system is expected to not respond at some point, since the limits were already drawn; however, what matters is the slope with which the system degrades to reach this point. Does this mean that it will cause the system to hang or gracefully fail under high load? Will it recover data after being restarted?

- **Scalability testing**: In this type of testing, the system's current behavior is studied to assess its capability to accommodate increasing demands. During this type of testing, the components that should be targeted to allow more load in the future are highlighted. Generally, these components are the ones that were identified as bottlenecks.

- **Soak testing**: As the name suggests, this is a rough plan to soak the system. It is achieved by running the system constantly for long durations. Generally, problems in allocating and clearing memory are uncovered.

- **Spike testing**: In this type of testing, we observe the system behavior against a full-blown usage scenario. Usually, we expect system usage to grow gradually, but in some real-life cases, access to the system is requested spontaneously by a great number of users; for example, after server restart.

Other performance testing types also exist. This chapter demonstrates the usage of Test Studio in order to implement load-testing plans. However, notice that with some adjustments to this plan and to the test execution settings, other nonfunctional performance testing types can be performed.

Measurements

The introduction has mentioned two key metrics for measuring system performance under load, which are response times and throughput. Test Studio has its own translation and elaboration on these metrics, which are gathered during load tests, in order to provide the user with important data to be utilized in post-analysis. Later in this chapter, we will see the other metrics that Test Studio can monitor while running load tests.

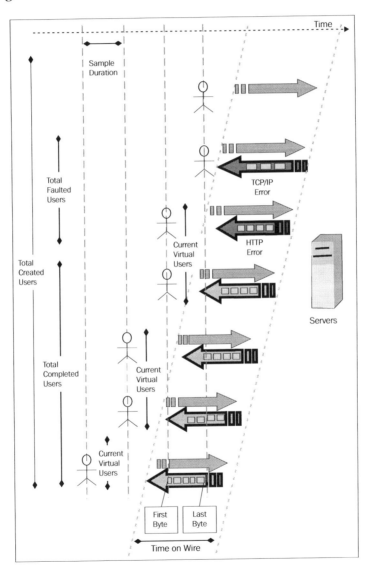

Simplified version of a load test over time

The previous diagram is a simplified illustration of a typical load test. We are going to traverse it from left to right to see how each component and measurement fits in the load testing picture. On the left-most part of the diagram, we have the system users. On the rightmost, we have the servers whereas in between the various arrows reflect the communication taking place between the two ends.

The actors represent the virtual users which simulate real life system users, and they are responsible for initiating the application HTTP requests to the server. Hence, there are no true browser sessions created throughout the execution of the load test; rather, there are HTTP requests and responses. The total number of virtual users created by Test Studio over the entire test-execution duration is called **Total Created Users**. Among these users, some will have their transactions successfully completed while others will receive TCP/IP errors in their results. The former subset is called **Total Completed Users** whereas the latter is called **Total Faulted Users**. Finally, we also have **Current Virtual Users**. They correspond to the number of users that are active during the time of data sampling for the performance counters. In the preceding diagram, we have in total seven created users, four completed users, one faulted user, and one user with no response at all. As for the current virtual users, at the time of the first sample there was only one active user, at the time of the second sample there were two users, at the time of the third there were also two..

All communications are initiated from the client to the server via requests, whereas the server results are carried back via responses. Therefore, we have two additional metrics called **Requests sent per second** and **Responses received per second**.

Some requests do not always complete successfully and result in errors; thus we also have **Total errors** and **Errors per second**. The first metric counts all the HTTP errors that have occurred throughout the test execution, which corresponds to one in the preceding diagram. The second metric corresponds to the average HTTP errors per second, which is one divided by the total test execution duration in our case.

Normally, the request carries in its body the information required by the server to process. This brings up the issue of data size. Thus, the **Bytes sent per second** corresponds to the sum of bytes sent in the seven requests bodies divided by the total test duration. Similarly, the responses carry data in their body to be analyzed by the client side. This too has a measurement and it's called **Bytes received per second**, which is the sum of bytes received in all six response bodies, divided by the overall test duration.

In this chapter, we also talk about time metrics. The metric known average response time, which is the time taken for the first byte to be received, is referred to as Time to first byte in Test Studio. So, the average time for receiving the first byte for all requests initiated by all virtual users is called **Average time to first byte**. On the other hand, the response time will stand for a particular period of time included between request initiation and receipt of the last byte of response. Subsequently, the **average response time** is computed as the average of HTTP requests and response times for all virtual users. The last metric is **total time on wire**, which corresponds to the addition of all the time spent on wire during all requests.

Load testing in Test Studio

After applying performance testing on one web test at a time and after measuring the underlying system's metrics, Test Studio extends these possibilities by simulating multiples of this request and multiples of the user executing it. During such scenarios, a network of users will be created and managed so that they perform the anticipated activities. This is all achieved with Test Studio's ability to multithread sessions and to simulate a load on the tested server.

The following section starts by understanding various Test Studio load components architecture, communications, and responsibilities to prepare for the load plan illustrated and executed afterwards inside Test Studio.

How it works

This section describes Test Studio 2012 R2 Version architecture, and the way it works in order to achieve a correct simulation of real-life system usage in terms of users and application transactions. Nevertheless, Test Studio does not confine to this only since the simulation alone is certainly barely revealing anything. It is mostly about the underlying metric numbers. Hence it is critical to have access to the necessary KPIs and a calculated set of metrics in order to accurately interpret the results. Test Studio is internally equipped with adequate services, providing all the functionalities mentioned earlier, which we are going to see in detail.

Similar to other tests, **Test Studio IDE** is the workspace that presents the capabilities for constructing the load tests and designing their load strategy. It also serves as the portal that initiates test execution and communication with other remote Test Studio services. The **Load Controller** is the Test Studio load simulation manager. This component is responsible for closely managing the load execution and orchestrating all load agents. The **Load Agent** is the component that controls the virtual users that produce the load traffic. Depending on your load-testing plan, you might want to have more than one load agent distributed on different machines with different specifications to imitate a real-life environment. Finally, the **Load Reporter** is the component that records the load test. It connects to the Load Controller in order to retrieve statistics and save them in a SQL database. The last section of this chapter deals with external reports and will explain the tables of this database.

To be able to make use of the components mentioned earlier, they will have to be installed on the target machine first. The following link belongs to the Telerik online documentation for Test Studio and explains how to install Test Studio services:
`http://www.telerik.com/automated-testing-tools/support/documentation/`
`user-guide/load-testing.aspx`.

As with performance testing, in order to successfully run your tests, all Test Studio services must be running correctly. Launch Test Studio services configuration manager from the start menu by going to **Start | All Programs | Telerik | Test Execution | Configure Load Test Services**.

After the window opens, make sure all services are running and the **Start** button is disabled. For every service, you can optionally change the network interface and TCP/IP port number. Most likely, the different load components will not be present on the same machine. Therefore, you have the flexibility to change the hosting machine.

The configuration manager section for Load Controller is shown in the following screenshot:

Designated Load Controller:

Host: [▼] Port: [8012 ⬍]

Configuring load controller

The following screenshot displays the section concerned with the **Reporter** service. This part of the window allows editing of the SQL database used by the Load Reporter. Note that in case the database name is changed, the newly provided database must contain all the tables used by the Reporter instance. This means that Test Studio will not create the missing database object, if any. Hence, in summary, there are two ways to guarantee a proper reporting database, either by letting Test Studio create one for you during installation or by downloading the relevant scripts from this link: `http://www.telerik.com/automated-testing-tools/support/ documentation/user-guide/load-testing/generating-reports-from-sql- database.aspx`. Once the database is created, the final step is to pass the newly created database parameters to the configuration window, as shown in the following screenshot:

Reporter Database Connection:

Instance:

Database: TestStudioReportingDB

Authentication

○ Windows Integrated Authentication
◉ SQL Authentication

Login Name:

Password:

Configuring the reporting database

The last section of this window holds the properties for the logfile. This file is used by Test Studio to write down logs from the different load services. Optionally, logging can be enabled or disabled using the fields shown in following screenshot. This logfile can grow large rapidly, so it is preferable to enable the logging option only for troubleshooting purposes.

Trace Log:

☑ Enable logging
Log File: C:\Program Files (x86)\Telerik\Test Studio\Bin\Load-Log.txt ...

Configuring logging

Load test planning and execution

In this section, we will see the structured load testing process, which begins by setting the expectations around the system usage in real life. Hence, before using Test Studio load capabilities, we are going to walk through a sample plan that was exercised on the BugNet application used in the previous chapter. After defining the KPIs that need to be monitored, the load characteristics for this plan will be implemented step by step.

The Planning and design phase

As with any testing type, the load-testing process should be thoroughly planned in order to bring the testing work closer to the real usage of the application. This phase includes estimation of the different variables that parameterize load testing. The principle elements that are going to dominate our estimates for this section are the users and their types of activities.

Defining goals

Some goals were extracted based on the objectives and expectations drawn for the project when nonfunctional application performance was tackled. These goals help in assessing objectives and avoiding materialization of key concerns by keeping an open eye.

The first goal is related to response time, where no request is allowed to exceed 2.5 seconds for any type of transaction, since this will cause the user to abandon the operation. The second goal is related to HTTP errors, where we allow at most five errors per second. The third goal tackles the issue of efficiency in handling transactions by the server—we seek to achieve at least 50 transactions per second.

So how will the preceding goals behave when the system is exposed to certain loads?

These loads consist of numerous combinations of transactions coming from different user types. Hence, the purpose of the next section is to narrow down these combinations by designing user workloads.

Designing workloads

Designing workloads starts firstly by estimating the projected number of users that are going to use BugNet.

Secondly, it proceeds by approximating the share that each transaction partakes of the overall usage of the system. Knowing also that transactions are categorized with the types of users (enumerated in the previous chapters), the estimated shares must also take into consideration the percentage of each user type of the overall number concluded in the previous step.

The estimates derived from the BugNet application are contained in the answers to the following series of questions:

- What is the projected number of users?

  We are considering each project hosted on BugNet will have 100 members divided into membership groups, as appearing in the following table. On an average, we expect to have 10 projects for a deployed BugNet version.

  The member distribution inside a group is as follows:

User types	Estimated numbers
Project Administrator	1
Quality Assurance	44
Developers	44
Reporters	11

- What is the percentage of concurrent users?

  The estimated percentage of concurrent users are as follows:

User types	Estimated percentages
Project Administrator	5%
Quality Assurance	50%
Developers	35%
Reporters	10%

- What is the length of user sessions?

  The estimates length of user sessions are as follows:

User types	Estimated session length (min)
Project Administrator	30
Quality Assurance	300
Developers	120
Reporters	60

- What is the percentage of each activity for each user type?

  The estimated percentage of each activity for each user type is as shown in the following tables:

- ° Project Administrator:

Activity types	Estimated percentages
Logging in	20%
Configuring BugNet settings	10%
Creating and editing projects	50%
Creating user accounts	20%

- ° Quality Assurance Engineers:

Activity types	Estimated percentages
Logging in	20%
Posting incidents	30%
Updating incident details and commenting on an incident	45%
Performing queries	5%

- ° Developers:

Activity types	Estimated percentages
Logging in	20%
Commenting on incidents	70%
Performing queries	10%

- ° Reporters:

Activity types	Estimated percentages
Logging in	20%
Performing queries	80%

After performing the calculations, the following total percentages are extracted for each activity:

Activity types	Estimated percentages
Logging in	20%
Configuring BugNet settings	0.5%
Creating and editing projects	2.5%

Creating user accounts	1%
Posting incidents	15%
Updating and commenting on incidents	47.5%
Performing queries	13.5%

Defining test cases

The preceding estimation serves in deducing the baseline tests. In fact, the left column of the last table corresponds to the list of tests to be used further on in load testing. The operations of logging in, creating user accounts, posting incidents, and performing queries were already automated in the pervious chapter, and they map to `Perf_Login`, `Perf-1_NewAccount`, `Perf-2_NewIssue`, and `Perf-3_PerformQuery` respectively. In addition to these tests, the following sections are going to make use of other powerful capabilities available inside Test Studio in order to automate the remaining tests, such as updating and commenting BugNet incidents.

The implementation phase

During implementation, we take the base tests and make sure they are present in an automated version inside Test Studio. Afterwards, we plug in all the estimated numbers in the test designs. For this purpose, we are going to discover next a new template made available by Test Studio in order to perform load testing.

Start first by creating the folder that is going to hold all the subsequent tests. Rename it as `Load Tests`. Under this folder, add a new test based on the **Load Test** template depicted in the following screenshot and call it `Load-1`:

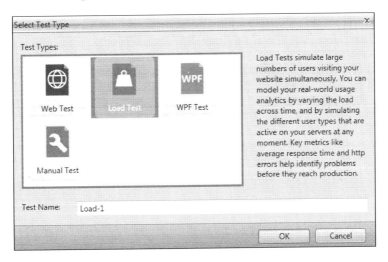

Creating a load test

Double-click on the added test to enter its edit mode. The first step starts by configuring the environment in which the test is going to run. This means we are going to specify the different Test Studio services that will handle and manage test execution. Subsequent to this, we reach the actual creation of the test requests and the specification of the planned load.

Configuring services

From the **Steps** ribbon, click on the **Environment** button appearing in the following screenshot:

The Environment configuration button

This button opens the workspace that is shown in the following screenshot:

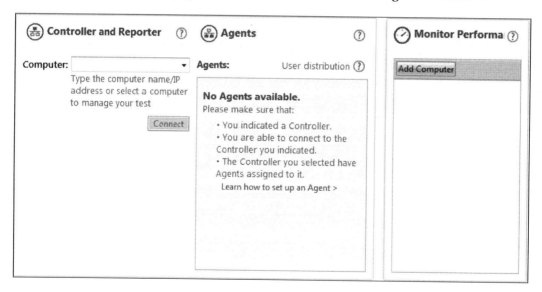

Load test workspace

We start from the first pane to the left, which is responsible for configuring the Controller and Reporter machines.

As mentioned earlier, the Controller will manage the test execution whereas the Reporter will handle the test results and their storage inside the database. The following screenshot shows the section related to specifying the machine hosting these services, where the connection to it was successful:

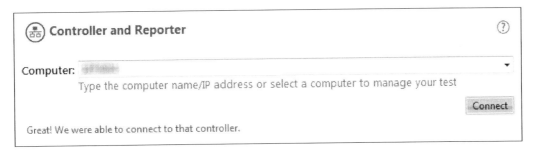

Configuring the machine hosting controller and reporter services

It is in the **Computer** field that the specification of the machine name or IP is entered. After filling it, the connection must be validated, so click on the **Connect** button. If the connection was successful, the label in green will be displayed as shown in the preceding screenshot. The connection has to be successful for us to proceed. Some reasons why the connection cannot be established are:

- Misspelling the machine name or IP
- The services are not started
- The services and Test Studio release versions are different
- Network settings problem

The **Agents** pane, which corresponds to the middle pane, displays the detected agents. During the execution of the load test, the Controller will evenly distribute the virtual users across the available Load Agents. The following screenshot is a sample of how Test Studio lists the test agents inside this section:

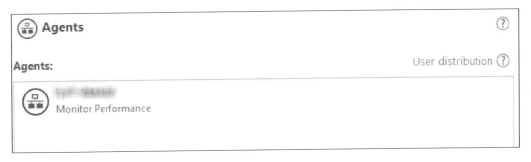

Load agents

As a result of our work, the ribbon has an indicator to relay to us whether all connections were successful. The green circles shown in the following screenshot signify that the services are reachable; on the other hand, a red circle suggests a failing configuration, which requires further investigation.

A successful connection to load services

The last pane, the **Monitor Performance** pane, enables us to add the list of computers to be monitored. The *Measurements* section of this chapter has introduced some metrics calculated implicitly by Test Studio. Thus, after deriving the performance deficiency points, KPIs are then used for troubleshooting the results and identifying the root causes. So, as we did with performance testing, we are going to select the performance counters to be monitored throughout the test execution. The following screenshot shows the performance monitoring workspace:

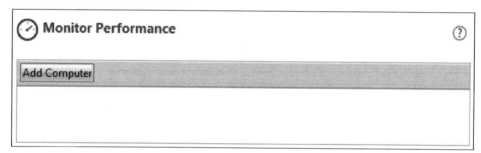

Configuring computers for performance monitoring

Click on the **Add Computer** button appearing in the screenshot. Following this, the **Monitor Performance** window shown in the following screenshot is invoked:

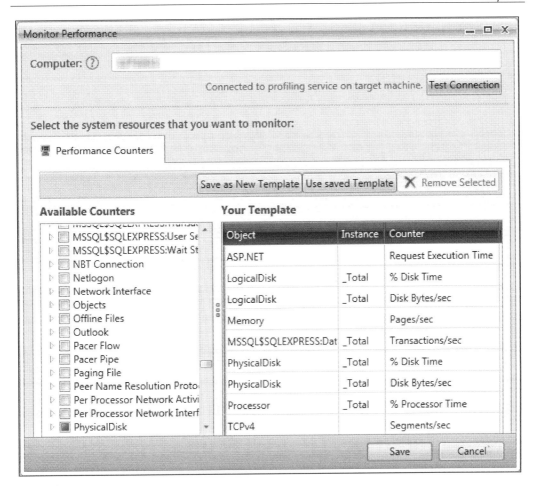

Choosing performance counters

To configure the computer, enter the name or IP of the machine to be monitored in the **Computer** field and then click on the **Test Connection** button to confirm that the target machine is reachable.

The next step is to add the counters that need to be monitored. The **Performance Counters** section shows a list that correspond to the **Windows Performance Monitor** counters that are native to Windows systems. We will select the same list of performance counters used in the previous chapter, which was saved in a template. So, browse for the BugNet template after clicking on the **Use Saved Template** button.

Click on the **Save** button and notice how an entry is added under the list of monitored computers.

With this, we have wrapped up the environment configuration.

Designing tests

The design stage comes after the test environment setup. We have arrived at the
Design button of the **Steps** ribbon, shown in the following screenshot:

The Design button

This stage comprises of two main steps: defining user profiles and specifying the
corresponding test settings. The left pane, titled **Define User Profiles and Workload**
and shown in the following screenshot, will receive the user activities planned in
the first phase. These activities will be saved in the form of HTTP requests and can
be created or supplemented using four different ways, as we will see. Following the
completion of these activities, we specify the Test Studio **workload**, which maps to
the estimated percentage of users out of the overall targeted number of virtual users.

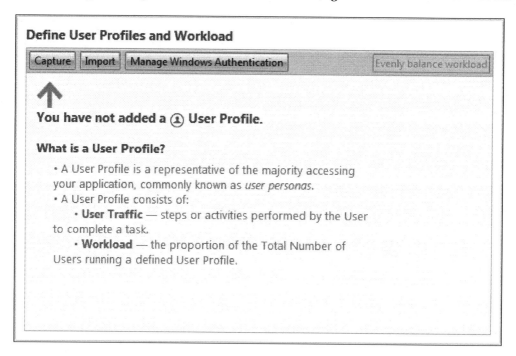

Profile and workload panel

To record a new test or to import an already created web test, click on the
Capture button.

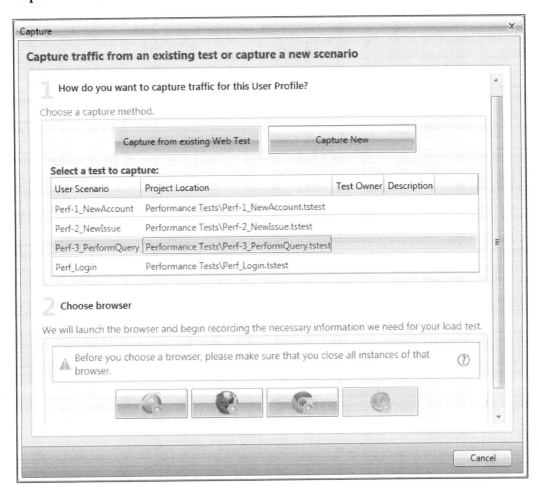

Capturing a new scenario

The **Capture** window is invoked and displays two options. Hence, to capture traffic
for a new test, the **Capture New** button should be clicked. This will launch a new
browser instance of our choosing and record the traffic for the requests initiated
during the session. Alternatively, click on the **Capture from existing Web Test**
button to import an existing test created using the web template.

On clicking on the **Capture from existing Web Test** button, the **Select a test to
capture** section is enabled as shown in the preceding screenshot. This section will list
the web tests created in the previous chapter. Select **Perf-3_PerformQuery**.

Knowing that browser types can also influence the performance of requests, this window offers a choice between multiple supported browsers. So choose the Internet Explorer icon from the **Choose browser** section.

Once a browser type is chosen, Test Studio will automatically execute the test steps in order to record the underlying HTTP traffic. An **Edit User Profile** window is invoked on the execution termination and has the **Dynamic Targets** window open directly on top of it. The latter window contains variables used by BugNet to generate information for the replayed requests. The dynamic targets are variables with assigned values sent from the server to the client. Subsequently, they will be used by the client, where it will generate further requests by passing these values as parameters. Test Studio automatically detects dynamic targets and displays them in a list as shown in the following window:

Selecting dynamic targets

In order to observe more closely how these variables work, we will take the example of the row highlighted in red.

The **Dynamic Target** column holds the name of the variable. The **From** column holds the request ID where the dynamic variable will be located in its response. The **To** column holds the request ID where the dynamic variable is used as a parameter. Finally, the **Original Context** column displays how this variable appears in the response. Before we see these column values inside the list of requests, we need to close the **Dynamic Targets** window. However, prior to this and in order to correctly replay the requests from the virtual users, we need to make sure these parameters are resent to the server; so select all variables displayed in the window and click on the **Done** button. While automating your tests, the best way to decide whether or not to include a target is to ask the developers. They will provide correct answers on the criticality of adding these variables as dynamic targets.

At this point, we have the **Edit User Profile** window enabled. The **Name** field carries the test name. The **User Traffic** panel to the left has the list of all the requests that were recorded during execution. The following screenshot shows a snippet of the requests list, where the 50th request is highlighted:

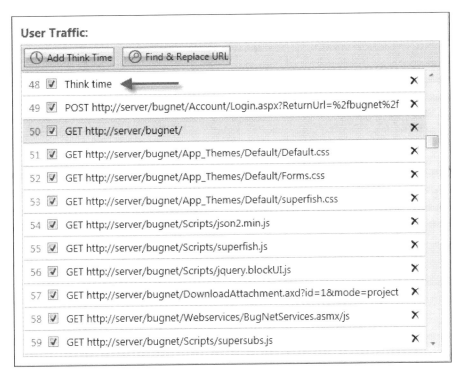

Load test user traffic

The **Dynamic Targets** window says that we should be able to find the value under the **Original Context** column in the response of the 50th request. The following screenshot shows the response, which is reachable by selecting the request and clicking on the **Response** tab inside the right-hand side pane that displays the details:

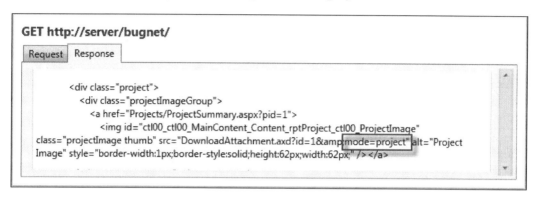

GET http://server/bugnet/

Request | Response

```
<div class="project">
    <div class="projectImageGroup">
        <a href="Projects/ProjectSummary.aspx?pid=1">
            <img id="ctl00_ctl00_MainContent_Content_rptProject_ctl00_ProjectImage"
class="projectImage thumb" src="DownloadAttachment.axd?id=1&amp;mode=project" alt="Project
Image" style="border-width:1px;border-style:solid;height:62px;width:62px;" /> </a>
```

The Response tab having the dynamic target

The **Response** section contains outlined text that confirms the sought value. This value is passed as a parameter in request number 57, which is shown in the preceding screenshot.

The **Edit User Profile** window also offers another capability. Usually, when using an application in real time, there are certain delays on the client side that are not comprised in any time latency spent over the different application components. These delays correspond to the time taken by the user to think, which normally occur between UI operations performed against the screen. This inactivity at the client side represents the time taken by the user to analyze and prepare for the second action. Fortunately, Test Studio has a notion for this type of time and materializes it with **think time** steps. The previous screenshot for **User Traffic** contains this step and it is at position 48.

By default, Test Studio will insert the think time steps between the test steps. The think time details can be adjusted after selecting it. Again, the right-hand side pane will display the details as shown in the following screenshot. The **Duration** property stands for the idle time whereas **Deviation** is the factor of randomization added to the former property. This means that for the same **Think Time** step, the idle time can be any value between 7 and 13 seconds.

Setting the think time range

Click on the **Save** button to finish the creation of the user traffic that corresponds to performing a query web test. Repeat the same steps to import the following tests.

- `Perf-Login`
- `Perf-1_NewAccount`
- `Perf-2_NewIssue`

The second alternative for adding user profiles is through importing an already existing web test or previously recorded fiddler traffic in the SAZ files. This can all be performed through the **Import** button of the **Define User Profiles and Workload** panel. The following window opens after clicking on the **Import** button:

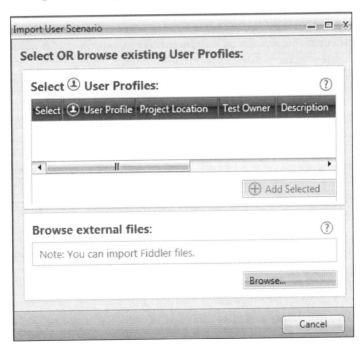

Importing external user scenarios

Click on the **Browse** button and attach the file called `Updating and Commenting incidents.saz`, which is produced from the fiddler after carrying out a test to edit the comment for an already posted bug on BugNet.

To sum up, we have now created five different activities for various BugNet users. The user profiles are not completed before we specify the corresponding workloads. Under the **Workload** column, adjust the slider for each test to comply with the following screenshot. The values were extracted from the `User types` table generated during the planning phase.

User Profile		Workload		Delete	User Identity
Perf_Login	✏	▭	20%	✕	▾
Perf-1_NewAccount	✏	▭	1%	✕	▾
Perf-2_NewIssue	✏	▭	15%	✕	▾
Perf-3_PerformQuery	✏	▭	15%	✕	▾
Updating and Commenting incidents	✏	▭	49%	✕	▾

Specifying workloads for user profiles

The preceding screenshot also shows a **User Identity** column. When the scenario to be automated requires Windows authentication, you can create identities using the **Manage Windows Authentication** button and then assign them from the combobox. When the test executes, it will impersonate the user with the assigned Windows identity.

The final stage of the implementation phase is to set up the behavior of virtual user creation.

In some cases of load testing, you might want to test a full-blown scenario, where all users log in concurrently and start carrying out their tasks. Such cases appear in spike tests, which was explained near the chapter start. These situations could occur, for example, after restarting the web server in the middle of working hours. Once the application becomes available again, all the users that had open sessions will rush to log in in order to resume their work. However, this is not always the case. Normally, we will detect the sessions being incremented bit by bit until reaching a saturated number. In fact, this is useful to observe the application's nonfunctional behavior in handling a growing number of requests throughout its usage. We are going to see next how to make this happen inside Test Studio.

1. The following screenshot shows the right-hand side panel of the **Design** work area:

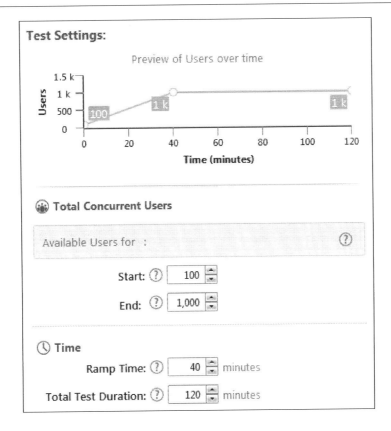

Test Settings:

Preview of Users over time

Designing virtual users over time

The first section of this panel is a dynamic chart line that automatically updates following the modification of the numbers appearing in the sections underneath. The **Total Concurrent Users** section has two variables. The **Start** field holds the number of parallel users that will start executing the user profiles as soon as the test is ready to start sending requests. The **End** field holds the maximum number of users that will be reached and maintained throughout the remaining time of the test. The period of time during which the number of users increases from start to end is ambiguous until now. It is specified in the **Time** section by setting the value for the **Ramp Time** field. This value represents the initial duration through which the creation of virtual users will grow from 100 to hit 1000 users. These numbers are extracted from the *Designing workload* section of this chapter, where they correspond to the number of estimated project members and the number of estimated project members multiplied by that of the estimated number of projects respectively. In our case, we need 40 minutes for the number of virtual users to be saturated, which is the estimated time required for employees (represented by virtual users) to log in to the BugNet in real life. Finally, the test will run for 120 minutes (two continuous hours of various BugNet activities), where each activity type will execute according to the designated percentages.

The Execution and analysis phase

During this phase, additional test settings are specified at the level of the executing instance before we actually run the test. We will start by instructing Test Studio how frequently we wish to have our performance counters sampled. Afterwards, we proceed to the goals assignment.

This section is the last step in load test creation and execution. We are going to discover the last button in the **Steps** ribbon, shown in the following screenshot:

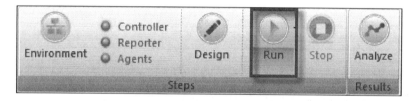

The Run button for load tests

Click on the **Run** button to enable and edit the run settings.

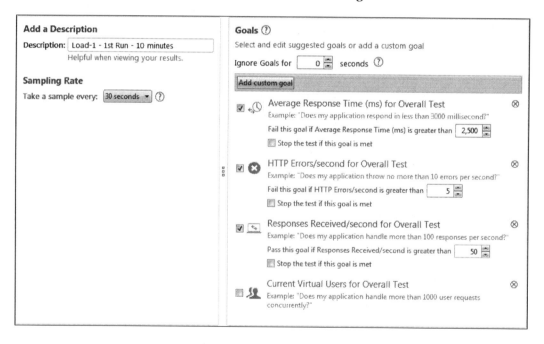

Execution settings for load tests

The left-hand side panel contains the **Description** property, which is a free input field allowing the user to enter information about the specific execution instance in text. The **Sampling Rate** dropdown allows the selection of the intervals at which the sampling is going to take place. In this example, the test will run for 10 continuous minutes, where performance data will be recorded every 30 seconds and saved for later analysis.

The right-hand side panel is responsible for specifying the goals, where four are originally displayed by Test Studio in an inactive state. They will not have any effect on the execution unless we check their corresponding checkboxes. Therefore, the preceding screenshot shows some entries that have been enabled to reflect the goals defined in the *Defining goals* section of this chapter. Based on these numbers, Test Studio will, by default, only alert the user and color the metrics that do not satisfy these thresholds in red. Optionally, we can choose to abort the test execution if any of the underlying rules is violated. This depends on how critical the goal is.

Other metric rules can be added on top of the default goals list by clicking on the **Add custom goal** button. The ensuing window will allow you to build your own verification expression and again choose whether there is a need to interrupt test execution in case it is not satisfied. The following screenshot shows the pool of goal operands that can be chosen:

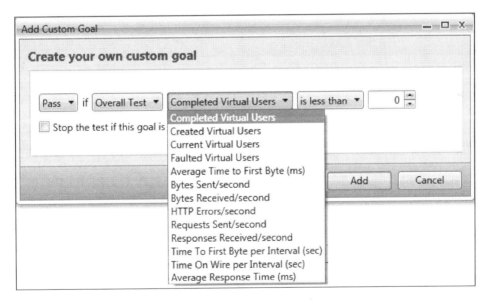

Adding custom goals

Click on the **Run this test** button and wait until the execution finishes.

We have now entered the analysis phase. The data gathered during execution will be available to use after clicking the **Analyze** button of the **Results** ribbon.

The Analyze result button for load tests

A built-in automatic reporting mechanism is available inside Test Studio under three contexts. The **DASHBOARD** view has a summary of the metrics seen in the *Measurements* section of this chapter. The following screenshot shows an example of a run result for this load test:

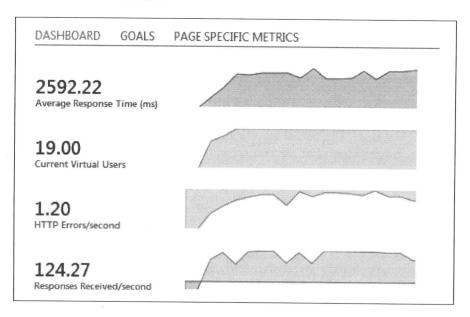

The Dashboard view of test results

Notice how the average response time is colored in red since it has surpassed the designated threshold. The curves corresponding to the other metrics are colored in green, which means that they lie in the targeted goal range.

The **GOALS** tab shown in the preceding screenshot holds a more detailed view of the assigned goals. It compares the actual numbers against the targeted ones for every goal. Finally, the **PAGE SPECIFIC METRICS** tab offers very important information at a page level. The total errors and the average response times are calculated for each URL and displayed in a grid view.

Other test result tabs are also available in case we want to further examine the relation between the average response time and the virtual users, investigate why there has been a steep rise in HTTP errors, or troubleshoot the sudden fall in responses received over the entire test execution duration. Additionally, we may want to see how the performance counters that were assigned in the test design stage are acting. We may also want these metrics to contribute to some complex charts. And finally, as executions are being re-run after performance adjustments, we would like to compare the resulting curves from each run on one graph. In these cases, we are looking for more advanced charts and Test Studio offers these capabilities through its custom charts.

While on the **Analyze** tab, the left-hand side pane has the list of test executions. Each execution entry holds the date and time of execution and two other buttons, as depicted in the following screenshot:

A test execution entry in the Analyze tab

The magnifier (the top button in the preceding screenshot) contains the dashboard, goals, and page metrics for a single run, which have been described earlier. The chart line (also highlighted in the preceding screenshot) gives the ability to construct user-defined charts. Click on this button; a collapsible panel appears. It contains the list of metrics automatically measured with Test Studio in addition to the counters that were manually initially selected for monitoring purposes. For a more focused analysis, they can be filtered by any of the set of monitored machines through the **Filter by computer** combobox.

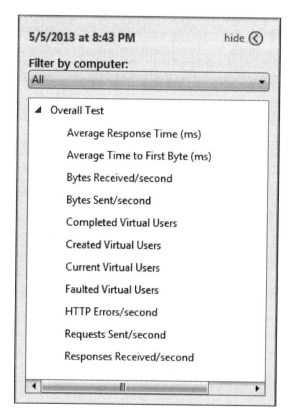

The performance metrics chart panel

The first chart that we are going to build draws the correlation between the response time and concurrent virtual users. Select **Average Response Time, Current Virtual Users**, and **Created Virtual Users** from the metrics panel to enable them. The resulting chart is shown in the following screenshot:

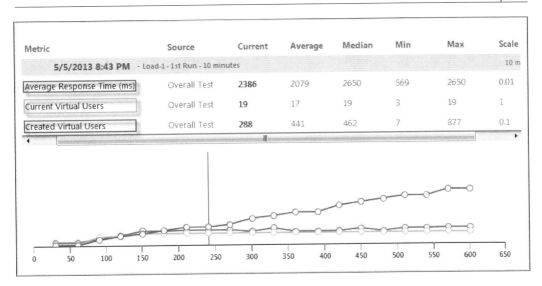

Metric	Source	Current	Average	Median	Min	Max	Scale
5/5/2013 8:43 PM - Load-1 - 1st Run - 10 minutes							10 m
Average Response Time (ms)	Overall Test	2386	2079	2650	569	2650	0.01
Current Virtual Users	Overall Test	19	17	19	3	19	1
Created Virtual Users	Overall Test	288	441	462	7	877	0.1

The response time with respect to virtual users

The horizontal axis corresponds to the time measured in seconds. It starts at 0 and ends at 600 seconds, which corresponds with the 10 minutes specified for the overall test execution duration. On this graph, we have three plotted curves. Each stands for a certain metric and is recognizable by its color.

At first, notice how it takes 2 minutes for the gradually increasing number of current users to reach its maximum—starting at second 30 and ending at second 150. The lowermost blue curve corresponds to the current virtual users, and it stabilizes after reaching the maximum number of intended users during the load test. This means that at any point greater than 150, the number of concurrent active users involved in application transactions corresponds to the maximum value. The purpose of this ramp-up behavior is to simulate the real-life usage of the system and study its capacity to process transactions from an incremental load injected users.

During the overall test execution, the created virtual users will deprecate after accomplishing their designated BugNet operations. Meanwhile, Test Studio will counter this user declination with the creation of additional ones to maintain the overall number of concurrent users throughout the test duration. This is where the created virtual users' line on the chart comes into the picture. This is the uppermost line colored in green and as expected it should be strictly incrementing from start to end to make up for the destroyed virtual users. Another hidden implication also lies behind the total created virtual users' line, where the greater the number of created users is, the faster the application will process transactions. This is because Test Studio will have to create more users to compensate for the destroyed ones.

Finally, the response time middle line in red represents the time spent on the client side while awaiting the receipt of the last byte of the response. Sudden spikes in the line could hint at overloaded situations, which require further investigation in order to isolate the component that is causing the bottleneck. Response time charts also help in finding the tipping point, over which the system will no longer be able to process requests. Moreover, the trend of these lines is useful in expressing the scalability, where the system is assumed to be more scalable if the line increases in a flat manner. Steps in the response time lines can signify dangerous behaviors since the number of users and response times are not regularly proportional.

We are going to dwell just a bit more on this chart to examine some statistics already calculated by Test Studio. Notice that the table has many headers related to some key statistical information: **Average**, **Median**, **Min**, and **Max**. They are intuitive metrics and provide useful information, as designated by their titles. For example, the response time average is **2079** milliseconds; its lowest value was **569** and its peak point reached **2650** milliseconds. The median is equal to **2650** milliseconds and it occurs at second 330. This point is found on the horizontal axis after summing the regular middle point to the warm up time at the beginning. The warm up time displays neither user creation nor request execution. Another handy column is **Current**. As we slide the vertical slice line over the horizontal axis, this column will be dynamically populated with changing values corresponding to the intersection of each curve with the bar. In the preceding chart, at approximately 240 seconds, the current virtual users had already reached its peak, the created virtual users that far was **288**, and the response time for the executing request was **2386** milliseconds.

The second chart we are going to build represents the amount of responses received per second. To clear any line already present on the chart, either click on the corresponding metric again to deselect it or click on the **x** button at the end of the row in the chart table to remove it. Clear **Created Virtual Users** and **Average Response Time** and replace them with **Response Received/second**. The following chart shows the resultant graph after updating the metrics:

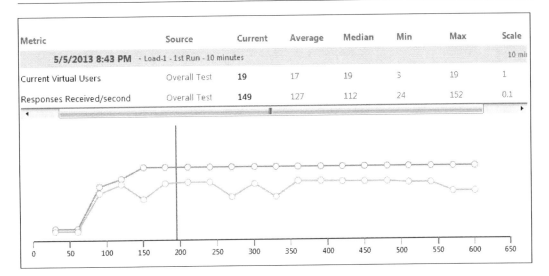

Metric	Source	Current	Average	Median	Min	Max	Scale
5/5/2013 8:43 PM - Load-1 - 1st Run - 10 minutes							10 min
Current Virtual Users	Overall Test	19	17	19	3	19	1
Responses Received/second	Overall Test	149	127	112	24	152	0.1

Responses per second with respect to the current virtual users

So far we have restricted our charts to results captured during one execution. Test Studio's great advantage in reporting is that it enables the ability to easily compare multiple runs against each other. This is why it will always keep the execution results for future reference.

So as the improvements are applied to the components causing bottlenecks, it is time to plot the repetitively captured KPIs generated from this component on one chart. For this purpose, we will use Test Studio custom charts once again.

Firstly, make a new run of the same test. The **Analyze your results** pane in the **Analyze** view now holds two entries sorted by ascending order based on the date value. Enable the metrics panel for any of the execution runs. Locate the node that represents the machine that was chosen for performance monitoring and select the metric corresponding to the total processor time. Repeat the same steps for the other run. This will cause both curves to be plotted on the same chart, as shown in the following screenshot:

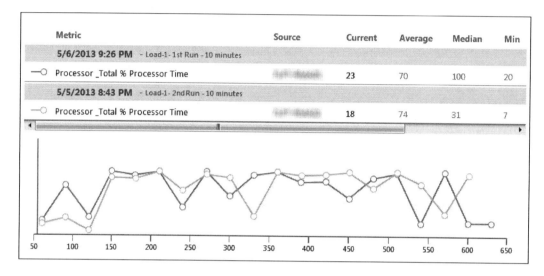

Comparing two executions

The upper section has the table displaying the lists of the runs that participate in the chart whereas the lower section contains the two lines corresponding to the processor time behavior in each run.

Database reporting

The customization and analysis of the load results is not limited in Test Studio since in addition to the user-defined charts that we have just seen, Test Studio extends its reporting power to SQL server too.

During the services configuration stage, a section was available to set up the SQL database that is going to be used by the reporting service in order to record the data indicators that are being captured. The following screenshot describes the reporting database:

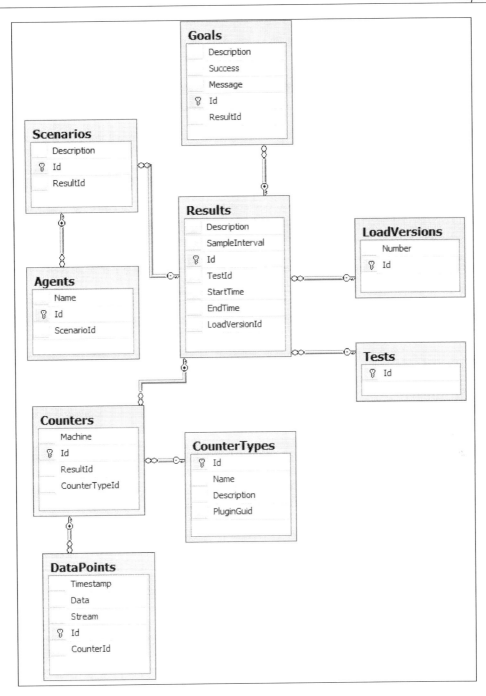

The reporting database diagram

The following list explains the usefulness of each type of data present inside the various tables:

- **Tests**: This table contains the list of tests created using the load template and are uniquely identified by their GUID

- **LoadVersions**: This table contains the Test Studio load versions managing load testing

- **Results**: This table contains the results for each execution instance (recognized by its `Description` field, which maps the `Description` column in the table) and they mainly map to the `Tests` and `LoadVersions` primary keys

- **Goals**: This table has the goals (recognized by their `Message` column) that were assigned for each test at the design stage, and since they can vary per execution instance, they mainly link to the Results table primary key

- **Scenarios**: This table contains the load testing scenarios

- **Agents**: This table has the list of Test-Studio-installed load agents

- **CounterTypes**: This table has the predefined list of performance counters (recognized by the `Name` column) that can be monitored during load execution and which were available while preparing the environment of a load test

- **Counters**: This table has the list of counters that were effectively selected for performance monitoring throughout executions for all tests; since they can differ for every execution instance, they depend on the `Results` table primary key

- **DataPoints**: This table contains the actual values gathered for the counters in each executing test instance, so they depend on the `Counters` primary key

Creating reports

This pool of rich test results along with their distribution among the SQL tables provides the power to perform any suitable comparison in the context of our analysis. For example, the following chart represents the percentage of goals that has been met out of the original number of assigned goals. This percentage is applied for all the execution instances of a specific test.

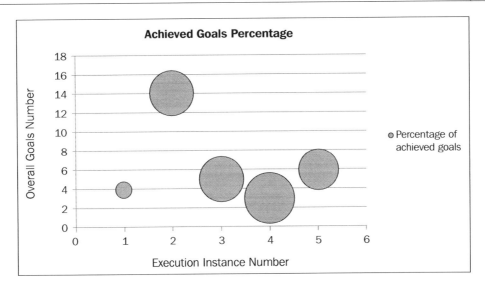

The percentage of achieved goals chart

Three types of variables are used to draw this chart. The horizontal axis represents a number increasing from one to six. It represents the number assigned for each load test execution instance. The vertical axis has the number of goals that was set for each of these instances. The **Percentage of achieved goals** calculates the number of goals that passed with respect to the overall number. They are represented on the charts by the blue bubbles. The size of the bubble helps to visually capture performance discrepancies between the multiple executing instances of the test.

Finally, the **T-SQL(Transact-SQL)** query that was used to retrieve the underlying chart table is as follows:

```
SELECT Results.Description,
COUNT(Goals.Description) AS NumGoals,
SUM(CONVERT(Decimal, Goals.Success))/COUNT(Goals.Description)*100
   AS percentagePassed
FROM [TestStudioReportingDB].[dbo].[Results] INNER JOIN Tests ON
   Results.TestId = Tests.Id
INNER JOIN Goals ON Results.Id = Goals.ResultId
WHERE Tests.Id = '149C299B-E5D6-45B1-9F82-2FDA040D144E'
GROUP BY Results.Description
```

Summary

This chapter has walked us through the design and implementation of load testing plan, as well as performance metric gathering, which we have achieved entirely with Test Studio features.

Afterwards, we have seen how to configure the various load services for Test Studio in order to set up the correct environment for our load tests to run. The Controller, Reporter, and Load Agent services were discussed in detail.

The chapter also demonstrated in detail the plan that is going to be applied to the application under test, which was used in the previous chapter, BugNet. The plan has covered estimates related to projected number of users and types of activities. With these elements, we have built the workloads for the users.

With the theoretical information ready, the chapter then proceeded by actually exhibiting all the load testing features inside Test Studio. It has gone through the steps for configuring Test Studio properties for a load test. The steps consisted of firstly setting up the environment on the load test level, which comprises Load Agents, Controllers, and Reporters. Secondly, we designed the user profiles, which are reflected in creating user activities along with their associated percentage in contributing to the overall activity load. Thirdly, also in designing, we saw how user settings are tuned to simulate real-life usage of the system by the virtual users. Fourthly, we saw how to run the test, which required performing a few steps before actually initiating the test execution and were related to sampling intervals and determining goals.

Lastly, we have seen analysis and reporting in Test Studio by plotting test performance metrics and performance counters for one or multiple test executions for the same load test. The very last section of the chapter explores the database created and continuously updated by the Test Studio Reporter for each run.

In addition, the functional and nonfunctional testing was addressed, where we had applied them on two types of application technologies: WPF and ASP.NET. The next chapter deals with the latest trend, mobile development. As with any other programmed application, this too needs testing. Test Studio can be helpful here too, as we will see when we demonstrate how it can be used to test your iOS application.

9
Mobile Testing

"The clients like our application! With the mobile app boom, we want to support a lightweight version on smartphones to boost our business and keep our users satisfied." This in fact was the target for this week's team meeting, which has surely brought with it automated testing.

Therefore, this chapter shows you how the Test Studio automation solution extends to cover mobile-device application testing by demonstrating the following feature list:

- Deploying Test Studio components
- Creating automated tests
- Executing automated tests
- Analyzing test results
- Syncing to the web portal
- Administering and managing the local test projects

iOS testing inside Test Studio

So you are developing this application, doing some developer testing, and running it over and over again and adding some enhancements here and there, but still do not think this is enough? Well, you are right.

- How do you really understand the quality of what you are offering?
- How do you ensure the same user experience irrelevant of the device?

The answer is to incorporate automation into your testing strategy!

Test Studio is not only a solution to the quality of your desktop and web applications but its iOS version also takes care of your native, web, and hybrid apps.

Test Studio for iOS also acts as a feedback tool, which keeps the developers and users involved in the same loop of continuous suggestions and enhanced releases. Hence, Test Studio provides the means by which the users can convey to the developers their experience and wish list either through integrated e-mailing mechanism or the cloud.

Unhandled errors are also an important resource for aiding developers to keep themselves aware of the application flaws uncovered during real-time usage. So, Test Studio also presents the possibility to automate the delivery of crash reports produced by the application right to the developer's inbox or web portal.

Test projects created within Test Studio can be seamlessly run against your application deployed on an iPhone, iPod touch, and/or iPad. These tests are portable and ready to be extended and executed on any of these devices wherever you are located.

Portability extends over the artifacts developed inside Test Studio, for example, the projects, test scripts, test results, and so on. This data can be either transported to another device allowing you to resume your testing from there or shared in the cloud for real-time monitoring and follow up.

The remaining of this chapter exhibits the preceding features by offering step-by-step instructions to guide you through the entire testing process ranging from the environment setup and requirement deployments, creating test projects, and syncing and monitoring in the web portal. Finally, we wrap up with the data management section, which describes how to administer the database containing the test projects and how to transfer it between devices.

Requirements

Prior to testing your iOS application, there are some requirements that should be met to be able to use Test Studio. We start with the environment requirements. Your application should be developed with the following requirements in order to successfully use Test Studio:

- Mac OS X 10.7+
- XCode 4.2+
- iOS SDK 4+

Once you have met these requirements, we can then move to the testing requirements, which are summarized as follows:

- Test Studio for iOS
- Test Studio file bundle

The Test Studio app for iOS is going to host the test creation and execution against the application under testing. It can be directly downloaded from the App Store on any of the supported devices. It is available for free and doesn't require jailbreaking or unlocking of your mobile device. The following link has the details for downloading Test Studio from the app store:

`https://itunes.apple.com/us/app/test-studio/id523796105?mt=8`

As for the file bundle, it contains the following items and can be downloaded from this link: `http://www.telerik.com/community/license-agreement.aspx?pId=969` using your Telerik account:

- `Test Studio Extension`: This folder has the libraries that should be compiled with any application that is going to be tested with the Test Studio app.
- `Test Studio CI`: It contains the tools to create coded tests for your application.
- `Test Studio Simulator`: It has the scripts to deploy Test Studio to the simulator, where you can simulate the creation and execution of your tests against the application before taking things to the actual iOS device.
- `Documentation`: It has the help information for using Test Studio on iOS which is also available online.
- `Demo Applications`: It contains a native UIKIT-based and a web application compiled with `Test Studio Extensions` and is ready to be used for testing.

Deployment

For this chapter, we are going to demonstrate the features of Test Studio on an open source application called Switchy. It can be downloaded from the following link:

1. `http://xcodenoobies.blogspot.com`

Switchy is a native UIKIT-based application and it provides a series of various switches that can be collectively controlled with two buttons. The **Force On** button will cause all the switches to toggle on whereas the **Force Off** button will reset them to their off state.

Main screen of the Switchy application

UIKIT-based or hybrid applications need to be compiled with Test Studio libraries so that the application becomes visible to the recorder. So how do we compile Switchy with these libraries? Open the application with **XCode** and follow these steps:

1. Using **Finder**, open the TestStudioExtension folder found inside the Test Studio file bundle downloaded earlier.

2. Open the iOS folder residing there and then inside it locate the two files highlighted in the following screenshot:

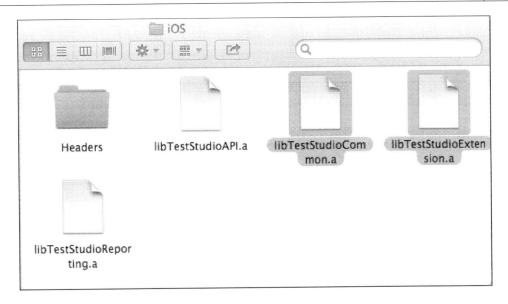

Test Studio extension libraries

3. Drag the `libTestStudioCommon.a` and `libTestStudioExtension.a` items to the opened Switchy application inside **XCode** , as shown in the following screenshot:

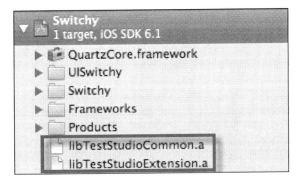

Adding extension libraries to the application

4. In the resulting ensuing window, choose **Create folder references for any added folders** as follows:

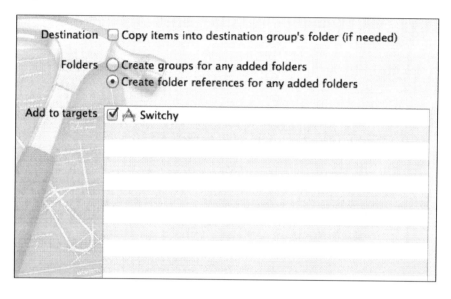

Creating references to the libraries

5. Click on the **Finish** button.

6. Select the project node inside the **Project Navigator** window to display the **Targets** section as shown in the following screenshot:

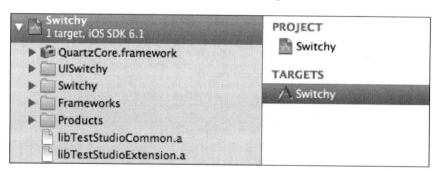

Displaying application Targets

7. Go to the **Build Settings** tab shown in the following screenshot and then look for the **Linking** section.

8. Add this text `-all_load` for the **Other Linker Flags** option:

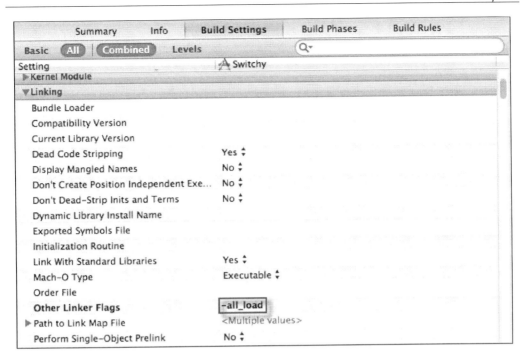

Linking Test Studio extension libraries

9. Go the **Info** tab and expand the **Document Types** section as shown in the following screenshot:

10. Click on the plus button and then fill in these values:

    ○   **Name**: tstest

    ○   **Types**: com.telerik.tstest

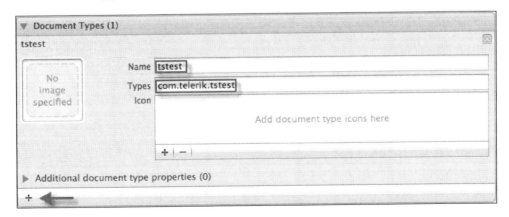

Adding document types

11. On the same tab, expand the **URL Types** section.

12. Click on the plus button and fill the various fields as follows:

    ○ **Identifier**: com.telerik.automation

    ○ **URL Schemes**: tsSwitcher

    ○ **Role**: Editor

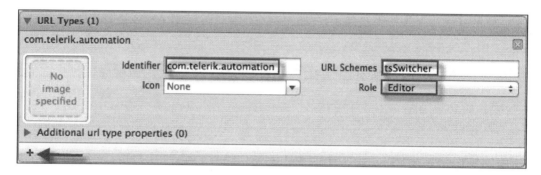

Adding URL types

After this step, the application is ready to be used with Test Studio iOS.

Simulator

XCode supports, by default, iPhone and iPad simulators. In order to use the Test Studio app on an iOS application running inside the simulator, a python script needs to be run. Hence if the following script does not run, Test Studio will not be deployed on the simulator and you will not be able to carry on the automation of your application through the simulator:

1. Launch the terminal window on your machine.

2. Using the cd command, browse for the TestStudioSimulator directory inside the downloaded Test Studio file bundle. For example, if the folder is saved on the desktop, type the following commands sequentially inside the terminal window:

```
cd Desktop
cd "test studio for ios"
cd teststudiosimulator
```

3. The script that we need to run is called `installteststudioinsimulator.` `py` and is present under the folder currently open in the terminal, so type the run command as follows:

```
python installteststudioinsimulator.py
```

This will cause a script to run and eventually make the Test Studio app accessible from the simulator. Make sure that no errors are returned and the operation is successful before moving on to the next section.

Automating tests

Testing can be now conducted on Switchy without the need to do any modifications to the source code. The preceding deployment steps are all what is required to make the application UI open for Test Studio. This means that the iOS version will not rely on any positional information, such as screen coordinates to perform the UI actions, but rather it can recognize the various UI elements involved in the execution. Hence, Test Studio uses object base recording and execution, which makes test authoring richer and more comprehensive on one hand and the execution more reliable on the other.

This section creates a test project for Switchy and gradually takes you through the test steps of creation, verification, execution, analysis, and result debugging.

Creating tests

Test authoring can begin after we run the solution in the simulator. From there we can start the Test Studio app through which we will access Switchy and carry out our testing.

In **XCode**, choose **iPhone 6.1 Simulator** from the list of available target devices and then click on the **Run** button:

Choosing a simulator to run

This will cause an iPhone interface to be launched with a running instance of the Switchy application. Click on the iPhone home button to go back to the desktop and then start Test Studio. The following screenshot shows the first view corresponding to the Test Studio main menu:

Test Studio running on a simulator

In this section we are going to tackle the **Testing** option, therefore, click on it to enter the test creation phase. At this stage there are no created projects, so the first step consists of clicking on the circular button shown in the following screenshot to create one:

Creating test projects

In the **Create Project** view, perform the following steps:

1. Name the project as `Switchy_Test`.

2. Click on the **Save** button.

3. Test Studio directly puts you on the tests view, which also does not contain any entry, so click on the circular button again to create a test.

4. In the **New Test** view, enter `T1-SwitchOn_Successful` in the **Test Name** field.

5. Click on the **Choose Target App** button.

Note that the next time you attempt to create a project or a test the circular button will not exist, so alternatively click on the plus button available in the lower-right corner of the screen.

Two options are listed as shown in the following screenshot. They consist of either starting a web-based recording session, in case the testing was intended against a mobile web application, or a native-based recording session, in case the testing is going to be made against a native application compiled with the Test Studio's extension libraries. In our example, we will go for the second option. So how do we assign Switchy as our target test application?

Upon pressing the **Other...** option, Test Studio begins a lookup for all local native iOS applications compiled with the Test Studio extensions. When the search is completed, Switchy will be present within the list. Click on it and then on the **Save** button. The next time you attempt to create a new test, the Switchy app will be directly loaded inside the list of options.

Choosing target application

The steps view is opened where nothing is currently displayed. The procedure for the test case that we want to automate is as follows:

1. Drag the first switch to the right.

The expected result is that the **On** label should appear inside the switch.

Again, click on the circular button located in the middle to start adding steps. This will cause Switchy to be launched in the recording mode. The recording mode is characterized by the **Recording** label at the top of the screen in addition to the red outline enclosing the whole application interface. Start executing the test by switching on the first control. As the UI actions are performed on the screen, Test Studio will be adding the corresponding steps. The next step consists of creating verification steps to assess whether the **On** label has appeared. In order to do so, we will retrieve the list of default verifications based on the element to be verified. For this purpose, pull up the collapsed toolbar at the bottom of the screen to show the recording toolbar menu illustrated in the following screenshot:

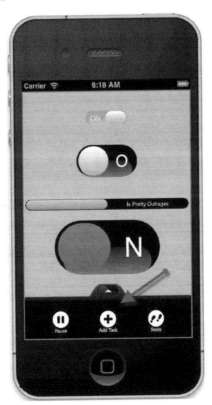

The recording toolbar

Click on the **Pause** button and then on the **Add Task** button. The toolbar collapses and Test Studio enters its wait for a screen input. This means that the element upon which the next click is applied is going to be used as the verification target. So click on the **ON** label. The **Tasks** view is enabled with a list of actions and verifications as depicted in the following screenshot:

Inserting verification steps

The upper section has a list of predefined verification steps related to the **ON** text label. The first expression is built using the `switch` statement, where ON is represented by 0. The second expression verifies the label text value.

The lower section, **Browse All**, has a complete list of available actions and verifications with respect to the object. Click on the corresponding disclosure arrow to bring the full list into view (for the **Actions** section) as follows:

The available actions of UILabel

For the **Verifications** section, a rich list of the element display and other characterizing attributes contributes to the verification expressions:

The available verifications of UILabel

In our example, we are limiting the verification to **text isEqualTo "ON"**, so select it by clicking on it. With this action, Test Studio is going to take us back to the application screen, where if we wish to resume our recording we can by clicking on the **Record** button from the toolbar. Having no further steps to automate, click on the **Steps** button to finish the recording.

The recorded steps are illustrated in the following screenshot:

Saving test steps

The **Abort** button will stop the recording and cancel the added steps during this recording session (any previous steps will stay intact). Hence, click on the **Save** button to save the steps.

Execution

After completing and saving the recorded steps, we have the option to edit them. While on the test steps view, click on the **Edit** button located in the upper-left corner of the screen. Two buttons will bind to every step as follows:

Editing a test step

The first button to the left removes that particular step from the list of steps, whereas the button at the far right allows you to shuffle their order. The way to do it is to hold the button, drag it, and then release it at the end position.

At the moment, we do not need to make any changes, thus, click on the **Done** button and then on the play button of the test toolbar as shown in the following screenshot:

Running the recorded test

After the execution ends, the **Result Details** view is directly displayed as follows:

Test execution results

The **Overall** section has the execution summary describing the overall result state, duration, and time of execution. The **Device Details** section has the device summary (in our case, the simulator), and the **Step Results** section has the sequence of steps with the execution result for each. The first step which toggles the switch has passed, so has the verification.

Click on the **Test Results** button to go back to the list of results executed, and then click on **Close** to regain the steps view.

At any point, if we want to view the list of results for a specific test, the last button of the test toolbar will open the results list.

Testing on the device

Early on, we have mentioned that authored tests can be executed on the device itself and this is in fact only two steps away, given that your device is already provisioned for development. The first step consists of connecting your iOS device to the machine. Once tethered up, the second step is to change the active scheme selection from the iPhone simulator to the connected device. Following this step, you will be able to resume creating, editing, and executing the tests on the device itself.

Debugging tests

So far we have been receiving only passing results for the executions. However, what if a test fails? What does Test Studio have to offer with regard to troubleshooting the failures? This is what we will see in this section.

Firstly, we need to incur such failures. Therefore, go to the test again and click on the arrow for the verification step, **text isEqualTo "ON"**. The following details are displayed:

Editing step settings

Click on the **Operation** option to edit the verification rule and change the **Target** text value to **OFF**. Click on the **Save** button and run the test again. This time we are expecting our test to be unsuccessful and the results come to confirm it.

As usual, Test Studio directly marks the failing step. Click on the disclosure arrow for the verification step to go into the error details. The following screenshot shows the information about the failure that has occurred and thus a hint on how to fix it.

Step failure details

Based on the **Verification failed for comparison, 'ON' isEqualTo 'OFF'** clue, we now know that we must go back and check why we were expecting an **ON** label to appear inside the switch while the actual label is **OFF**. Go back to the test steps and revert the verification value to **ON**.

Test elements

Test Studio, here again, grants test execution a strong advantage, which is reliability. Implicitly, it drops the option of misidentifying any object from the list of root causes associated with a certain execution failure, because it does not rely on any positional or visual information. This means that replaying tests will never fail because an object was simply relocated or resized.

Wait on elements

Knowing that Test Studio recognizes and understands the nature of UI elements, it spends a default period of time trying to relate an object's find expression to a UI element. Hence, if the expression involves tapping a switch, Test Studio will try to find the switch element within a period of 3 seconds after which it asserts that the element is missing.

Suppose that we want to test the **Force On** button's behavior for the Switchy application. The functionality for this button is to simply turn on all switches. However, with the new Switchy build a few code changes have been introduced, which have caused some background processing to take place while the switching action is running. These modifications have affected the speed of this feature. Subsequently, a label was added to describe the switching progress. Initially when we click on the **Force On** button, the label says **Switching on in progress**. When the processing finishes behind, the label reports back by displaying: **Action has completed**. In order not to keep the user idle, the added internal processing is made through an asynchronous call, which permits the user to carry on other operations through the interface.

So, we come up with the following test case in order to test the forcing switches on the Wait on elements feature:

Procedure:

1. Click on the **Force On** button.

The expected results are:

1. All switches are toggled on
2. A label appears at the top of the screen: **Action has completed**

Let's make a few modifications to the application in order to simulate this situation:

1. Open the application in **XCode**.
2. Open the `ViewController.xib` file, and add a label and delete its text.
3. Open the `ViewController.h` file and add a definition for the label as follows:

```
@interface ViewController : UIViewController
{
    Switchy *sw1, *sw2, *sw3, *sw4, *sw5;
    IBOutlet UILabel *switchesState;
}
```

4. Open the `ViewController.m` file and alter the definition of the `turnOn` method to add the code that will dispatch a new thread responsible for setting the end value of the label after spending 5 seconds of waiting time:

```
switchesState.text = @"Switching on in progress";
    [sw1 setState:YES];
    [sw2 setState:YES];
    [sw3 setState:YES];
    [sw4 setState:YES];
    [sw5 setState:YES];

    dispatch_queue_t queue = dispatch_get_global_queue(DISPATCH_
      QUEUE_PRIORITY_LOW, NULL);
    dispatch_async(queue, ^{

            [NSThread sleepForTimeInterval:5];
            switchesState.text = @"Action has completed";
    });
```

5. From the `ViewController.xib` file, add a reference of the label to the `switchesState` string.

   Launch Test Studio and then go to the project tests view and create a new test named `T2-ForceON_Successful`. Select the target application to be Switchy, save your selection, and perform the following steps:

6. Click on the **Force On** button.

7. Insert a text verification step on the **switching on in progress** label.

From the second step settings, accessible through the disclosure button, also change the **Operation** property's value to **text isEqualTo "Action has completed"**, after clicking on this property's disclosure button. The final test will look as follows:

The steps of the T2-ForceON_Successful test

Unexpectedly, if you run the test as it is now it will fail on the second step. If we click on the disclosure button, we will notice that the cause of the error is as follows:

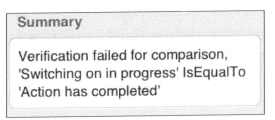

Summary of the verification step error

Unlike what the error says, the updated text label is in fact appearing on the screen, however, not before some delay. This delay is greater than the default wait on the verification, which means that Test Studio will execute the second step before the asynchronous processing behind the force on button command ends. Ideally, we would want to either instruct Test Studio to wait on the specific label for more than 5 seconds or introduce a wait before the verification step.

Let's first try to increase the wait on the verification steps label text. Therefore, open the test steps inside Test Studio by performing the following steps:

1. Click on the disclosure arrow of the second step to drill down into its details.
2. On the invoked settings, click on the **Operations** option.
3. Set the wait setting to **6** seconds as shown in the following screenshot:

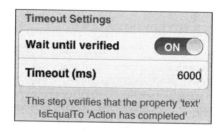

Changing wait time on step

4. Click on the **Save** button.
5. Run the test and notice how this step now passes.

Alternatively, as briefly mentioned previously, we can insert a standalone wait step as follows:

1. Click on the record button, which corresponds to the first in the test toolbar.
2. Choose the **Just Launch the App** option.
3. Once the application is started, click on the **Steps** button after dragging the recording menu upward.
4. In the **Edit Steps** view, click on the plus button in the upper-right corner.
5. The **Add Step** view has the **Wait** option as shown in the following screenshot, which can be used to simulate the wait:

Adding the Wait step

6. Click on the step disclosure arrow.

7. Adjust the time to **6000**.

8. Click on the **Add** button.

9. Click on the **Edit** button and drag this step to the second position.

10. Click on the **Done** button.

11. Click on the **Save** button.

12. Run the test.

Notice how a delay is introduced before the first red outline appears around the string label. This behavior corresponds to the verification step and specifically to Test Studio's first attempt in verifying the text label.

Locating elements

Switchers have another way of communicating their state to the automated tests. The isOn property tells whether the switch is in the On or Off state. Therefore, we can rely on this property to verify the outcome of the automated tests. As usual, using the tasks feature we can highlight and add verification against whatever UI element we are seeking. Nevertheless, capturing the switcher object itself necessitates higher precision to be able to pinpoint it from within the pool of surrounding controls and containers. The subsequent example uses the **Elements** option accessible during recording in order to overcome this problem.

From the tests view, select the first test, T1_SwitchOn_Successful. Once you are on the steps screen, click on the record button and then choose **Play and Continue**. Following this command, Test Studio will run the test and will then pass the control to the user once completed:

1. From the toolbar, click on the **Add Task** button.

2. Click anywhere inside the grey area away from any apparent UI element.

3. Click on the **Elements** button as shown in the following screenshot:

The Elements button

4. The following screen appears:

Selecting an element

The upper section has the UI element we are positioned on and is outlined in red. In our case, it is the **UIView** element selected in the **Sibling** section. In order to drill up to the UIView parent, click on the button having the **UIWindow** label. This label changes dynamically depending on the item selected inside the siblings list.

Click on the **UIView** disclosure arrow. The list of the UIView children is retrieved with the first element selected and outlined in the upper section. Select the first available **Switchy** entry by performing a single click on it. Notice how the application view in the upper section is scrolled up to fit the corresponding Switchy object into the view.

This is exactly the object we want to build the verification against and which would have been barely possible without this feature. So to finish adding the verification step perform the following steps:

1. Click on the **Select** button.

2. On the **Tasks** screen, click on the **Verifications** disclosure button.

3. Select the first verification **isOn isEqualTo "YES"**.

4. On the recording screen, click on the **Steps** button.

5. Click on the **Save** button and run the test.

Web portal

With the growing number of applications undergoing internal testing and even external testing during beta testing, it becomes cumbersome for a manager to track all the automated tests, results, feedback, and encountered problems by test engineers and beta users scattered in different geographical locations. The web portal is the manager's gateway to track all the mobile apps' status during their lifetime.

Through the web portal, you can:

- Know the quality of the applications through the **Testing** view.

- Know how the users find your application through the **Feedback** view.

- Know the number of crashing errors through the **Crash Reports** view.

- Let others collaborate through the **Contributors** view.

Registering an application

Applications participating in the web portal must be registered first. As web portal owners, we will use Switchy as an example on how to register an application:

1. Log in to the web portal with your Telerik account on `http://my.teststudio.com`.

2. Go to **Settings** by clicking on the button highlighted in the following screenshot:

Registering a new application

3. Go to **Reporting Applications**.

4. Click on the **Register New Application** button also found in the preceding screenshot.

5. In the ensuing **Add New Application** window, edit:

   ○ **Application Name** to `Switchy`

   ○ **Type** to `iOS`

   ○ **Bundle Identifier** to `com.emirbytes.switchy.Switchy`

   ○ **Allow anonymous access** to `True`

 The **Allow anonymous access** option will make the Switchy application available when sending feedback of type, **One Time**. The **Feedback** section explains this feature in a more detailed way.

6. Click on the **Add** button.

7. Click on **OK** to close the result message.

8. Click on **Done** to finish adding the reporting application.

Testing

The web portal has a tab dedicated for viewing automation projects and tests that have been created against your applications. Data can be synced from your local device and once they are uploaded they will then be accessible from the web portal. To explore the syncing feature, let's first fix the web portal settings of Test Studio as follows:

1. Run Switchy from **XCode** and launch Test Studio.

2. On the main menu screen, choose **Settings**.

3. On the **Settings** screen, click on the web portal disclosure button.

4. The **Web Portal** window prompts you to first log in with your Telerik account, so click on the **Log In** button.

5. In the invoked login window, enter your Telerik username and password and then click on the **Log In** button.

6. Once your credentials are verified, a window prompts you whether you would like to move the present projects to the account you just used for logging in as follows:

Moving projects to account dialog

7. The profile for this account will be used to sync data to the web portal, so select the **Move My Projects** option.

Test Studio now takes you to the **Web Portal** window giving you the ability to switch between the local and the newly created profile. Keep the selection as it is, in order to proceed with syncing the data for the Switchy_Test project, which has been moved to this profile following the event of our choice in the previous step.

Click on the disclosure buttons to examine the details for the projects included in each profile.

To initiate the syncing process, go back to the main menu and choose **Testing**. In the **Projects** view, click on the syncing button found at the lower-left corner of the screen as follows:

Syncing projects

Once syncing completes, you can log in to your web portal to view the project that was pushed into the test projects grid, which is viewable from the **Testing** tab:

Testing	Search here...		
Project Name		Tests	Failed Results
Switchy_Test		2	1

Synced project on Web Portal

To drill down to the tests, double-click on the **Switchy_Test** entry:

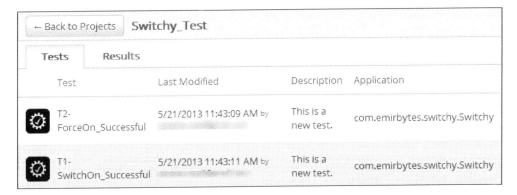

Synced tests

To view the results, click on the **Results** tab, whereas to view the test steps double-click on any of the tests.

Contributors

Contributors can be managed by the account owner of the web portal. These people will be able to surf through a project web portal by choosing the corresponding account from the dropdown at the top of the screen.

For now, only one account is available. In order to invite contributors to it, execute the following steps:

1. Click on the **Contributors** tab from the menu.
2. Click on the **Invite Contributors** button.
3. Enter the contributor e-mail address and invitation message.
4. Click on the **Invite** button.

The contributors to whom the invitation have been sent and accepted will appear inside the grid.

Feedback and crash reports

Feedback and crash reports are two special features offered by Test Studio allowing the application's managers and developers to be continuously informed about users' opinions, suggested enhancements, and confronted problems. Using the deployed version of Test Studio on the simulator, we will see how to invoke these features on the Switchy application.

Configuring settings

For this section, we will need to configure the default target e-mails for the described features. The steps are as follows:

1. Run Switchy in **XCode** and open Test Studio.

2. Choose **Settings** from the main menu.

3. Scroll down until the **Feedback** section (as shown in following screenshot) appears:

Feedback and crash reports configuration screen

4. Enter the default e-mail address that is going to receive the e-mails containing the user's feedback in the **Email** field of the **Feedback** section.

5. Enter a default e-mail address in the **Email** field of the **Crash Reports** section.

6. Optionally, send a copy of the e-mail to the Telerik development team by toggling on the **Send to Telerik** option.

The Feedback option

So what did you think of Switchy?

"The application code design is pretty neat! The UI displays nicely on my iPhone and the colors are cool, but I prefer to see the switches ordered by width!"

Hmmm, why not send that to the developer. On the Test Studio main menu, choose the **Feedback** option. The next view has three available options as shown in the following screenshot:

The Feedback screen

Switchy comes under the native iOS application, so choose **Native App**. Had it not been compiled with the Test Studio extension library, we would have chosen the **One Time** option, which allows sending a general feedback about a native or web application that was registered with the allow anonymous feedback option checked to true.

It is time to assign the target application, so choose Switchy. After that, the application launches where a feedback toolbar is appended at the bottom as shown in the following screenshot:

The Feedback toolbar

To create a message, follow these steps:

1. Click on the **Compose** button.
2. By default, a snapshot is taken for the application in its current state so click on it to zoom on a certain area.
3. The view is reverted back to the application interface, so click on any point on the screen and then drag to draw an outline around the required region.
4. Click on the **Done** button to finish your selection.
5. In the textbox that appears, enter the feedback message text.
6. Click on the **Done** button to save the text and then on the **Save** button.
7. Finally, click on the **Done** button in the feedback toolbar.

Notice that the composed message did not leave your local machine yet. It is rather saved in your outbox along with other feedback messages that might have been created during the same session. This way you have the flexibility to delete some messages after clicking on the **Edit** button, or perhaps edit their content by clicking on the feedback message disclosure arrow. The following screenshot shows an example of two feedback messages:

Queued feedback messages

There are two ways to inform the application developer with the messages and they are reflected in the two buttons **Email** and **Upload**.

The e-mailing option consists of combining all the current feedback messages and sending them to the e-mail address specified in the Test Studio's settings.

The uploading option actually pushes the feedback messages to the web portal. In order to be able to use this option, the **Web Portal** settings must be configured and Switchy must also be a registered application. Once completed, the uploaded feedback messages will appear in the web portal under the **Feedback** menu option.

Crash reports

Here, we are concerned with unhandled errors that occur while Test Studio is running your application. After a crash occurs, a pop-up window will prompt you, whether you want to send a report to the concerned parties as follows:

Sending the crash report dialog

If confirmed, an e-mail interface will be launched having the error details inside the message body. In addition, the **To** field will be automatically populated based on the options specified in **Settings**. Hence, if a default e-mail exists in the **Crash Reports** section, this e-mail address will be directly added. So is the case for the Telerik e-mail which is also configurable as we have seen.

Sending crash reports does not have to be left up to the user's decision. This information can be acquired implicitly from the crashed application without any user intervention. This is achieved by embedding calls to the TSReport iOS library found in the Test Studio file bundle, which hosts services for crashes and user feedback. In order to employ these services a few steps are required at three levels, which are as follows:

- Web portal configuration
- Application configuration
- Code implementation

The web portal configuration for the crash reports requires the application to be registered as a reporting application.

The application configuration requires two steps in addition to the deployment setup procedures carried out at the beginning of this chapter:

1. From **XCode**, select **Switchy** from the list of **Targets**.
2. Go to the **Build Settings** tab.
3. Locate **Header Search Paths** under the **Search Paths** section, enter `$(SRCROOT)/TestStudioExtension/Headers`, and make sure that the `TestStudioExtension` folder exists under the solution's root folder.

4. Go to the **Build Phases** tab and expand the **Link Binary With Libraries** section.

5. Click on the plus button and add a reference to the `libTestStudioReporting.a` library found under the `iOS` folder of the Test Studio's extension file bundle folder downloaded earlier.

Finally, the code implementation consists of the following steps:

1. Open the `AppDelegate.m` file from **XCode** and add this line of code in the **Import** section in order to add a reference to the Test Studio's reporting class: `#import <TestStudioReporting/TestStudioReporting.h>`

2. Locate the `application:didFinishLaunchingWithOptions:` method.

3. Add the following line before the `return` statement:

```
[TSReport setupWithAPIKey:@"API_KEY" appId:@"APP_ID"];
```

4. To get the **API_Key** and **APP_ID** parameters for the registered Switchy application, log in first to the web portal.

5. Click on the **Settings** button.

6. Click on the **Reporting Applications** tab.

7. Click on the **Edit** button having the pen icon.

8. A window similar to the one depicted in the following screenshot will open:

Register application information

9. Copy the keys and substitute them with the corresponding parameters of the `setupWithAPIKey` method.

10. Add these lines of code after the `setupWithAPIKey` method:

```
NSError *error = nil;
If (![TSReport installCrashHandlerWithMode:TSCrashHandlerModeSile
nt error:&error]) {
    NSLog(@"This is an automatically sent error: %@", error.
localizedDescription);
}
```

The first parameter for `installCrashHandlerWithMode` is the method called `TSCrashHandlerModeSilent`, which offers the capability of sending crash reports implicitly whenever they occur without the user's intervention. Instead, you can choose `TSCrashHandlerModePrompt` to imitate the regular behavior explained earlier, which consists of asking the user's consent to submit the crash report.

Data management

In Test Studio, portability is not a feature that confines only to testing your application seamlessly on the various supported devices, but it also permits transferring local database used by Test Studio over multiple machines. By opening `iTunes` and locating the database residing under the Test Studio's `Document` folder of the Test Studio App, this database can be moved to your local machine and vice versa. The following sections demonstrate how you can administer your database by creating backups and then merging them into an existing active database.

Configuring settings

Only test projects belonging to profile can be transferred among devices, therefore, we must switch to the local profile before proceeding with the following steps:

1. On the Test Studio main menu, choose **Settings**.
2. On the **Settings** screen, click on the **Web Portal disclosure** button.
3. From the **Teams** option, select **Local**.

At this point, there are no projects under the local profile, however we will proceed with this example to demonstrate database sharing. In order to create projects, choose **Testing** from the Test Studio main menu and create projects.

Database backup actions

Go back to the **Settings** screen and scroll down to the **System** section shown in the following screenshot:

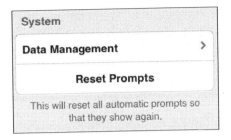

Managing databases

Click on the **Data Management** disclosure button, and then from the **Data Management** screen choose `TestStudio.sqlite`. The **Database** window is invoked where the first section displays the database summary.

The **Local Actions** scope allows backing up the database to your local machine, so click on the **Backup My Database** button. A pop-up window warns the user that only non-synced projects presented in the **Local profile** section will be backed up. Click on the **Backup My Database** button. The backup is processed and the result is displayed on the **Data Management** screen under the **Backups** section as follows:

List of backed up databases

The **Global Actions** scope has the **Reset My Database** button, which will reset the entire database including all profiles. If you do not have a backup of your database, the data will be lost. Hence do not click on it for now!

Database restore actions

On one hand, backups can be restored by firstly selecting the targeted timestamp and then performing the provided actions. Select the backup outlined in the preceding screenshot. The **Database** view is invoked also with actions acting at two levels.

The **Local Actions** scope affects only the local non-synced databases. The **Merge Into My Database** button will attempt to add the backed up projects to `TestSutio.sqlite`. If the backed up project doesn't exist in the local database, it will be directly added. If a version already exists, the newer version will be preserved. The **Delete Database** button will only delete the selected backup.

The **Global Actions** scope affects the entire database, meaning all profiles and projects. Therefore, the **Overwrite My Database** button will totally replace the existing database with the backed up version.

Summary

This chapter has put you through the complete process of assessing and testing the quality of your mobile App with Test Studio. It started off by guiding you on how to acquire and deploy the needed components on an iOS simulator which hosted our work for the rest of the chapter.

The Test Studio iOS version was used to test a developed application after having compiled it with the Test Studio extension libraries. We used an open source application called Switchy, against which we have built a testing project, tests, and steps and added verifications using predefined tasks. The steps were then executed in Test Studio, where we analyzed their results in passing and failing situations. Some unexpected behaviors driven by asynchronous method calls were examined and solved by using the wait feature. We also saw the element's feature, which helped us to overcome situations where the target element is inaccessible or easily delimited on the application UI.

Furthermore, as a web portal account owner, we saw how to access this portal and register the Switchy application. Using Test Studio, we created feedback messages and saw how crash reports work. Finally, we used the sync feature on the created data to make everything available in the cloud.

Finally, the last section showed us how to back up, merge, or overwrite projects by manipulating the local database using the available local and global actions, which affect the local and global profiles respectively.

The next chapter will reveal some tips and tricks that could be employed to benefit our tests with more flexibility and responsiveness in relevant situations.

10
Tips and Tricks

Introduction

No meeting today! You are sitting in your chair thinking how you can tweak the automated tests to make them more efficient.

This chapter leaves you with some key ideas that, depending on your automation context, can be important and usable in solving the arising problems. These ideas revolve around test reusability and are mainly tips on enhancing automation maintainability within Test Studio, which are as follows:

- Reusing the same test in the regular and data-driven mode
- Creating extension libraries
- Data binding find expressions
- Passing variables between tests

Maintainability

At the beginning of this book, we looked at test reusability as a strategy for enhancing maintenance. We tried to minimize duplicating the same functionality in multiple tests and even in the constituent steps. The test maintainability topic was frequently present in the examples throughout this book mainly because of how much it affects test durability and effectiveness over time in addition to how much it lowers the automation cost. The simplest scenario which describes all the aforementioned characteristics is when having the login functionality implemented inside a number of tests. If at some point in time the login window is redesigned to allow the choice between Windows or regular member authentication before being able to input the credentials, then all the automated login functionality scattered among the tests should also change! Hence, your tests:

- Lack durability, since they are vulnerable to changes outside the functionality they are testing

- Lack effectiveness, since they become useless if they do not function

- Require high maintenance cost, since they require a great amount of time and effort to be updated as changes are introduced

This chapter continues on this topic by illustrating two more methods that can be used to substitute a repeated logical group of steps with external calls, either to other automated tests or to extended libraries.

The first option seems familiar. We have already seen how to use the **Test as Step** Test Studio feature to invoke external tests in the form of a step in the calling test. In addition, we have particularly seen how a non data-driven test calls a data-driven test, a data-driven test calls a non data-driven test, and finally how a data-driven test calls another data-driven test. Nevertheless, notice how each test type had to be called in its defined context. This means that data-driven tests, when acting as a caller or a called test, had to be associated directly or indirectly with a data-driven table so that they run correctly. Similarly, a non data-driven test cannot be dynamically associated with data-table values where, if needed, the test has to undergo a manual conversion. In conclusion, this behavior takes away the flexibility of dynamically reusing the same test in data-driven and regular contexts.

Making a test work for both data-driven and hardcoded input

The scenario starts where you, as a tester, were responsible for automating the `File Info` feature and were handed the functional manual test scripts. As you were looking through them, you noticed that they all revolve around setting some values for the UI elements. So you decided to apply a time and effort saving design which treats each subprocedure as a separate component in order to enhance the long term maintainability and reusability.

 Subprocedure is a term introduced in *Chapter 2, Automating Functional Tests* referring to a block inside a test case procedure constituted from the UI element's readiness verification steps and the UI operation's steps on that element.

So the solution stipulates creating an independent WPF test for each subprocedure as shown in the following diagram:

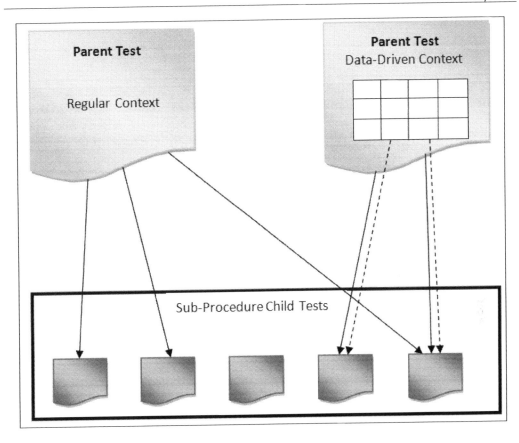

Reusing child tests in parent context

An arrow means that a parent test calls the child test with an arrow head. A dotted arrow means that the child with the arrow head is bound to one of the parent data table columns.

This design works fine for regular tests. But when the time comes to apply the same methodology on a data-driven test, you face a problem! In terms of theory, you want to use the second data-driven model mentioned previously, a data-driven test calling a non data-driven test, where you bind the parent test to a global data table inside the parent test and using the **Test as Step** feature, you add the needed child independent tests that will receive the input from the parent. So far, this is feasible. But what really happens is after binding the child test steps to data-table columns, they are always going to expect some values to be passed on from the parent. So how will the subprocedure tests behave when called again in the regular context? They will end up throwing exceptions because at runtime, the bound table column must have an existence and should always be initialized before reaching the last step.

We don't want to end up tying the subprocedure child tests to data sources. So, should you proceed by creating the same set of child tests for both data-driven and regular modes? The following example describes a workaround for this problem.

First, make sure that the `authorization` parameter is set to `False` in the `settings.xml` file found inside the `File Comparer` application's `bin` folder. Let's begin by creating a WPF test called `Func-6_FileInfo_Create_Successful_Reg`. For this test, record the creation of a file without filling the **Creator Name** field with any value. Then open the `Op_FileInfo-FillCreatorName` test created earlier and add a scripted step. Drag it into the `If` block such that it executes before the scripted step that is bound to a data table column. Update its implementation to:

```
string val;

try
{
    val = (string)GetExtractedValue("Creator Name");
}
catch
{
    SetExtractedValue("Creator Name","Mark Moore");
}
```

In this code, we are making use of the two methods provided by Test Studio that allow us to manipulate test variables. The `GetExtractedValue` method is supposed to read the value saved in a variable to which the caption is passed as a parameter, whereas the `SetExtractedValue` method provides the means to set the content for a variable. So, in our scenario, when the `try` block executes, it will result in an exception since the `Creator Name` variable is null. Consequently, the `catch` block executes and in turn uses the `Create Name` variable, but this time to set its content to `Mark Moore`. Thus, when the next steps executes, it will set the field value to `Mark Moore`.

From the test properties pane, locate the **Data** section and unselect the **InheritParentDataSource** checkbox.

Go back to the `Func-6_FileInfo_Create_Successful_Reg` application and using the **Test as Step** button, add the `Op_FileInfo-FillCreatorName` test. Run the test and notice how the **Creator Name** field is populated with the hardcoded value. To rerun the test with the `Func-6_FileInfo_Create_Successful_DB` test, revert the state of the **InheritParentDateSource** checkbox to true and run the test. This time the value populated in the **Creator Name** field is the one retrieved from the `Paul Johnson` database.

Extension libraries

Further on the subject of reusability and maintenance, Test Studio offers the possibility of creating unified functionalities through library extensions. In the first chapter, we have seen how to override a useful function after test completion to add custom logging based on the overall test status. Now, suppose that this has been appended to the automation guidelines where every test has to supply this feature. Currently, the way to go about it is to edit test by test and implement the `OnAfterTestCompleted` function. This is of course a weary task (there is no need to mention that), and with this specific guideline amendment, all the subsequent tests will have to undergo the same feature change. So the solution resides in centralizing this functionality and making it dynamically available for the present and forthcoming tests.

Extension libraries can be employed to hold the targeted functionality. After designing and compiling such a library, we will add it to the Test Studio plugins. Hence, whenever any of the events related to the preceding functionality or any other similar one occur, our overridden versions will be seamlessly called in all the tests. Extension libraries are created within Visual Studio by referencing some of the Test Studio libraries and extending them.

For this purpose, start Visual Studio and create a project of the type `Class Library`. Name your project `TestStudio.Extension`. Now perform the following steps:

1. Add references to the following four libraries:
    - `ArtOfTest.WebAii.dll` found under **Telerik | Test Studio | Bin** of the `Program Files` directory
    - `ArtOfTest.WebAii.Design.dll` found under **Telerik | Test Studio | Bin** of the `Program Files` directory
    - The `System.Runtime.Serialization` .NET library
    - The `System.Windows.Forms` .NET library

2. Add the following namespaces after the `using` block statements:
```
using System.IO;
using System.Data;
using System.Data.OleDb;
using System.Windows.Forms;
using ArtOfTest.WebAii.Design.Execution;
```

3. Update the class definition to implement the `IExecutionExtension` interface as follows:

```
namespace TestStudio.Extension
{
    public class TestStudioExtention : IExecutionExtension
    {
    }
}
```

4. Right-click on the `IExecutionExtension` class and choose the **Implement Interface** option from the context menu and then choose **Implement Interface** again from the child context menu list.

   With this action, a complete list of functions that can be implemented is listed as follows:

```
OnAfterTestCompleted
OnAfterTestListCompleted
OnBeforeTestListStarted
OnBeforeTestStarted
OnInitializeDataSource
OnStepFailure
```

In our example, we will customize the handling of list startup, test startup, and steps failure.

The `OnBeforeTestListStarted` function is called before a test list starts execution. For this event, we need to:

- Enable all test annotations, custom and native, in order to visually debug and compare the steps description to the actions driven on the screen
- Enable the logging for these annotations to be able to refer to them even after tests have executed
- Query windows event log and replicate any error to the test list log

The `OnBeforeTestStarted` function is called before a test starts. We will use this event to demonstrate how our version of the execution library is called in our example. Therefore, for this function we will call the log method to write a custom message.

The `OnStepFailure` function is called whenever a step executes and results in a failure. In this case, we are interested in verifying some of the system state conditions. Hence we will query the system information to assert if there exists a live connection to the machine.

To start implementing the preceding functions, remove the `throw new NotImplementedException()` statement for all the functions and update some of their implementations in this way:

1. For the `OnBeforeTestStarted` function, add the following log line:

   ```
   executionContext.Manager.Log.WriteLine("Reading from extension
   library");
   ```

2. For the `OnBeforeTestListStarted` function, add calls to firstly enable the display and logging of both kinds of annotations and secondly query the event log for errors:

   ```
   list.Settings.AnnotateExecution = true;
   list.Settings.AnnotationMode =  ArtOfTest.WebAii.Core.
   AnnotationMode.All;
   list.Settings.LogAnnotations = true;

   list.Settings.QueryEventLogErrorsOnExit = true;
   ```

3. For the `OnStepFailure` function, add a call to log the connection status:

   ```
   executionContext.Manager.Log.WriteLine("Connection status: " +
   SystemInformation.Network);
   ```

4. For the `OnInitializeDataSource` function, add `return null`. Although this function will not receive any custom implementation, it has a `DataTable` return type and therefore must always have a return value. This does not apply to any other method (they should be left empty if not used).

Notice how the `executionContext` parameter object was utilized to access the runtime objects used by Test Studio throughout the test execution. The `Manager` object is an example and it holds references to other important objects such as `Wait`, `Settings`, `Desktop`, `Applications`, and so on. The `Log` object is also referenced by the `Manager` object and is frequently used in our examples.

Once the implementation is complete, compile the solution and copy the generated library from the solution's `bin` folder. Paste the copied library inside Test Studio's `Plugins` folder found under **Telerik | Test Studio | Bin** of the `Program Files` directory.

Accordingly, we will create a test and a test list inside Test Studio to demonstrate the behaviors we just implemented. Add a WPF test under the `Automated Test Scripts` folder and name it `Func-15_FileInfo_Extended`. Record the following steps to simulate the creation of file's metadata:

1. Go to the **File Info** tab.
2. Enter `Test Automation Guidelines` in the **File Name** field.
3. Enter `Paul Johnson` in the **Creator Name** field.
4. Choose the **DOC** extension.
5. Set the **Effort** field to 7.
6. Click on the **Create** button.

Then using the hover over the highlighting feature, add an incorrect verification against the submission result as follows:

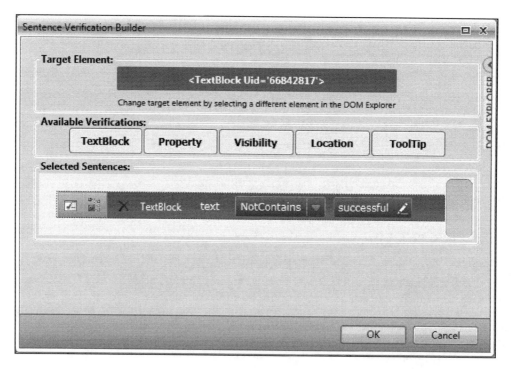

Adding a verification step

As depicted in the following screenshot, Test Studio will alert you with a message explaining that the constructed verification does not reflect the current text state. Since we are deliberately adding this step to satisfy the preconditions that will trigger the execution of the `on step failure` function, click on the **Yes** button:

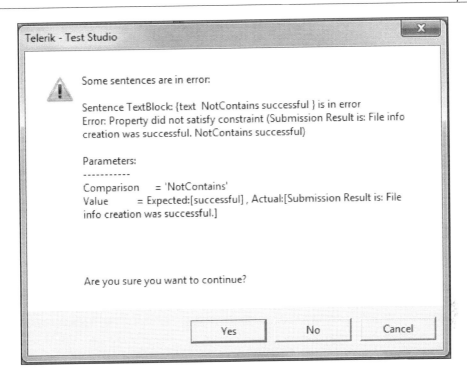

Test Studio alert window on erroneous verification steps

Go to the **Lists** tab and create a new list named `List_Extended`. Add the preceding created test to it and then run the list.

The default log folder is called `WebAiiLog` and is found on your `C:`. Browse for this folder and then open the first showing text document after sorting the file entries in a descending order based on the modified date. Notice how the log starts with our custom **[Trace] : Reading from extension library** message which ascertains that the execution is made according to our modifications. The runtime annotations appear next in the list which ends at the verification step. Finally, the last line is **[Trace] : Connection status: True**, which means that the `on step failure` method executed and the network status was successfully printed.

Data-driven design

Throughout this book, we have seen how data-driven design is highly efficient for adding dynamicity and multiplicity to test automation. Its usage was revealed in two contexts: when binding either a regular test step or a verification step to a data table column. Making use of the power of this feature in other contexts can also be useful.

Parameterizing the find element's expressions

Chapter 4, Maintaining Test Elements has focused on the default expression used by Test Studio to locate interface elements. It has elaborated on some strategies to add more robustness to these expressions by basing them to the known nonchanging attributes. Out of these strategies, we have seen a built-in Test Studio feature called chained expressions which was demonstrated through an example which attempts to locate a cell inside a data grid. The following screenshot previews this example and describes the solution which involves hardcoding values at the leaf level of the chained expression:

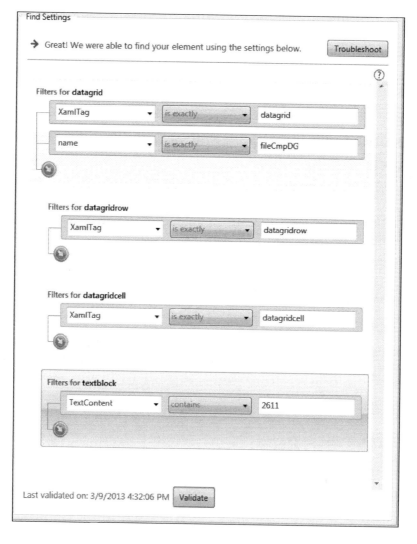

Chained expression in Find settings

Notice how the `TextContent` operand takes a text value equal to `2611`. We will see how this restriction denies us the possibility of binding this test to a data source. So let's assume we have the following test case to automate, which eventually will be tied up to a data source, by performing the following steps:

1. Go to the **History** tab.
2. Choose the **4/29/2013** date from the combobox.
3. Right-click on the `Func-1_FileCompare_Equal_Successful_In1.trx` entry (which is contained under the first column).
4. Click on **Display Details** from the context menu

The expected result is that the **Details** window contains the text, **In1**.

In a data-driven context, the test case that follows will be tied to a data source by performing the following steps:

1. Go to the **History** tab.
2. Choose the **4/29/2013** date from the combobox.
3. Right-click on the `Func-1_FileCompare_Equal_Successful_In2.trx` entry (which is contained under the second column).
4. Click on **Display Details** from the context menu.

The expected result is that the **Details** window contains the text, **In2**

In the third step of the procedure, if we intend to follow the same strategy of chained expressions to implement the find expression of the cell to click, we will hardcode the last `TextContent` operand to the cell content. Therefore, we will lose the flexibility of varying the destination cell at runtime by varying the cell text value. In this section, we will see how to make data-driven chained expressions.

Inside Test Studio, add a WPF test under the `Data-Driven Tests` folder and name it `Func-16_History_ContextMenu_Successful` and then execute the following steps:

1. Record the steps contained in the first test case.
2. From the **test editor** panel, click on the **Local Data** button.
3. Create the table shown in the following screenshot:

	File Name	File Details
1	Func-1_FileCompare_Equal_Successful_In1.trx	In1
2	Func-1_FileCompare_Equal_Successful_In2.trx	In2

The Func-16_History_ContextMenu_Successful local data table

4. Select the step corresponding to clicking the cell inside the data grid that should be similar to **RightClick on CFileTextblock**.

5. Following this action, locate the highlighted element in the **Elements** pane and right-click on it, then choose **Edit Element** from the context menu.

6. In the ensuing **Find element** window, click on the **Find in the Live Version** option and then on the **Choose Test Step** button in the **Existing Test Step** section.

7. In the **Test Step Selector** window, choose the preceding designated step and then click on the **Select** button.

8. Test Studio will run the test up to this step and enable the **Find Settings** window.

9. Update the first two chained expression sets as follows:

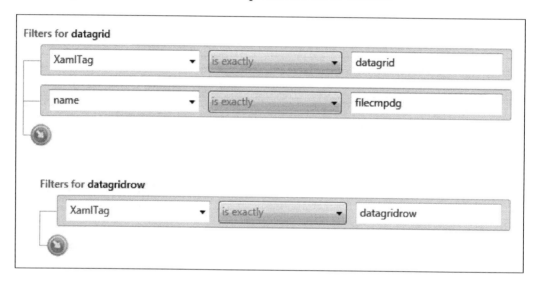

Updating chained expressions for a data grid cell text block

10. Add another embedded level and change the operand to TextContent. A combobox will be enabled for the value field. Expand it and choose **File Name** as shown in the following screenshot. The **File Name** option corresponds to one of the columns created earlier inside the local data table. For each iteration, the TextContent operand will be assigned the value of the active row. During execution, Test Studio will try to locate this text inside any data grid row.

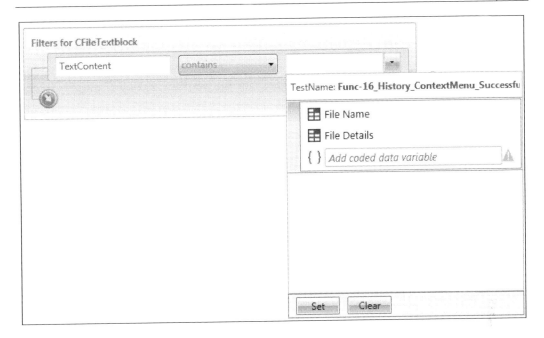

Binding text content property inside chained expressions

11. A warning message pops up informing the user that the instant validation against the existence of the element can no longer be made since there has been a data binding, so click on **Ok** and then save the changes.

12. Save your changes and close the **File Comparer** active window.

Now that we have transformed the process of finding a cell into a dynamic activity, one problem still hinders the successful execution of the test. The test verification step has a hardcoded value as well. Here comes the role of the **File Details** column. Therefore, to convert the data-driven step, perform the following steps:

1. Select the verification step from the test editor workspace.

2. In the **Properties** pane, locate the **Data Driven** section and expand the combobox for the **Bindings** property.

3. Select **File Details** for the value property and click on the **Set** button.

Run the test and notice how the clicks on the data grid cells occur in different places during each run. The overall passing status of the tests also asserts that the verifications were successfully updated with the changing data.

Variables

Other than the regular usage of variables, Test Studio particularly allows them to be used as information carriers among the several test steps. On one hand, we have seen how to control them through the IDE using the binding property, and on the other hand through code by using the `SetExtractedValue` and `GetExtractedValue` methods. Are the variables only confined to the execution scope of a single test?

Passing variables between tests

While creating most of the tests, we made use of the custom `LogResult` method showing its result after the log messages. While applying the reusability scheme, you notice that this method is replicated all over the tests and therefore constitutes a maintainability threat. So you start taking actions to abstract its definition away from all the tests. Theoretically, you would want to create a test A which is alone responsible for holding the definition of this method and hence receiving alone any future changes concerning its functionality. Afterwards, you want to replace all the internal coded steps currently implementing the `LogResult` method with a call to test A. However, how would you vary the string passed as a parameter to test A and thereafter to the `LogResult` method inside?

Test Studio offers flexibility in variables creation as we have seen in the first data-driven example of this chapter. During the compilation stage, it allows the usage of uninitialized variables either through test steps binding or code. So during test crafting, there is no validation with regards to the variable's existence. However exceptions will be thrown at runtime if the variable is not initialized by that time. This section makes use of this flexibility to solve the problem at hand.

For this example, we will need two WPF tests called `Func-17_PrintSubmissionResult_Successful` and `Op-Common_Log` respectively.

For the `Func-17_PrintSubmissionResult_Successful` test, perform the following steps:

1. Start recording.
2. Click on the **Compare Files** tab.
3. Select the **Default** radio button.
4. Click on the **Compare** button.

5. Hover over the highlighted button and use it against the **Result** label.

6. From **Quick Tasks** of the tab element menu, select **Extract – verify text content matches 'The files resulted in equal comparison'** by double-clicking on it.

7. Stop recording.

8. Expand the step properties and update the value for the `DataBindVariableName` field from `CompareFilesTextblock` to `logString`.

`logString` is the name of the variable to be used as the parameter to the embedded test. For `Op-Common_Log`, add the following coded step:

```
var text = "String to print is: " + (string)
GetExtractedValue("logString") + Environment.NewLine;

using (System.IO.FileStream fileStream = new System.
IO.FileStream(@"C:\File Comparer Files\Log.txt", System.IO.FileMode.
OpenOrCreate, System.IO.FileAccess.ReadWrite, System.IO.FileShare.
Read))
{
                fileStream.Seek(0, System.IO.SeekOrigin.End);
                byte[] buffer = new byte[text.Length];
                buffer = Encoding.UTF8.GetBytes(text);
                fileStream.Write(buffer, 0, buffer.Length);
                fileStream.Close();
}
```

The first statement in the preceding code uses the `getExtractedValue` method to extract the value of the `logString` that is passed at runtime by the parent test. The remaining code in the method opens the logfile and writes the content of the variable to it.

Go back to the `Func-17_PrintSubmissionResult_Successful` test and using the **Test as Step** feature, add a call to the `Op-Common_Log` test. Make sure that the added step is the last.

Run the test and after it finishes execution, open the logfile referred to in the `Op-Common_Log` test. Notice how the inner test successfully receives the tab name and prints it to the file as follows:

```
String to print is: The files resulted in equal comparison!
```

Summary

This chapter has built on top of the concepts acquired through all the previous chapters to create more flexible solutions in order to resolve various automation difficulties.

Overall, we have seen four sample problems and gone through their solutions step-by-step. Their purpose was to achieve better maintainability by reducing code duplicity as much as possible. To achieve this, we firstly used the same child test in regular and data-driven contexts. Secondly, we implemented some of the startup and completion methods through the development of pluggable extension libraries. Thirdly, we have created find and verification strategies for a data-driven element. Fourthly, we have seen how to unify the calls to methods characterized with their global usage by all project tests.

Configuring BugNet

In order to configure a BugNet application for testing, log in with **Username** `admin` and **Password** as `password` and then perform the setup detailed in the following sections.

Creating user accounts

1. Hover over the **Admin** option from the toolbar and click on **User Accounts**. Create the user account depicted in the following screenshot. For the password, enter 1234567and then click on Add New User.

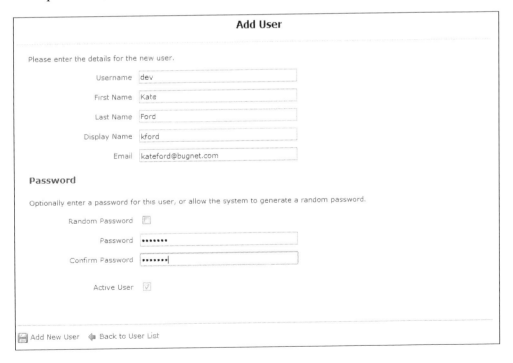

Adding a dev user

2. Create the user account depicted in the following screenshot. For the password, enter `1234567` and then click on **Add New User**.

Add User

Please enter the details for the new user.

Username	tester
First Name	Tom
Last Name	moore
Display Name	TheBugHunter
Email	tommoore@bugnet.com

Password

Optionally enter a password for this user, or allow the system to generate a random password.

Random Password	☐
Password	••••••
Confirm Password	••••••
Active User	☑

Adding a tester user

Creating a project

1. Hover over the **Admin** option from the toolbar and click on **Projects**.

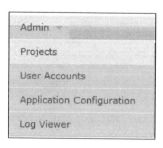

Admin ▾

Projects

User Accounts

Application Configuration

Log Viewer

Navigating to Projects

2. After the project page loads, click on the **Create New Project** option. The following images show the step-by-step instructions for creating a BugNet project . For each step, enter the information shown in the following screenshot:

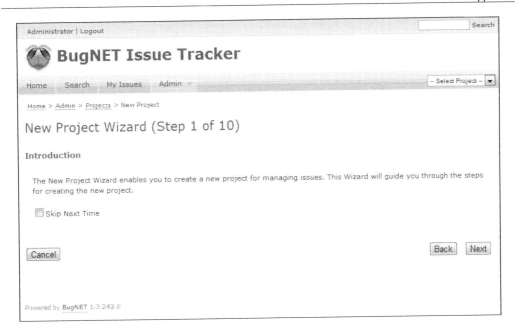

The New Project Wizard page

3. Click on the **Next** button.

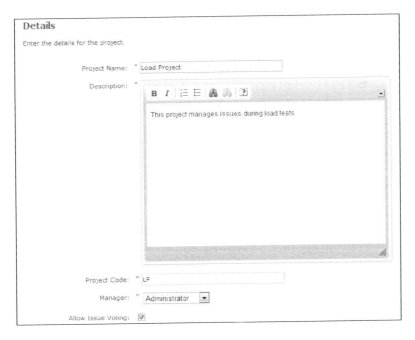

The Details page

4. Enter the relevant details and click on **Next**.

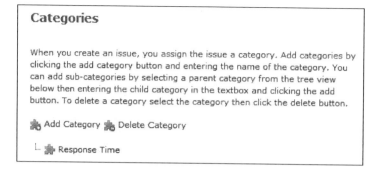

The Categories page

5. Click on **Add Category** and then click on **Next**.

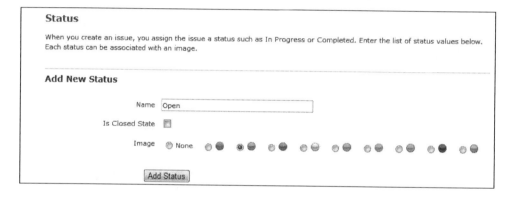

The Status page

6. Click on **Add Status** and then click on **Next**.

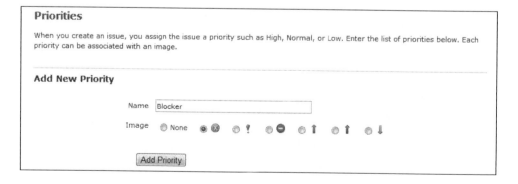

The Priorities page

7. Click on **Add Priority** and then click on **Next**.

The Add New Milestone page

8. Click on **Add Milestone** and then click on **Next**.

The New issue page

9. Click on **Add Issue Type** and then click on **Next**.

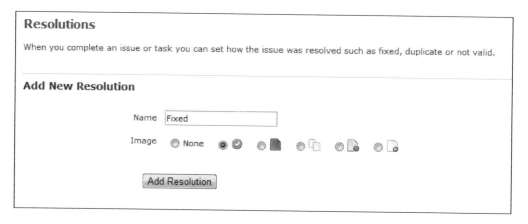

The Add New Resolution page

10. Click on **Add Resolution** and then click on **Next**.

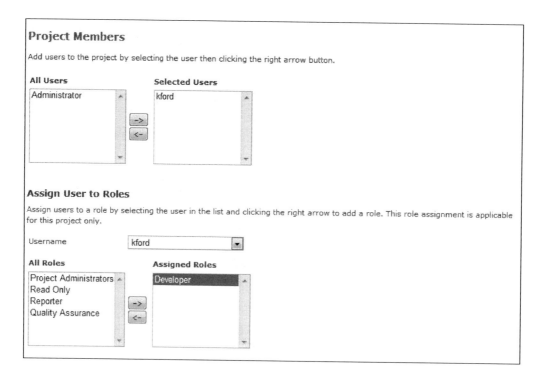

Adding the first user to the project

11. Add a user by following the steps in the preceding screenshot and click on **Next**.

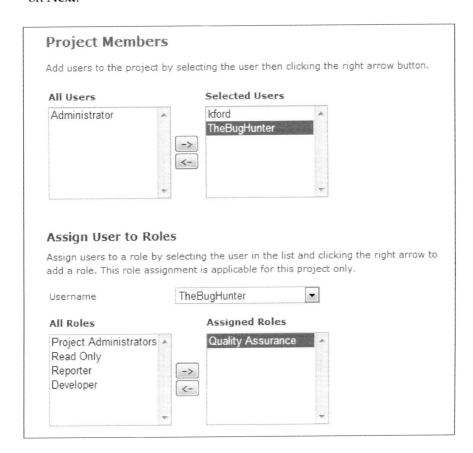

Adding a second user to the project

12. Add another user in the same way and click on **Next**. On the last page, click on **Finish**.

Index

history view 247
overview mode 242, 243
execution errors 64-68
execution metrics
    for last run 215-217
    over time 218, 219
execution phase, load testing 256, 272, 273
execution settings 69, 70
exit criteria
    about 9
    evaluating 10
Export button 128
Export Dialog node 132
Export label 127
Export ribbon 158
Export to Visual Studio option 181
extension libraries 331-335

F

Fast Forward label 170
Fast Forward Manual Test dialog 161
Fast forward test button 161
feedback
    about 315-319
    default target e-mails, configuring 316
File Comparer application
    about 15, 25, 161
    file metadata, creating in manual
        tests 153-156
    Import Results tab 215
File Comparer Login window 168
FileComparer.Test node 27
File Compare tab 223
File Details column 339
File Info tab 126
File Info Upload Feature 194
File Name text field 149
filtering
    options 133, 134
Find.ByAutomationId method 147
Find.ByExpression method 147
Find class 146, 147
FindLogic expression 122
FindLogic property 122, 134, 136

Find Settings window 142
Force On button 305
functional test automation 13

G

Gather Computer Performance
        Data window 242
GetExtractedValue method 330, 341
Get Latest Version option 183
Get Specific Version option 183
goals table 282
GQM (Goal Question, Metric) paradigm
    URL 207
gridIndex 56

H

HistoryTextblock 122
history view 247
HTTPProxy checkbox 206
hybrid tests
    about 159-164
    refactor tests 164, 165
    repository maintenance 167

I

IExecutionExtension class 332
implementation phase, load testing
    about 259, 260
    services, configuring 260-263
    tests, designing 264-271
implementation phase, performance
        testing 234-241
Import Manual Step window 157, 186
Import Results tab 215
InheritParentDataSource property 237
iOS testing
    about 285, 286
    deployment 287-292
    requisites 286, 287
    simulator 292
isOn property 309
ISTQB (International Software Testing
        Qualification Board) 9

U

UIWindow label 310
Undo Pending Changes option 183
UnexpectedDialogAction 204
Upload Files button 29
usability testing 21
user accounts
  creating 343
using block 164
using block statement 331

V

Validate button 144
Validation Failed label 40
values
  extracting, to variables 53-59
variables
  about 340
  passing, between tests 340, 341
  values, extracting 53-56
verification steps
  about 35-38
  inserting 38-40
versioning 176-181
View Class button 44
Visual Studio
  integration with 181
  report integration 211

W

Wait on elements feature 305-308
web portal
  about 311
  application, registering 311-313
  contributors 315
  testing 313-315
Web Test 27
workloads 231
workloads, load testing
  designing 256-258
WPF Test option 27, 161
Writeline method 59

X

XML data source
  columns, bringing to XML
    attributes 102-104
  importing 100
XML data source binding 100

Thank you for buying
Learning Software Testing with Test Studio

About Packt Publishing

Packt, pronounced 'packed', published its first book "Mastering phpMyAdmin for Effective MySQL Management" in April 2004 and subsequently continued to specialize in publishing highly focused books on specific technologies and solutions.

Our books and publications share the experiences of your fellow IT professionals in adapting and customizing today's systems, applications, and frameworks. Our solution based books give you the knowledge and power to customize the software and technologies you're using to get the job done. Packt books are more specific and less general than the IT books you have seen in the past. Our unique business model allows us to bring you more focused information, giving you more of what you need to know, and less of what you don't.

Packt is a modern, yet unique publishing company, which focuses on producing quality, cutting-edge books for communities of developers, administrators, and newbies alike. For more information, please visit our website: www.packtpub.com.

About Packt Enterprise

In 2010, Packt launched two new brands, Packt Enterprise and Packt Open Source, in order to continue its focus on specialization. This book is part of the Packt Enterprise brand, home to books published on enterprise software – software created by major vendors, including (but not limited to) IBM, Microsoft and Oracle, often for use in other corporations. Its titles will offer information relevant to a range of users of this software, including administrators, developers, architects, and end users.

Writing for Packt

We welcome all inquiries from people who are interested in authoring. Book proposals should be sent to author@packtpub.com. If your book idea is still at an early stage and you would like to discuss it first before writing a formal book proposal, contact us; one of our commissioning editors will get in touch with you.

We're not just looking for published authors; if you have strong technical skills but no writing experience, our experienced editors can help you develop a writing career, or simply get some additional reward for your expertise.

Sonar Code Quality Testing Essentials

ISBN: 978-1-849517-86-7   Paperback: 318 pages

Achieve higher levels of Software Quality with Sonar

1. Take full advantage of the Sonar platform and its visual components to track code quality and defects

2. Create step by step software quality profiles that match your needs

3. Real world examples that use Sonar efficiently to assess quality and improve Java code

iPhone Applications Tune-Up

ISBN: 978-1-849690-34-8   Paperback: 256 pages

High performance tuning guide for real-world iOS projects

1. Tune up every aspect of your iOS application for greater levels of stability and performance

2. Improve the users' experience by boosting the performance of your app

3. Learn to use Xcode's powerful native features to increase productivity

Please check **www.PacktPub.com** for information on our titles

Python Testing: Beginner's Guide

ISBN: 978-1-847198-84-6   Paperback: 256 pages

An easy and convenient approach to testing your Python projects

1. Covers everything you need to test your code in Python

2. Easiest and enjoyable approach to learn Python testing

3. Write, execute, and understand the result of tests in the unit test framework

4. Packed with step-by-step examples and clear explanations

JavaScript Testing Beginner's Guide

ISBN: 978-1-849510-00-4   Paperback: 272 pages

Test and debug JavaScript the easy way

1. Learn different techniques to test JavaScript, no matter how long or short your code might be

2. Discover the most important and free tools to help make your debugging task less painful

3. Discover how to test user interfaces that are controlled by JavaScript

4. Automate your testing process using external testing tools.

Please check **www.PacktPub.com** for information on our titles

43926098R00209

Made in the USA
Lexington, KY
18 August 2015